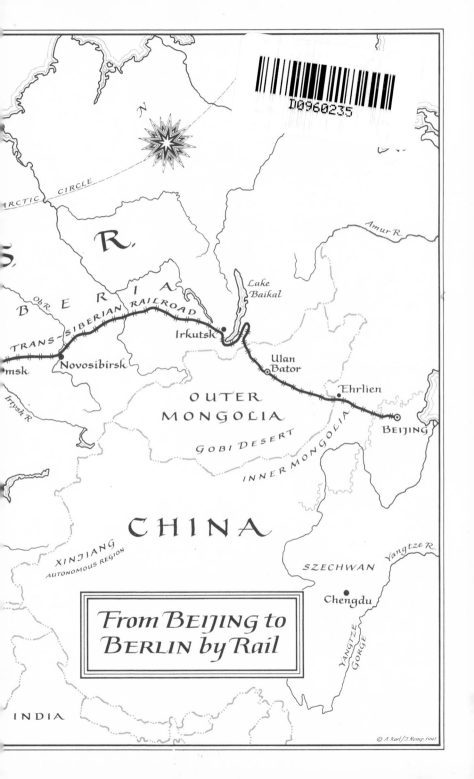

From BEIJING to
BERLIN by Rail

© A. Karl / J. Kemp 1991

WALL TO WALL

BY MARY MORRIS

Vanishing Animals
and Other Stories

Crossroads

The Bus of Dreams

Nothing to Declare:
Memoirs of a Woman Traveling Alone

The Waiting Room

Wall to Wall:
From Beijing to Berlin by Rail

MARY MORRIS

Wall to Wall

FROM BEIJING TO BERLIN BY RAIL

NAN A. TALESE

D O U B L E D A Y

New York   London   Toronto   Sydney   Auckland

PUBLISHED BY DOUBLEDAY
a division of Bantam Doubleday Dell Publishing Group, Inc.
666 Fifth Avenue, New York, New York 10103

DOUBLEDAY and the portrayal of an anchor
with a dolphin are trademarks of Doubleday,
a division of Bantam Doubleday Dell Publishing Group, Inc.

Grateful acknowledgment is made to the following for permission to quote from copyrighted material:

"The Mending Wall" by Robert Frost, from *The Poetry of Robert Frost*, edited by Edward Connery Lathem. Copyright 1930, 1939, © 1969 by Holt, Rinehart & Winston, Inc. Copyright © 1958 by Robert Frost. Copyright © 1967 by Lesley Frost Ballantine. Reprinted by permission of Henry Holt & Company, Inc.

"Questions of Travel" by Elizabeth Bishop, from *The Complete Poems 1927–1979* by Elizabeth Bishop. Copyright © 1956 by Elizabeth Bishop. Copyright © 1979, 1983 by Alice Helen Methfessel. Reprinted by permission of Farrar, Straus & Giroux, Inc.

"The Last Supper" by Osip Mandelstam, from *Osip Mandelstam: Selected Poems*, translated by Clarence Brown and W. S. Merwin. Copyright © 1973 by Clarence Brown and W. S. Merwin. Reprinted by permission of Atheneum Publishers, an imprint of Macmillan Publishing Company.

Library of Congress Cataloging-in-Publication Data

Morris, Mary
Wall to wall: from Beijing to Berlin by rail/Mary Morris.—1st ed.
p. cm.
1. Morris, Mary—Journeys. 2. Novelists, American—20th century—Journeys. 3. Railroad travel. I. Title.
PS3563.O87445Z478 1991
818'.5403—dc20
[B] 90-21848
CIP

ISBN 0-385-41465-X
June 1991
First Edition

1 3 5 7 9 10 8 6 4 2

THIS BOOK is dedicated to the people of China, the Soviet Union, Eastern Europe and elsewhere who have struggled to bring down walls; to my family, living and dead, for the stories they told; and to my husband, Larry O'Connor, for all the obvious reasons; and to Kate so that one day she may understand.

ACKNOWLEDGMENTS

MANY PEOPLE helped me to write this book. I am very grateful to my friends and colleagues who provided me with sources, materials, and careful readings, including Michael Kimmel, Annette Jaffee, Robert K. Massie, Susan Eve Jahoda, Martha P. Trachtenberg for her research which proved invaluable, Samuel Zimberoff for his stories, and Bessie Malkov and my parents, Sol and Rosalie Morris, for sharing with me what they remembered. I am grateful to my agent Amanda Urban for her help, Nancy Adler for her logistical support in New York while I was writing from afar, and Cristina Corsini of Distinctive Travel for her assistance with the travel arrangements. And I am most grateful to the librarians at the Santa Fe Public Library who provided me with innumerable books and let me keep them for extended periods of time.

I want to thank my editor, Nan A. Talese, as always for her editorial insights and general support, and Larry O'Connor, for his concern and encouragement, for his careful editing, spelling expertise, and general nurturing during the writing of this book.

And finally I want to thank the many people I met on this journey—on the trains, in restaurants, through various contacts—who spoke with me openly, often at great risk to themselves, who trusted me not to betray them, and who gave me information I could not have gotten by any other means. In most cases I have disguised these individuals, even though this may no longer be necessary. I am grateful for their courage and I hope that this work will in no way betray their trust.

AUTHOR'S NOTE

SINCE I JOURNEYED to China, the Soviet Union, and Germany in 1986, much has changed. When I traveled, democracy and free enterprise were being spoken of openly in China, glasnost and perestroika were just beginning to grow current in the U.S.S.R., although Sakharov still languished in Gorky and the Berlin Wall was quite intact. Since then, there have been the crackdown of the democracy movement and the abuses of human rights in China, the remarkable altering of the Soviet state, the opening of the Berlin Wall. I have been deeply moved by many of the recent developments and deeply saddened by others. As some walls have come down, others, perhaps more solid than before, have gone up. While this work is a travel memoir, it is also a travel history. But I am not a historian nor a political theorist. What I have written about in these pages is what I witnessed in 1986, a time when these countries were on the brink of promise and change. The world I saw then is not the same world now, but the hints, the suggestions of what was to come, were already in the air.

Before I built a wall I'd ask to know
What I was walling in or walling out.
And to whom I was like to give offense.
Something there is that doesn't love a wall.
  That wants it down.

—ROBERT FROST, *Mending Wall*

The Great Wall

FROM THE OUTSIDE, on a tree-lined residential street of Beijing, the Mongolian Embassy didn't appear as if it would present any problems. It stood serene with its brown stucco façade, the color of the desert I longed to cross—a low wall of scrub pine and pink gravel driveway, an open gate, reminiscent of an Italian villa. The moon-faced girl with the sleek black hair and a reddish complexion greeted me at the gate with a faint look of recognition. This was my third visit.

The first time I had come to this gate was just as she was locking it three weeks before. I'd grasped the bars like a monkey, pleading silently with her. The embassy was open for visas only a few hours a week. In order to cross Mongolia on the Trans-Siberian Express as I intended to do, one needed a Mongolian transit visa, and the only place in the world to procure one for the traveler wandering with no tour guide to show the way was at the gate where I stood. The first time, I had been sent away and told to return in two days' time. I had returned obediently on schedule and was informed that I had to leave my passport for twenty-four hours, which was impossible because the next morning I was to depart at dawn for Chengdu.

I had spent several weeks traveling through a steamy Szechwan Province where I viewed disconsolate pandas in dingy concrete-and-steel cages, flying to Tibet where I had experienced the wonders of the Jonking Temple, sailed through the massive arches of the Yangtze gorges, dined on delicacies and touched silks in Shanghai, all the time thinking that the one thing I truly wanted might elude me—the stamp on my passport that would enable me to enter the land of my Russian ancestors by rail.

I wasn't even sure why I needed this visa. I had been told that they lock the train at Ulan Bator so that in transit passengers cannot suddenly decide to disembark, though later I learned this was not true. But the fifteen dollars per person they charge for a transit visa apparently provides a substantial income to the Mongolian government, which is the true reason for its requirement.

This time the moon-faced girl ushered me through the gate into a small guardhouse where I handed her my passport. She fondled it, opening it, looking at my picture, then at me, studying the stamps from its many journeys. "Come back tomorrow," she said.

"Tomorrow," I repeated. "Tomorrow is Saturday," I said, knowing that the gate would be locked.

"Tomorrow," she said. I stared into her placid face, at her Central Asian rustic beauty. She was a descendant of the roving Tatar tribes, the great khans, the fiercest conquerors history has known. United under Genghis Khan in the thirteenth century and ruling over much of Asia and Europe for some two hundred years, the Mongols spread their terrible conquest from Eastern China to Poland. Indeed, in my own family of former Jewish peasants males are sometimes born with the "mark of the Tatar," a blue spot at the base of the spine from an elongated coccyx, a genetic trait that made Genghis Khan sit far forward in the saddle. My own brother was born with the blue spot which faded shortly after birth, the vestige of rape and inbreeding during the Tatar reign eight hundred years ago.

Now this Mongolian woman who was in a sense both enemy and ancestor stood with my passport, my fate in her hands.

I found myself folding my hands before my face, in a Buddhist supplication, a blessing, a prayer. "Tomorrow," I said, "I'll be back tomorrow." I walked away from her backward, then headed down the quiet Beijing street.

□   □   □   □

Ever since my grandmother told me about being buried alive, I have wanted to travel to the place where the little graves were. To find, if not the town, at least the part of the world my ancestors came from. I have been on many journeys, but I always wanted to go to the place of my grandmother's stories.

My grandmother, Lena Malkov Zimbroff, came to America from Russia, from a small village in the Ukraine, when she was twelve years old, and she told me stories of Cossacks and pogroms and the flight to America. It is my maternal grandmother I speak of. I had other grandparents, of course. My mother's father was a redhead with a fiery temper that killed him years before I was born. My father's parents were little people who lived in darkened rooms that smelled of oily soup and aging breath.

But my mother's mother was a teller of tales, a dreamer with translucent blue eyes that made me think not of the marbles the boys played with in her alleyway, but of globes and oceans and distant lands. She told me of the small graves dug in the backyard of their home some thirty miles north of Kiev, in the district of Chernigov *("Chernigov gibernia,"* my grandmother called it), on the outskirts of the town of Nezhin.

When the Cossacks rode into town—those fierce marauding men who were in part remnants of the Tatars (the name Cossack deriving from the Tatar word *kazak* or "free man")—mothers trembled, clasping their children in their arms. My grandmother told me of a young cousin skewered on a saber, of another swept away in a torrent of hoofbeats. To protect her children, my great-grandmother buried them in the ground with reeds sticking out of their mouths.

With a misty look in her eyes, my grandmother told it to me this way. She told me that she had to lie down on her back in a tight, moist hole of earth. It was dank and slimy and the dampness penetrated her clothing, entering her flesh. Then my great-grandmother stuck the reed in her mouth and frantically hurled dirt over her daughter's face for she had eight children to bury in this way. When she was done, she smoothed the grave while Lena clutched her fingers to her side, clamped her eyes shut and awaited the end of her burial alive, wondering what would happen if her mother were captured, if she never came back. When my grandmother told me this, my mouth tasted of soil. I found it difficult to breath.

Whenever there was a pogrom (which might have been every six months or every two years) and the Cossacks rode into town, this was what my great-grandmother did until one day she looked at her oldest daughters, teenagers now. They were beautiful and they had outgrown their graves. That was when they decided to leave.

Even though she lived in downtown Chicago, my grand-mother's house was the first foreign country I ever traveled to. The whispers in thick, impenetrable tongues, the smells of baking breads and savory fruit stews, the fairy tales—they all came from another land. In a wistful, mysterious voice my grandmother told me Russian folktales—of Baba Yaga, the cannibal witch, or Jack Frost whose embrace was death, or the girl turned into a firebird, her feathers spreading beauty across the land as she died in the talons of the evil prince. Marushka, she called me, after the firebird girl.

And in that same voice, conspiratorial almost, she told me of a village, a girlhood, a flight to America—stories more compelling to me than the made-up kind. They came as if they'd floated out of the paintings of Chagall, un-bound by gravity, rising in the air and settling, forever it seems, into my memory. A cow, a young man, his bride, a baby tossed into the air. Mud-lined streets, yelping dogs. At times the stories took a dark turn. The young man is wrenched from his bride; the dog is buried alive in the mud. A saber pierces the child suspended eternally above her mother's arms.

She told me of the cousin jailed for political reasons, and of her own daily trips to the jail with baskets of food. She described traipsing through the mud, the filth seeping into her shoes, while the cousin languished there. She never knew what became of him once she'd left Russia for good. She told me of the Cossack man who was kind and gave children bits of bread. Then one day he carried off a girl from the village and no one ever saw her again, though everyone said she wanted to go.

In all her stories, made-up and real alike, the meek triumphed, wrongs were made right, the beautiful, the great survived. It was a child's world, one I came back to again and again. Its bleak history was lost to me. Nothing really bad could happen here.

My grandmother made things up. I don't know if half of what she told me is true: if I really had a cousin who was lawyer to the czar, another who married Trotsky's daughter and is living somewhere in Scandinavia, and yet another who discovered a way to keep the Leaning Tower of Pisa from falling down. It is possible all the stories were pure invention, but none stayed with me more than the image of my grandmother buried with a reed in her mouth, the clatter of hoofbeats overhead.

In contrast to the Mongolian Embassy, the Chinese International Travel Services office felt as if I had walked into a commodities exchange. Or a run on a bank. The hot, airless room was stuffed with people, most of them shouting. Europeans in jeans with dirty rucksacks, Eastern Europeans in dark polyester suits and ties, British standing taken aback, Central Asians in their caftans and skullcaps were all jockeying for position, shouting, waving vouchers, trying to grab the attention of one of the many Chinese bureaucrats who shouted back at them, snatched vouchers, disappeared, came back, disappeared again, sat at their desks to have lunch, came and went, saying over and over again, *"Mali, mali."* We don't know. We don't know.

My heart sank. It did not seem possible that the ticket I had prepaid in New York, which according to my travel agent had to be picked up in Beijing, would find its way to this office and into my hands, enabling me to board the train early next week. Already this had been a journey of obstacles, some of greater dimensions than I had even begun to imagine, and now it seemed as if this one more thing would stand in my way.

I found what appeared to be a line, cozied up to the person ahead of me, and stuck there until after a long wait a neurasthenic Chinese young man stared at my voucher, then at me, as if I were somehow to blame for his trouble. He motioned for me to wait as he wandered off. Then he came back and motioned for me to sit down.

I sat on the ground beside two men. They wore burlap caftans, small skullcaps, and sandals strapped to their feet. Their features were more reminiscent of people from Arabia than China and I recognized them to be Chinese Muslims from Central Asia. These were the descendants of the Arabs and Persians who traveled the ancient Silk Route as merchants or mercenaries. I didn't want to stare, though they were a type of person I'd heard about but never seen before.

Instead, I took out a small notepad and a fountain pen and began to write. As soon as I moved the pen across the page, I felt them staring at me. The one next to me in particular had his eyes almost on my page. I paused, looked at him, then handed him the pen. First he tried to write with his left hand, as I had done, and his friend began to laugh. Then he tried to write with his right hand and his friend laughed some more. They laughed and laughed, then gave the pen back to me.

Next the man beside me made a sweeping motion with his hand that encompassed all of Asia, afterward giving me a questioning shrug. I thought for a moment, putting my hand to my chin. I picked up the pen. I drew a rectangle, four wheels, and a track. The man stared at my train. He appeared puzzled. Then he smiled a toothless grin. He nudged his friend. They both pointed at the drawing. Then they were shaking my hand, introducing themselves. "Moskau, Mecca," the man beside me said. I pointed to myself. "Moskau," I said.

In dream journeys I had imagined crossing the Hindu Kush, retracing Marco Polo's steps. I had stared at maps of the South Seas, of Madagascar, and made and remade my journeys as many times as I'd made my bed. I dreamed of desolate outbacks, solitude on a mountain pass. But the trip I always wanted to take was the one to the place where the little graves were. "Childhood," Graham Greene has written, "is a non-cerebral, thus mapless little journey." I carried the place within me, buried, a place for me of dreams.

In 1986 I was invited to China with my companion of several years to tour the country under the auspices of the Chinese Friendly Contact Association. I had first debated seeing China in this official fashion, but then it began to occur to me that I could use that as a jumping-off point to take the trip I had always wanted to take. While I would have preferred taking the train from Vladivostok to Moscow, there was a China route.

I pleaded with my companion to accompany me. In the years we had been together, we'd hardly had a vacation. But there were concerns on his side. A conference in Sri Lanka he wanted to attend, a demanding ex-wife, difficult teenage sons. Night after night we discussed it and finally I made up my mind. I would leave him in Shanghai, traveling on to Beijing and then across Asia. I would visit the area of the Ukraine where my family originated. Then it was my intention to fly home from Moscow. I would do the journey on my own.

For months I planned the trip. I had everything arranged, as was necessary when traveling to the U.S.S.R. in 1986. But on the morning of April 28, ten days before I was supposed to depart from New York to Beijing, something on the morning news made me pause. Technicians at the Forsmark Nuclear Power Plant, sixty miles north of Stockholm, had reported a troubling blip across their computer screen, this signal indicating an abnormally high level of radiation. Frantic engineers ran every check they could on their own reactor, fearing a problem there, but could find none. Meanwhile farther to the north, in other parts of Sweden, Denmark and Finland, similar readings were being taken. Somewhere a mysterious source of radiation was spilling across Scandinavia.

A study of prevailing wind patterns confirmed their fears. Air currents had been whipping up from the Black Sea, across the Ukraine, over the Baltic and into Scandinavia. As the Swedes and other northern countries turned their suspicions to their powerful and stony neighbor to the east, the Soviet Union met their demands with silence and denials.

All day I followed the news. Then at 9 P.M. Moscow time, a Soviet newscaster read a four-sentence statement as follows. "An accident has taken place at the Chernobyl power station, and one of the reactors was damaged. Measures are being taken to eliminate the consequences of the accident. Those affected by it are being given assistance. A government commission has been set up." Then he shuffled his papers and turned to a story about the Soviet peace fund.

On the news a red, pulsating circle, like an agitated heart, reached out from Chernobyl, its circumference pounding at the edges of Chernigov and Nezhin in the Ukraine and Gomel in Byelorussia, where my great-grandfather was born, the region north of Kiev that was my intended destination, that I had spent my childhood dreaming about. As the worst non-military nuclear disaster in history unfolded, I had ten days to decide. No one knew yet the extent of the injuries, deaths, evacuations, long- and short-term effects. Its realities were cloaked in secrecy.

The advice of friends divided sharply along gender lines. All my women friends of childbearing age who knew I was approaching forty and wanted to have a child told me to stay home. All my male friends, except for the family doctor and my Russian shoemaker, told me to go ahead. "It'll be interesting," they all said.

I spoke with a journalist who had written on nuclear fallout. He said it was still too early to predict the extent of the radiation and that the half-life of that kind of radiation was very short. Possibly by the time I was to travel there it would just be like getting a few extra chest X rays. He suggested I travel with a Geiger counter and a dosimeter, for measuring how many rads I was getting. "But then a Geiger counter is heavy," he said, "but a dosimeter is pretty light." He said I could get one in those electronics stores around Pennsylvania Station. He also advised me to avoid eating while in the Soviet Union.

I was laughed out of every electronics store in New York, but I packed an extra duffel bag full of Eastern Mountain trailpack dinners (beef Stroganoff, sweet-and-sour chicken, Sloppy Joes), a pot and a heating coil (though I didn't know what I was going to use for water), iodine pills, two dozen cans of sardines, beef jerky, high-energy candy bars, fruit juice in cans, canned tuna, crackers—determined to go to the Soviet Union despite the dangers, and live out of my duffel. On schedule in early May, we departed New York for Beijing and I had not altered my plans to travel to the Ukraine.

The Chinese International Travel Services office wasn't emptying, but people were coming and going. European tourists exited smiling, tickets in hand. Students in denim jackets who looked sweaty and spent, as if they'd just left the furnace cities of the Yangtze, were now laughing, smiling, tickets about to arrive. My Chinese Muslims heard their names called and scurried to the counter, leaving me sitting there, not saying good-bye.

I decided that if I stood up something would happen faster, so I got off the floor. No one seemed to notice me. I got back in line. The man who had taken my voucher had disappeared and now that I was faced with the obstacles before me, the journey seemed wrong, impossible from the start. I should have known this before leaving New York. It was ill-fated. Star-crossed.

Suddenly the neurasthenic Chinese man who had taken my voucher appeared and beckoned me to follow him through a maze of back corridors, darkened stairways that smelled faintly of cooking oil and boiling rice. The voices of amused bureaucrats rose like canned laughter. I puffed up six flights, careful to count in case this was not my last time here. We came to a dingy office, unlit, with a dark linoleum floor. A woman sat at a desk reading what appeared to be a novel. A man in a corner was dreamily practicing his tai chi. The bureaucrat who led me thrust my paper in their face. They looked at my voucher as if being shown a street address in a city they'd never seen. *Mali, mali,* they said. We don't know. We don't know. But the man practicing his tai chi stopped, looked again at my voucher. "Monday," he said. "Ticket here Monday."

It was Friday and Monday was two days before I was to leave. The weekend without ticket or visa stretched before me like a vast, barren plain. Making my way downstairs, I slumped against a wall. It occurred to me now that I was not going anywhere. That I could sit on the floor of the Chinese International Travel Services office, the traveler ghost, and watch others come and go, but somehow I would never go anywhere again.

DEJECTED, I wandered down Jianguomenwai Avenue—the official façade of Beijing—past the Beijing Hotel; then I cut over to Wangfujing Street, the main shopping street in Beijing. "Wangfujing," meaning "the Well of the Princes' Residences"—this street of storefronts selling cheap underwear, pirated cassettes, mascara and lipstick, polyester shirts —was once a thoroughfare of palaces. Little alleyways jut off the main artery with names like Pig Market and Lantern Market Street that are remnants of the imperial past, reflecting trades that no longer exist.

I paused at an electronics store before mountains of cassettes, transistors and batteries. The voice of a romantic Chinese singer pealed into the street. A crowd only of men in white shirt sleeves and dark pants stood transfixed by the dour female newscaster who read the news on a black-and-white TV, a map of the world behind her.

Then I wandered into China's number-one department store, oddly reminiscent of Filene's Basement. All the clothes were piled in large bins, mostly unfolded. Women picked through the piles of shirts with puffy sleeves, lacy fronts, the kind I wore occasionally in junior high, decades ago. They admired the ruffles, the soft round collars. The men's shirts were more traditional, in white and blue. Women tested lipstick on the backs of hands. All these accoutrements of Western self-centeredness and capitalism were unthinkable a decade ago, but now a shopping frenzy was going on that reminded me of the Chinese International Travel Services office, and I departed, heading for the gentler residential streets.

Once you have left behind the buildings of state, the

wide imperial highways and the commercial arcades, Beijing might as well be a village, still living in the ancient, agrarian past. Leaving Wangfujing, I entered the maze of side streets, courtyards and alleyways that make up the heart of Beijing. Here women in skirts with anklets or knee-high stockings squatted by the side of the road, their crotches revealed. The children had bows in their pigtails, many with gauze over their faces, red or yellow, to protect them from the dust that blows across the Gobi. Old men with long white facial hairs sat in front of houses in navy blue suits, canes in hand, toothless, nodding. Babies, often in plastic sun visors, played at their feet, diaperless, in slit-open pants so that the child can relieve itself whenever and wherever it chooses.

The smell on these side streets was of aging meat, urine, dust. The heat was strong. Women peered at me as they tipped their babies so they could pee. The streets seemed lined with toothless grins, rusting bicycles. The houses consisted of boards hammered together, while molting birds sang in cages. Thick, elephantine plants engulfed the entranceways where young girls with dark, inscrutable eyes swept.

I peered into living rooms, bedrooms, as I passed. It is something I have done at various times in my life and it brings me an odd, voyeuristic pleasure. Looking into the lives of others. Trying to imagine how they live. As if the walls that separate us are torn down. I can speak their language. I am invited in. Instead I see concrete floors, barren rooms with perhaps an old calendar or a poster on the wall —a Chinese rock star or the Yangtze Gorge, neither of which the resident will probably ever see. Unmade beds stand beside kitchen tables piled with bowls of rice. An ancient woman swats flies.

I thought of my companion whom I left behind in Shanghai. He would return to New York via Tokyo, then depart for Sri Lanka. I would travel across Asia, to Berlin and then New York, alone. I could see his face as we parted, assuring me that he would be at the other end. But now, peering into the lives of the Chinese, I wondered what they would think if they could suddenly peer into mine. A man too busy and perhaps untrue. A woman in need. The prospects for a family fairly small, vague as the troubled image in a crystal ball that won't come clear. I had traveled the world on my own for years—the Middle East, Europe, Latin America. But now suddenly, here in China, a fatigue came over me and I felt as if I could not go on for another minute alone.

I came to a Chinese apothecary, the kind I'd seen in the provinces. On one side behind a white marble table stood the pharmacists in white coats, looking quite earnest. Behind them were neat rows of white bottles of medicine. Antibiotics, chemically induced cures. On the other side of the apothecary an old man sat, a serene, yet whimsical look in his eye. He wore the generic navy blue suit that now seemed vintage Chinese, his beard a long white strand, his glasses thick around beady eyes. Before him was a glass cabinet filled with oddly shaped tubers, antlers and horns, desiccated insects, twigs, barks, weeds, and the leaves that made up the ancient cures of Chinese medicine.

People went in, some to the modern, Western medicine side, others to the old man for the ancient cures. The elderly tended to go to the old man, the young to the Western side, but there were exceptions to the rule. I smiled at the pharmacists in the white coats, but went to the old man with the long white beard strands.

Before some of his cures were little cards, written in a shaky English scrawl, to my surprise. I found potted deer antlers, pearl cream, a do-it-yourself acupuncture kit, strong and healthy tablets, recovery of youth tablets, staunch-bleeding wild ginseng, ginseng royal jelly, moisten one's throat tablets, anti-obesity pills and general weakness herbs.

The herbalist smiled at me. With his hands he showed

me how some cures you grind, some you boil and drink. With some he made a bitter smile. With others he rubbed his tummy in a satisfied way. I indicated I was traveling by making several circling motions around an invisible globe and then I dropped my shoulders in a tired slouch. Like a deaf-mute I had come to China to learn to sign. He nodded and laughed, pointing to the strong and healthy tablets. I purchased a small quantity. They looked like rabbit pellets. I would carry them with me for five thousand miles, never taking a one.

As I left the pharmacy, an old woman walked out of one of the houses, heading toward me. She hobbled with a cane; her tiny feet no more than three inches long rose like hillocks. I recalled descriptions I had read of the pain in the night when the bones break, of little girls screaming as their mothers bind them even more tightly. I felt my own feet beneath me and found myself walking even more briskly through the streets of Beijing.

THOUGH I had been avoiding this for weeks, I knew it was time to go to the U.S. Embassy and find out what the present travelers' alerts were on Kiev and the outlying regions. Perhaps I also had an ulterior purpose. After days alone in Beijing, I was gripped by a desire to speak my own language, to carry on a conversation, regardless of how mundane.

I reached the entrance to the embassy and a blond, crew-cut marine, standing very straight the way marines tend to do, asked for my passport. "I don't have my passport," I said. "It's at the Mongolian Embassy, getting a visa."

"I'm sorry," the marine said, "but we need proof of citizenship to allow you into the embassy."

"Do you think I'm Chinese?" I asked.

The marine laughed. "I'm sorry," he said, "but I need a passport."

"Sir," I said, standing very proudly, "I am an American citizen. I need to get into my embassy." Ask me about Mickey Mantle, I wanted to shout. Ask me about Walter Cronkite. Bruce Springsteen. Howdy Doody, thinking the marine must be about my age.

The marine grinned and shrugged. "Those are my orders, ma'am."

"Then can you get me an information officer? I need to talk to someone about Kiev."

He looked amused, then picked up the phone. A sandy-haired man arrived in khaki pants, shirttail out. He was sweating profusely in the heat of the day and he had the beginnings of a paunch, appearing like a good candidate for high blood pressure. His hair was thinning. He looked at me and sighed, then looked at the marine. "She can come with me." He gave the marine a dismissive flip of the hand, then led me into a small antechamber where we sat down on hot red vinyl couches. Rubbing his hands together like a resident therapist, he said, "How can I help you?"

"I have an itinerary that takes me to Kiev and Chernigov, which is outside of Kiev and thirty miles from Chernobyl. Do you have any current information about the situation in that part of the Ukraine?"

He looked at me as if I had just landed from Mars. "I've been traveling," I said.

He ran his fingers through his damp hair. "We have a travelers' advisory on Kiev. I personally would advise you not to go there. I definitely would not go to any outlying areas and I am certain the Soviets won't let you."

I had already worked out a plan in my head if this were the situation. I would go to Kiev, then rent a car to take me north. Even if I could not get as far as Nezhin or Gomel, at least I would see the area. "But I can go to Kiev . . ." Of course I knew I could go to Kiev. Just weeks before, the Soviets had issued the travel vouchers to take me there.

"You can go at your own risk."

"But what is the danger? Do you know the risk?"

"The Soviets have been very circumspect. We don't have all the facts. We don't know much about the conditions of the water and air. . . .   Do you know anything?" he asked me hopefully.

"You're the information officer," I said.

"Oh, we know what we read in the newspapers, but we don't have an exact report." Either he was lying or he was a fool.

"But I can go if I want."

"I don't think you can go outside of Kiev, but you can go to Kiev if you want." Now he was beginning to lose interest in me, finding me rather crazy, I think.

"Can you give me a fact sheet?"

"Well, I just don't have anything very informative . . ." He stared at me for a moment, then snapped his fingers as if a light bulb had just gone off in his head. "I'll loan you my copy of *Time* magazine," he said.

"Oh, that would be great," was my bemused reply.

"Here, I'll Xerox it for you. You decide."

I followed him to the copy machine where we both looked ill under the green glow. Then he thrust the pages into my hands, having grown weary of me by now, and wished me a safe journey. As I passed through the glass doors, I saw him shaking his head.

Stopping for a Coke at the soda machine, I sat on the steps of my embassy in the heat of a steamy Beijing summer day and read what I had not known before departing. That all pregnant women and schoolchildren had been evacuated from Kiev. The school year had ended early. Many Kievans had fled the city. The queues at the train stations to get out of Kiev continued to be long. Moscow and other cities were inundated with Kievans. People had been told not to drink water, to avoid milk products and leafy vegetables. They were told to wash often and keep their windows shut. The area north of Kiev had been evacuated. No one could travel there. According to the issue of *Time* magazine, the reactor was still on fire.

Why I wanted to continue on this journey remained a mystery to me. Even as I sat on the steps of the embassy absorbing for the first time the facts as they were known, my purpose seemed vague and unsure. My parents had pleaded with me not to go. "You aren't going, are you?" my mother asked in that same way she always phrased her statements, ending them with a question that inspired doubt. "He loves you, doesn't he?" "You're happy, aren't you?" My father, a man for whom oceans are filled with sharks, freeways with maniacs, took the more tempered businessman's approach, speaking to me as if discussing something with his broker. "Do you think it is advisable . . . Have you given any thought to staying home?"

But I am a person who has always searched for home. Goethe once said that writers are people who have the disease of homesickness, that being a writer is being on a constant search for the place where you belong. I have always longed for the place that was mine on the planet. Perhaps this made me restless, made me wander the earth, never putting down roots. Perhaps this is why I'm partial to tumbleweed, pack rats, and nomads, those who carry their lives around on their backs.

Once when I was living in the West I met a man who came from a valley called Puerto de Luna, Gateway to the Moon. He had lived in that valley all his life and his ancestors before him. He took me on a tour—the sinkholes, the decaying adobe churches, the path Coronado took as he searched for the City of Gold. He showed me the house in which he and his father before him had grown up. This landscape was his vision. This geography was in his blood. Everything he knew or loved he traced back to Puerto de Luna. Everything he remembered was here.

But my family are Jews, Russian Jews at that, and we have been called the wanderers of the earth, though our wandering was forced upon us not by nature, but by hardship and necessity. A purple plant with aimless reaching tentacles is named after us, the wandering Jew. My own family, which lived for troubled centuries on the steppes and farming land of the Ukraine, has been scattered like seeds and what is left dissipated in deaths, lawsuits, family feuds. It is only by chance that my tribe has landed where it has. I have heard of a psychological disability whose symptom is restlessness. The inability to stay put. The need to move on. It is the condition of a person who must flee, who cannot stay, yet who is always looking for somewhere to rest. Diaspora of the blood. I seem to be so afflicted, though perhaps it is the affliction of my race.

I have spent hours pondering where my own final resting place will be. If I were to die tomorrow, I have no idea where I'd go. A family plot in the Midwest, a place on the East Coast near the sea, or ashes sprinkled on a forest floor, tossed into Lake Michigan, or perhaps a Long Island cove. Yet I have a fear of fire and do not want to contemplate cremation even in death, but this seems an easier choice than to pick one place where I must lie.

Recently my mother informed me that there is no room for me in the family plot. A distant cousin with no particular claim has taken my spot, so my choices are limited even more. Besides, do I want to lie for eternity beside them? It is more like me to be tossed to the wind.

I have always admired those who know when they have come home. A woman once told me this story. She had been driving along a country road when her car broke down. She knew no one in the area so she got out and walked. She walked until she came to a long driveway lined with trees, and she could not see the house. She followed the driveway until she came to an old boarded-up farm-house with green shutters and a wraparound porch. The porch had a swing that looked out over a valley. She sat in that swing and rocked until the sky turned a pinkish-orange and the sun was setting. She knew that this was where she belonged. She has lived there ever since, some thirty years now.

But I am not that way. I have lived in too many places. I've seen too much of the world. At times I want the desert; other times the sea. I long for the changing seasons, but cannot say no to a Caribbean breeze. Sometimes I want the feel of asphalt under my feet; other times I long to breathe country air. I think I will never stop somewhere and say this is my home. This is where I belong.

The truth is that where I belong comes to me in my dreams, but I know I cannot go there. For years the image has always been the same, no matter what the dream, no matter where it takes me. In the jungles of Guatemala, the hill towns of Tuscany, the North African desert, it has al-ways ended at the same place. Tracks through the snow, leading down familiar streets lined with snowmen, sleds, children at play. These tracks take me back to Illinois, to Hazel Avenue, above the shores of Lake Michigan, and my childhood home.

The house is gone, long ago sold to a man who has married a woman half his age. An American flag flies on the lawn; white wrought-iron furniture, antebellum style, sits on the front porch. They have built a cage for a dog who howls into the night. I know this because when I am in Illinois I visit my neighbor, and from her house I spy upon my former life. I try to envision someone else sleeping in the room where my father tucked me in. Where I read my first books, whispered my first secrets to girlfriends on the phone. Now a stranger lives inside that life while I wander, searching perhaps still for the tracks that will lead me home.

CHEN BAO, a Chinese writer who was an acquaintance of a friend from New York, lived on the outskirts of Beijing and I made my way there in the evening. I walked through a narrow passageway that separated Chen Bao's rather large four-story house from another. Yelping dogs nipped at my heels. Plants lined this passageway. Old women and small children peered out at me. I rang and Chen Bao met me. He was a stout, broad-faced man with thinning hair and he greeted me with a wide smile. "It is good to see you," he said, as if he had known me for a long time. I was relieved to hear his English was quite good. "You see, ten years ago I couldn't say hello to you on the street. Now I can have you in my home."

He led me up a red linoleum stairwell four flights. The doors were open to other apartments as we passed. An old woman cooked at a gas stove. Two children were at play. An old man stared at me with frightened eyes which kept blinking as we passed. "We are very lucky, my family. We all live here together. My family and my wife's family. We have different floors, but we are all together. It is a very good arrangement."

We entered a living room that had been set up for tea, complete with small cakes and sweets. I gazed around me at the plastic bonzai and plastic plants which were everywhere —wisteria, evergreen, pineapple. A red velvet tablecloth was stretched across a table upon which we would have our tea. The room was decorated in Chinese lanterns with scrolls on the walls. It was the Chinese equivalent of an American home from the 1950s.

Chen Bao poured the tea. "Oh yes, we are very lucky. A decade ago, I could never have had you in my home. Why, it wasn't even my home during that time. Ten families were living here. You would not have believed the filth, the vermin . . ."

"Where were you?" I asked hesitantly. "Where were you then?" It appeared he wanted to talk about that decade of collective madness called the Cultural Revolution. It was the time when China wanted to purge itself of anything that showed signs of being tinged with Western privilege or thought. Scholars, scientists, doctors, officials, writers, artists—anyone in an elite profession was subject to reeducation by means of humiliation, ingenious torture (one district would boast of seventy-five new forms of torture), exile into the countryside. Tens of thousands were bludgeoned to death for playing the piano, keeping pets, reading novels. Anything viewed as personal, individual, self-centered was condemned as Western decadence. A generation of the country's most gifted thinkers and creative people was destroyed. By the end of it in 1976 at least a million were dead.

"Where was I? In the countryside, planting seeds. Actually I fared better than most. I was gone for seven years. Lost seven years. But I have done all right. I work for a newspaper. I write my own books. I have been able to get some of it back. Not like my father."

He paused again as I had begun to anticipate he would with each new direction he wanted to take, to see if I would follow him. If I wanted to go further. "Your father?" I asked.

"Yes, he did not do so well. He was a teacher of philosophy. He has not been the same. His mind is not the same. They made him kneel for days on broken glass. They did other things to him, things he won't talk about. I know they shaved his head and made him walk the gauntlet while they beat him with bats. But there are worse things you can do to someone. He was a man of principles. He believed what he taught. He was a kind of freethinker."

"Is he alive?"

"Oh, yes, he is alive. You saw him as we came up the stairs. But as you could see, he is not the same. But you know they persecuted everyone—stamp collectors, people who raised goldfish, who kept bonzai . . ." He waved his arm at his plastic plants.

"But that is over now," Chen Bao said. "We welcome foreigners. Our house is our own again. We live together. What happened is over. It will not happen again." Chen Bao sipped his tea, the complacent look gone and a more troubled one in its place.

Then he poured more tea as we grew silent, gazing into our cups, perhaps wishing we had never embarked upon this line of conversation. We were like two people who have been thrust into a premature and uncomfortable intimacy and suddenly we were aware of the embarrassing place to which it had led us. "That is over now," Chen Bao said, his face growing jovial again, passing me a cake. "Tell me about New York. Tell me what is going on in the rest of the world."

Upon returning to my room, I decided to phone New York. I wanted to talk with my companion, who had by now arrived from Japan. I asked the operator if I could place a call. I repeated my request several times until we got all the numbers right. She said she would call me back. I waited and waited, listening to a cassette of conversational Chinese, practicing the sound over and over through slight movements of my lips.

I cannot say that it was the happiest time of my life. I had been in an angry state, given to outbursts, rages, sudden tears. I was not getting younger and I had been with this man for over three years. What I thought I wanted with him—marriage, a child, a place of our own—had somehow eluded me. I had shut out others for his sake and now it all seemed to be a mistake. Because of him, I had built a barrier between myself and the world.

As I fell asleep that night waiting for the call that never came, I dreamed I was traveling by train through a foreign country that had fields of wheat. From the window of the train I watched the wheat as it blew in the wind. Each row was a different color—red, blue, gray, and green, repeated in the same pattern over and over again, but for some reason it did not surprise me to find wheat growing in these colors.

My companion is with me and at last we come to an enormous walled city. We enter and find ourselves in a central plaza. The plaza is lined with giant doors and the doors are painted in the same colors as the rows of wheat—red, blue, gray, and green. No one is there except the two of us, and we are surrounded by the walls of the city and by the enormous doors. He says he will go and find a hotel and he leaves me standing alone.

I stand before these giant doors, looming hundreds of feet high. I cannot reach the knocker, cannot reach the handles. I am left standing there for a long time, confronting these doors and walls. In the dream my companion never returns.

STRETCHING some four thousand miles across China's northeastern frontier, the Great Wall of China was built to keep the barbarians away—a task it failed to accomplish. Evil forces were said to dwell in the North, where the desert

—the void, the unknown—lay. To protect themselves from threats both real and imagined, the Chinese have traditionally turned their backs on the North. Yet the Wall, intended to contain those threats, did little to hold back the Mongol invasion of the thirteenth century. Still, the Great Wall remains the quintessential symbol of China and, in a sense, of the Chinese.

A few weeks previously I'd spent my thirty-ninth birthday climbing the Wall. With my companion, I'd walked its reconstructed ramparts, gazed across the North China plain. Now, under the assumption that I was leaving early the following week, I decided to return to pay my respects. Prior to getting the bus that would take me, I made my requisite visit to the Mongolian Embassy at 10 A.M.

At to the embassy, I stood, as anticipated, before a locked gate. I was kept from despair by the fact that a fellow traveler, a man in raggedy jeans and a dirty khaki jacket, a well-used rucksack dangling from his hand, stood shouting, "Hello, is anybody here?" in French. But the embassy gates remained ominously closed and I had the distinct sense that no one was home. Still, the presence of another human being made me think that they had told at least one other traveler to come back.

The Frenchman saw me standing there and said to me, *"Vous allez Trans-Siberia?"*

"Yes," I replied.

"June fourth?" he asked, now in an almost accent-free English.

I smiled. "So we'll be on the same train."

He shook his head. "I've had such a hard time getting this visa," he muttered.

His name was Pierre and he was French but living in Amsterdam where he played the saxophone. I told him I was American, traveling to Moscow. He said he'd been traveling in China for two months.

"But now," he said, "I'm afraid to go home."

"Why?"

"Chernobyl," he replied.

I was about to ask him more about his feelings of returning home in the aftermath of Chernobyl when the moon-faced girl from all my visits and a few of my anxiety-ridden nights came, jangling a large key with which she unlocked the gate. She motioned and we followed her into the dark, austere entranceway of the embassy. Here without ceremony or even a wait she handed him his passport and me mine. We both opened them at once and saw emblazoned there the red-and-blue stamp that would make our passage possible. I clasped mine like a child before a good report card. "So," Pierre said, picking up his knapsack, hoisting it upon his shoulder, buoyant now, "I'll see you on the train."

"Yes," I replied, thinking that in fact I would.

"We'll have plenty of time to talk then." He whistled as he walked away, making several Chinese stop and stare at the sight of a man whistling.

I boarded the bus, heading to the Great Wall, glad to be going somewhere if not yet on the train. Beijing had its claustrophobic side and I knew from my weeks of travel that the real China was not here any more than the real America was in Washington. Also I was trying not to think of what would happen on Monday if the travel services did not produce my ticket. Instead I let the excitement of this small adventure carry me—the people, some tourists, but many were Chinese tourists, boarding the bus to visit their wall.

The movement of the bus took us to the outskirts of Beijing, through the throngs of bicyclers (five million of them) to where the houses and apartment buildings dwindled to hamlets, finally into the countryside of rice paddies and small farms outside of Beijing. Farmers in broad-brimmed straw hats plowed with oxen. Children, scruffy and lean, in tattered brown shorts and T-shirts played with sticks and balls in their earthen front yards. They paused to wave at the bus as we passed.

I felt as if I could breathe again, away from the heat of the city which had grown oppressive. A breeze blew and I was content to stare outside, watching the rural landscape pass like some misty painting on a Chinese scroll.

Within a little more than an hour the Great Wall was in sight. I disembarked and joined the throng of tourists, for it was a Saturday and the crowds on the Wall felt more like the attendants to some major sporting event. All afternoon I climbed the Wall or sat on its parapets, watching tourists climb past me, or I turned and stared across the North China plain. I watched the Chinese scurry up and down this symbol of their nation, as much representative of who they are as, say, the Statue of Liberty is to America, or the Eiffel Tower is to France. I walked along the reconstructed part first, amazed at the old women with canes and those tiny bound feet climbing up and down the ramparts. Young Chinese couples in love walked tentatively hand-in-hand. I have never enjoyed tourist attractions, except to observe the curious breed of tourists they attract, but, perhaps because I was alone, I enjoyed walking among the throng.

Sitting on one of its parapets, I thought how this wall cut across the North China plain, along the rim of Inner Mongolia, until it reached the Yellow River, how for another thousand miles it snaked along the edge of the Gobi, then turned toward the distant province of Xinjiang until it came to an end along the ancient Silk Route at the Jiayuguan Gate. The age and scope of this wall are beyond comprehension. Even the man attributed with its construction—Qin, first Emperor and unifier of China—was merely connecting a series of already existing walls.

Qin, the Emperor from whom China draws its name (Ch'in), intended for his dynasty to endure for ten thousand generations instead of fourteen years, from 221 to 207 B.C. However, in those years Qin, a great warrior, managed to unify China. He was the ruler to whom Mao Tse-tung compared himself when he wanted to justify his tactics to unify the nation. Qin was proverbial in his cruelty. During his reign he burned books of the past and had scholars tossed into pits, to be buried alive. Mutilations, castrations, brandings and other forms of ingenious cruelty were commonplace occurrences during his reign.

Qin thought nothing of sending hundreds of thousands of laborers to their death as they connected a series of pre-existing walls to form what we have come to refer to as the Great Wall. The Wall stands twenty-five feet high and twenty-five feet thick at its base. Five horsemen can ride abreast along its ramparts. Stretching some four thousand miles along China's northeastern frontier, it is the largest structure ever built by man—the only man-made structure that can be seen by astronauts in space. Its purpose was to keep back the barbarians, but when the Mongols swept through in the thirteenth century the Wall was useless in holding them back. Built and rebuilt over generations, the Wall as we know it now was mainly reconstructed by the Mings, who ousted the Mongols.

But in order to understand this wall one must first understand something about the Chinese, as I had been trying to do for several weeks now. The Chinese have the oldest recorded continuous civilization (dating back four thousand years). They also have the world's oldest centralized state, dating back to Qin. Although spoken Chinese varies so much from province to province that a person from Canton literally cannot understand a person from Shanghai, its written language is uniformly the same and has been so for more than two thousand years.

The written language itself has been traced back to 1400 B.C. The ideographic script employs a character for every object and action. An abstract idea is created by combining concrete ones. Thus the Chinese notion of the world comes from a very specific, concrete place. To marry you make a socially desirable match. To choose a profession you make a pragmatic choice. To have a spiritual belief, you look at history and its lessons. To defend yourself, you build a wall.

The Chinese have always wanted to protect themselves from the North, the great land mass of Asia, and from the nomadic tribes they feared. Yet I could not help think as I wandered its ramparts that it represented something less substantial, a deep psychological fear. I thought of its builder, Qin, who had 270 palaces with tunnels connecting each one so that no one ever knew where he was sleeping. The Great Wall was his fantasy, or perhaps the projection of his paranoid thoughts.

Now this wall seemed almost a reflection of a collective paranoia—the need of a people to protect themselves not only physically, but emotionally as well. The Chinese do not seem to be a people who have much understanding of their fears. A recent study showed that while the Chinese have the lowest crime rate on earth, they are more afraid than Americans to venture out alone in the dark. Even in their personalities, they seem to live very much on the conscious level, hemmed in, unaware of their darkest dreams. Indeed, Western psychoanalysis does not work with the Chinese. They do not grasp the notion of revealing themselves. They tend to keep their feelings hidden, if they are aware of them at all. Yet fear of the unknown, the dark, the barren North, has historically been a national trait, reflected in modern times in the politics of terror.

The Chinese seemed to me at times like some ancient form of life, operating in the same way, say, an ant colony —another ancient form of life—might operate. Each with his function, his purpose. The individual is subsumed. Everything that happens is for the good of the collective race. And so this wall seemed to be the realization of a profound collective fear, like a child's fear of darkness. Some horror film in which the real horror is within, not without. In some Freudian way, it made sense to me that the culture

THE GREAT WALL 31

that had bound women's feet would build this wall. As if they thought they could contain what they could not control.

I had been having my own childlike fears of late, and so I felt a certain affinity for the Chinese and their "need" of this wall. Sleep had not been coming easily and when it did, I struggled with troubled dreams. I would wake shaking in the night, knowing there was no one I could speak with, no one I could call. No one who would understand me if I did. I felt somewhat like a prisoner, condemned by language and race, within a strange kind of solitude I had never known before.

I felt invisible in this scrambling crowd as they rushed up and down the ramparts and suddenly I found it more lonely to be in the crowd than to be really alone. I ascended to the northwestern part of the wall until I reached the end of the reconstructed part. There I looked out and saw miles more of wall, crumbling, with blue flowers growing out of its cracks. At the base, stones tumbled into the North China plain. A few boys had crossed onto the broken part of the wall, and I decided to do the same, leaving the throng behind. I climbed easily over the small barricade and put my foot on shaky stone, rough-hewn.

I walked for a little way, then found a place between two rocks where I sat down. Here I could imagine the soldiers of Qin guarding from the Wall's evenly spaced towers, scanning the plain for the barbarians who would rout them. In a distant tower, someone was playing a flute. The music rose eerily and was carried along the wind, weaving in and out of the Wall. No one was in sight and the music seemed to come from the wind itself.

The breeze was strong and warm and I turned my face to the north, to the flat and verdant plain that seemed to fade into a burnt sienna at the horizon where the edge of the Gobi lay. I stared in the direction of the north, across Asia, stared until I thought I could feel what it would be like to see Genghis Khan's men bearing down from the north, like my own worst fears, or to see a train leading me away across this same great plain.

It was late afternoon when I hopped a tourist bus heading back to Beijing via the Ming tombs. I had already visited the tombs several weeks before and was not anxious to return, but the tour bus was only making a forty-five-minute stop. Though the great rulers of the Ming Dynasty were buried here, I did not want to venture into the tombs again, to be caught up in the rush of tourists and of Chinese hungry for this proximity to their imperial past, amidst the dank, musty odors of the tomb.

Instead I opted for the garden aboveground and the cardboard hill of photographic fantasies where earlier my companion and I had been photographed in a cardboard airplane, vintage World War II. Now I tried on all the disguises—a princess, a warrior, a concubine. I stuck my head into the hole that put me astride horses crossing Arabia, in the bow of Viking ships. Here I could be a maiden in a harem or a reigning potentate. But in the end, with a strange compulsion to repeat myself, I opted for the airplane again. I climbed in and, as the photographer with buck teeth and thick glasses held up his fingers, trying to get me to smile, I soared for an instant solo, breathless and alone.

Forbidden City

SOMETHING WAS WRONG with my body, I thought, returning to the hotel. Fatigue seemed to flow through my blood. A weakness had entered my bones. I felt as if I were wrapped in gauze, as if I were floating down a river. Perhaps it was the heat and the dust of summer in Beijing or perhaps something really was wrong. I brushed this thought aside. Probably I am suddenly growing old. I have reached that point where the bones ache, the spirit languishes.

I put on the tape of conversational Chinese and let my body ease onto the bed. An overhead fan whirred and I closed my eyes, with no intention of sleeping. But I slept, then awakened, startled to find myself in darkness, famished and ready to go out.

I went to a restaurant not far from my hotel. Many of the restaurants I had frequented in Beijing were closer to the center of the city. They were accustomed to foreigners and their menus were transliterated and in some cases translated. But the restaurant I walked into was not this type.

It had concrete floors, about a dozen round tables with dirty, institutional tablecloths. The kitchen, which was part of this main room, had huge boiling vats containing rice and soups. The air was hot and steamy. Then there were various woks and frying pans. The chef was a tall, skinny Chinese man who was missing his front teeth. When he laughed he smiled a somewhat maniacal smile.

As I walked in, I stepped on rice and bones tossed on the floor by previous clientele. Finding nothing smaller, I took a large round table across from a Chinese family. There sat a husband and wife, who never looked at each other but stared into their bowls as they shoveled in their food, a small boy who was just past toddling age, two ancient grandparents, one of whom seemed to gaze blissfully into space, and a few other assorted people whom I assumed to be members of the extended family. I watched as the men at the table sucked bones and spit whatever did not please them onto the floor. Their table was literally piled with food, dishes on top of dishes, and one of the men kept shouting to the cook to make more. When he did this, the chef turned to the family and laughed his maniacal laugh.

I sat down and was handed a menu by a woman in a dirty apron who did not look at me. I opened the menu to find it was entirely in Chinese. Making a silent vow never again to travel to a country where I cannot speak or read the basics, I pondered my dilemma. The proprietress returned, pencil and paper in hand, prepared to take my order. Not knowing what else to do, I began to point. I pointed at the table of the family beside me. "I'll take that," I said, "and that," indicating a dish that looked like chicken with vegetables, "and rice." I pointed at a few things until the woman seemed satisfied, determining this was enough for me to eat.

Once she was gone, I turned my attention back to the Chinese family. Now the father was helping his little boy eat his rice with chopsticks. Patiently the father showed him how to hold the chopsticks, how to pick up rice, which kept falling into the boy's lap, and the boy kept scooping up the bits of rice with his fingers, thrusting them into his mouth. The elderly parents were smiling, chatting. One of the men across the table kept shouting, laughing. Then the whole table, except for the one oblivious grandparent, burst out laughing.

Food was put before me, but I could not find the strength to eat. Instead I watched as the father repeated his chopsticks lesson to the boy and now the relatives laughed less as the boy began to learn. Feeling myself like an orphan waif, I wanted this family to invite me to join them, but when they did not, I raised my chopsticks and slowly began to eat. The chicken dish I'd thought I was ordering turned out to be pork, something I rarely eat. It also seemed that I had ordered sea cucumbers, those slimy creatures the Chinese love, half-animal, half-plant that slither in the mouth. I picked at my food.

A beggar woman came into the restaurant. I kept thinking the proprietors would shoo her away, but instead they ignored her as she went from table to table, plucking whatever she could off pushed-away plates and from the floor. She paused at the family beside me and the father shoved a plate her way. She scooped what was on it into a burlap sack.

She came to me. She began taking food from one of my plates, stuffing it into her toothless mouth. Her face was wrinkled and looked as if it were covered with ash. She kept her eyes on me as she took the food, the way a cat might do.

Then she pointed to my plates. With a wave of her hand, she asked if I intended to eat. No, I shook my head, motioning for her to help herself. She opened up her sack and I stared inside. I thought of China with a billion mouths to feed, and this old woman foraging for food. I signaled for her to take it. She dumped all that was before me into her gunnysack and I watched as it fell into the dark, fetid bag, then she ambled away, her sack over her shoulder, filled with the day's pickings.

That night back at the hotel, I could not sleep. I wandered down to the lobby and found a corridor I had not explored. Here I found a door leading to a Chinese garden, and I walked inside. There was a small pagoda filled with fish, and lily pads floating on top of the water. Fifty young Chinese, mostly male, stood around the edges of this garden. Suddenly the lights dimmed and a strobe light came on. I stood stark still as the Chinese began to stir, huddling closer, backs against the wall. The few women who were in the room wore short but traditional skirts, no makeup, their hair combed in long tresses down their backs. They giggled, turning their faces away. I had stumbled into some Chinese version of a mixer at a disco.

Now the music came on. Dire Straits sang "Money for Nothing; Chicks for Free." I longed to jump onto the floor and writhe. I waited to see if anyone was going to dance, but they all stood, backs to the walls, while the strobe illumined their faces, bewildered, as if under interrogation.

I HAVE DONE what I can to trace my ancestry. There are no real records. There are ships' logs, immigration records. These are the facts from what I can discern: My great-grandfather came from Gomel, a town in Byelorussia, and later he married and moved to the Ukraine, into the Jewish Pale, to the district of Chernigov, somewhere outside the town of Nezhin, where my grandmother was born.

The history of the Ukrainian Jew is miserable and long. In the pogroms of the nineteenth century millions such as my own family fled, migrating to Europe, Palestine, the United States. In World War II a million and a half were slaughtered, including most of the Jews of Gomel. But before these events decimated the Ukrainian Jewish community, the Jews had lived in Russia for centuries.

After the destruction of the First Temple (587 B.C.), Nebuchadnezzar deported Jewish captives to Armenia and the Caucasus. Others came during the period known as the Diaspora (600 B.C. to 200 A.D.) when the Jews were forced to leave their land, and they migrated into Egypt, Europe, south into Ethiopia and Yemen, and east to Babylon. From

Babylon some crossed the parched deserts of Iraq, traversing the harsh mountainous regions of Persia until they arrived in the Crimea, in Georgia and Kazakh. From the Crimea and from Kazakh they wandered north and west, making their way into the Ukraine. Here they lived apart in small communities and worked as merchants, tradespeople, or farmed the land as peasants, living within the confines of the Jewish Pale of Settlement, the district within which the Jews were required to live.

Once the Jews arrived in the Ukraine, their problems hardly ceased. Though there were intermittent periods of peace and prosperity, hardship was a way of life. In each century thousands of Jews were slaughtered in pogroms. Gomel—where my own family's history begins—was the town to which many refugees fled during the Chmielnicki massacres in 1648 in which over 100,000 Jews were slaughtered. But the Cossack armies reached Gomel and about two thousand Jews were massacred. Eventually Jewish settlements were renewed here. By 1765 there were 685 Jewish families living in the city, many of them, such as my own family, belonging to that sect of Jewish mystics called Hasidim.

Nezhin, where my grandmother was born, was a simple town, not much more than a village really, but it was one of the centers of the tobacco trade. During the Chmielnicki massacres, all the Jews of Nezhin were killed. I believe that was when my ancestors fled to Gomel, where my great-grandfather was born. Later he would return to Nezhin where he would raise his family. But in 1881 and 1882, the year my grandmother was born, pogroms broke out again. Twelve years later, in 1894, with persecution continuing and the promise of America before them, my family left.

My great-grandfather brought Lena first, by ship to Canada, planning to send for his wife and the other children once they were settled. They traveled in steerage for thirty days. Lena was sick for the entire crossing. She thought she would never see land again. Most of the elderly and infirm were buried at sea. But at last the boat docked in Halifax. My great-grandfather made his way to Chicago because he had cousins there. It would be a few years before the rest of the family could follow, arriving through Ellis Island.

It is everyone's immigration story, really—I have a friend, descended from Hungarian aristocracy, who wound up in the hills of Montana. In Chicago, a small but emerging city on a seemingly endless prairie, the winters were difficult and my great-grandfather tended to pray rather than work. With his wife and eight children he lived in two rooms in a cold-water flat.

What I know is what people have told me, people mainly gone now. There is one great-cousin named Bessie, a teacher who never married. She remembers names like Gomel. She knows that her father was sent at the age of sixteen to London. There on the eve of Yom Kippur he slept on a park bench. In the morning he cursed his god and never went into a synagogue again.

Later he sailed for New York. When he asked his brothers in America for help, they refused him because he had given up his religion. When he was struck on the head and went deaf, they did not help him.

Bessie will only talk with me on the phone. She is frail and doesn't want visitors. She has a fond memory of my mother who she says once held her hand as they walked through the 1933 Chicago World's Fair. But other than that, Bessie says, the family rejected her father, made him the black sheep because he would not practice his religion.

But most of what I know—and it is vague at that—is what I remember. The facts of history are less vivid than what as a child I was told. I have pieced together what I can. *Chernigov gibernia,* my grandmother said. The district around the city of Chernigov. And Nezhin, my great-uncle Dave said. It was there, he told me, that he buried the dog alive in the mud. He told me this laughing, out of control. The dog struggled, he told me, but we buried it alive. Everywhere there was mud, he said. We had a cousin, a Bolshevik in prison there, and every day, Uncle Dave said, your grandmother and me, we brought him food in jail and we had to walk ankle-deep (he pulled up his pants leg to show me) in mud.

IT WAS SUNDAY and Wong had reluctantly agreed to meet me for an hour or so at the Summer Palace. Wong, a thin, frail-looking man with fine, intelligent features, worked in government and helped make arrangements for foreign visitors. He had arranged the official part of our trip. We had met several times briefly but had struck up a friendship. He had an affinity for contemporary American authors and said he would like to spend more time with me. However, actually getting together proved difficult. There were many demands on him, he had too much work, and in the end I sensed a hesitancy on his part.

Still, we met at the entrance to the Summer Palace, that bucolic setting which had been the summer home of the emperors of China. It was here that the last emperor was sent when he was banished abruptly from the only home he had ever known, the Forbidden City, in 1924. But the Summer Palace was as open, fertile and warm as the Forbidden City was enclosed, sterile and cold. It felt as a Summer Palace should feel, and I was happy to wander its grounds for the afternoon.

Wong and I strolled the paths along the edges of the lake where little boats sailed. We walked across narrow, arching bridges and paused to peer at family scenes, photo opportunities where young girls posed in crinoline dresses, boys assumed karate postures in kung fu jackets, grandmothers wrapped arms around resisting grandchildren. Here Wong, who had been talking almost non-stop about Norman Mailer, Henry Miller, and other writers prominent in literature courses at Beijing University drew a deep breath. He continued walking across the little bridge until we came to a gazebo on the other side. There he sank into a bench, as our gazes both drifted to the family scene.

"I have a little boy," he said at last. We had not spoken in any personal way before so I took this as an indication that he wanted to open up.

"How old is he?" I asked.

"He's three. Do you want to see his picture?" He reached into his wallet and pulled out a picture of a bubbly, smiling boy dressed in a short blue suit. He clutched the hand of a woman whose face was not in the picture.

"He lives in Shanghai. With my wife and my parents."

This confused me since it did not sound as if they were separated. "You are apart?"

"Oh, not in that way. It is because of our work units. She is a doctor and her work unit is in Shanghai. Mine is here in Beijing. We have been trying to get her transferred since my son was born, but we had to wait. Anyway, if they are moved here, then we have an apartment problem as well. My apartment is only one room, so we might have to wait years, maybe ten years for a bigger space."

"You can't just go and work in Shanghai? Or she can't just come here?"

"Oh, no, it's not like that at all. You can't just move around. You need a work unit transfer."

"But separating families?" I tried to fathom what it would be like—to have a child, but not be able to live with it—but I could not.

"I feel lucky," he said. "Some couples are apart for many

years. I think we will be together again soon, but then there are other problems. . . ."

Across the lake a new family had arrived. Another girl in a crinoline dress, clasping her grandmother's hand. Another father with a camera. There was a boy in a suit and tie. The father kept motioning him back closer and closer to the lake for the picture. "He's going to fall in." Wong laughed, but a sadness had come over both of us.

"What other problems?" I asked.

"You see, my son lives with my parents. If my wife and I were both in Beijing, with no grandparents to care for him, and our work schedules were very demanding—she often works nights; I am often away—then he'd have to go to boarding kindergarten."

"What's that?" I asked, thinking I already knew.

"It's a boarding arrangement for small children when the parents are separated or have long work schedules and cannot provide adequate home care."

"How old are the children when they board?"

"Oh"—Wong thought for a moment—"well, when they are three or so. They might start very young. So this is better—he has my parents; my wife is there. . . . I think about this all the time," he said. "I'm never sure what to do. But I see them forty days a year and my son has his grandparents and his mother. The father is dispensable, no? . . ." His voice trailed off. "Still, I worry. Last week he fell down. He was injured. He had to have stitches in his head. I couldn't tell how serious it was from here. I was worried. I couldn't sleep. My wife said it was just a few stitches, but still it is my son, my only child."

He stood up and we began to walk around the lake again. "You Americans have such a different family life, don't you?"

"Yes, it is different." I could not bring myself to say more to Wong, whose mood had now grown somber as he watched family after family line up for a photo opportunity across the lake. "Are you pleased you have a son?"

He laughed. "I am pleased I have a child. We are not peasants, you know. We do not drown our daughters," referring to the alleged practice in remote parts of China of drowning female infants, due primarily to the fact that female children when they marry leave home for good whereas male children remain and work, so the females are not a good investment. "We are happy to have a son. We would be happy with a daughter."

"Would you ever consider having another child?"

Wong, a man of perhaps not more than thirty, looked at me, shocked. "Oh, never. It would be impossible."

"Impossible?"

Again he laughed. "Well, not impossible," his double meaning clear, "but in terms of the state it is not possible. The second child would receive no public funds, no schooling, no health care. We could not do it. . . ." He smiled a bit wistfully, "I have my son and I am happy with this. What more do I need?" The small boy in the suit had stepped into the edge of the lake and his parents were shouting and laughing at the same time. Wong seemed to have lost interest in this scene and he looked away.

I had been feeling a pain in my neck, a stiffness in my back, the result, I assumed, of too much time on the road. I also felt weak, the general malaise which I had tried to explain to the Chinese apothecary. I had been told that there was an acupuncturist in my hotel, so before going out for the evening I decided to go.

I walked into a smoke-filled room. A soap opera was on the TV and two men and two women, all in white coats, sat watching the soap opera. One of the men was smoking a Camel. In the soap opera a woman cried, shouting in Chinese. I paused and looked at the TV. The woman clutched a child, pulling it away from the man. The child was screaming. It appeared as if the man had struck the child.

The man smoking the Camel pointed at me and spoke, waving his cigarette in the air. Hesitantly I pointed to my neck, my shoulders. He nodded. I showed him I was having trouble moving my neck—a problem of inner vision, a mystic had told me once, though I prefer to attribute it to an old injury from a fall from a horse. I was also fatigued and under stress.

I looked at this man more closely, for I was about to entrust myself to him. His greasy hair was slicked back, his face pockmarked. There were bloodstains on his jacket. Smoke encircled his head. I wanted to explain to him that I am lonely in this country where I do not speak the language; that my companion of many years is soon to be en route to Sri Lanka via New York and I am taking the train in search of my ancestral past, which, given the news and recent events, may never again be as it was. I cannot tell him of the weakness I feel in my body—the sense that I cannot complete this journey alone.

He motioned to the table and told me to lie down. The sheet was stained. Again there was blood. The man in the next bed groaned as needles went into his feet. I wanted to run screaming out of the room. The acupuncturist puts out his Camel and has me lie on my face. He sticks needles in my neck, my heels, into my shoulders. I am gripped with a sudden fear of needles in my eyeballs, my tongue. The pockmarked man heats bowls on a Bunsen burner. These he will cup on my back. The woman in the soap opera screams. Her child cries. Tears come to my eyes, but I cannot wipe them away.

THAT EVENING I met an acquaintance from New York, a professor of world politics who was teaching at Beijing University. We met in his austere dormitory room, consisting only of a desk and cot. Then we went to the cafeteria, where students sat poring over their books, shoveling food into their mouths with chopsticks. Some were milling about, speaking, but most were studying and even in the cafeteria there was a sense of Chinese seriousness.

The professor himself was Asian. I told him of my meetings with Chen Bao earlier in the week and my afternoon that day with Wong. He leaned forward and spoke to me very frankly and softly about China. "I came here with a very positive outlook," he said. "I was very, very pro-China, but it just doesn't work. The system is a failure. It contains the worst of capitalism (the old imperial order) and the worst of communism. The worst of capitalism because it is so class-conscious, so hierarchical. Rank is all that matters here—the cadre system, the work unit and so on. And the worst of communism because the Chinese want to exert complete control. The politics in everyday life is terrible here." He glanced around to see if anyone was listening before he continued to speak. "A student cannot come to my office without permission from his chairman. The chairman must know what the student wishes to discuss, when, where, why." He ran a hand wearily through his dark hair. "It just isn't working. And," he leaned ominously toward me, "I think it will get worse. I think we haven't seen the half of it yet."

He was, I thought, a somewhat cynical man. He had suffered some personal setbacks of late and I felt then that they were affecting his perspective. "But what about all the economic reforms?" I asked. "The attempt at a market economy. And what about what Chen Bao told me—how things are much freer?"

"Only to a point," he said, shaking his head. "And then you'll see. It will all change. It won't go any farther than that. It is a precarious balance here."

Late for a performance of the Chinese acrobats, I left him early, feeling a bit depressed by what he'd said. Then I hailed a cab. The cab stank of cigarettes and the man had deep tobacco stains on his fingers. But he was fairly young with slicked-back hair. I had been practicing my Chinese with tapes so I decided to try a conversation. "How are you?" I asked him.

To my surprise he replied, "I am fine. And you?"

"Good," I said.

"Where are you from?"

"New York," I told him, "America."

He laughed and smiled.

"You speak Chinese," he said.

"I am studying," I told him.

"Oh, that is good. That is very good."

The lights of Beijing went by and I felt lightheaded for the first time since I had been alone in China. It was as if I had suddenly found the Rosetta stone, deciphered the enemy's code, broken some terrible silence. A sadness came over me, for just as I was about to complete this phase of my journey I was beginning to feel at home.

Still, I was at a loss. I wanted to talk with this man more. To learn what his life was like. To ask questions, but I had exhausted my meager reserve of this arcane vocabulary and once again the Chinese became for me inscrutable. He dropped me off in front of the theater. "Enjoy our acrobats," he said. He waved as he drove away.

Just as I found my seat, the lights dimmed and there, in

the darkened, almost empty theater, I watched the acrobats. Women folded their bodies together like Siamese
twins in and out of each other, like lovers bending until one
became the other, legs and arms interlacing like vines. A
man shaped his body so that it fit through loops so tiny
that only my arm would have fit through. Another man
stacked glasses filled with colored liquid, one after another,
on top of his nose.

Act after act performed feats that appeared impossible—
not the kind we are accustomed to, such as doing back flips
or flying through the air. Here the movements were what I
had come to anticipate of the Chinese—controlled, exquisite, and in a certain sense pointless, yet perfectly learned.

Then came the one who amazed me most, the woman
who balanced the seven porcelain bowls, which she moved
from head to feet to her back and her shoulders while per-
forming acrobatics, gliding in and out of position like a
snake, on the head of her partner who did nothing but hold
her aloft, eyes in a fixed stare upon her during the entire
act. The acrobats, I knew, had spent their entire lives learning how to bend limbs, intertwine bodies, balance the
bowls, or even to stand perfectly still.

I was transfixed by the woman with the bowls, her
steady, reptilian movements, and her partner motionless below her. This was what they had trained for. This was all
they could do. I thought of China and the delicate balance
my friend had spoken of. How precarious it suddenly
seemed. The woman moved assuredly bowl to head, to feet,
to shoulders, to nose, but one false move and it would all
topple. I thought of my own precariousness, how fragile
life seemed. How far away from everything I was, not only
in distance but in feelings and time. Love itself was a kind of
a delicate act that could not be done alone; it was nothing
without the bowls.

MY GRANDMOTHER'S FATHER was a man named Isaac whom I have seen in pictures. A man with a long, dark beard, a sturdy body and, I am told, piercing blue eyes. For a living he peddled a cart of notions—shoelaces, pins, needles, buttons. When he was not working, which was most of the time, he prayed. He was, my mother told me, a handsome, austere, distant man.

His wife, my great-grandmother who had buried her children alive, was Chana Raisel, who bore him eight children, including three sets of twins, which does not include the many who died. In the old country they lived in a hovel. In Chicago, where they'd gone because of cousins on Chana Raisel's side, they lived in a flat with two bedrooms. On Saturday night Chana Raisel heated a tub of water and once a week they bathed.

Because Isaac peddled and made little money, his children went out to work. By the time they were eight, or nine, or ten, they were working in the sweatshops and factories and lumber mills. From the time she arrived in America, my grandmother sewed pillows in a sweatshop, as did the other girls.

Chana Raisel stayed at home and slaved. When she died, an exhausted, bitter woman, Isaac married again, a woman he was wedded to for twenty-six years, eighteen of them during my own mother's life. Her name was "she." "She" never came to my grandmother's house because "she" was a stepmother. His children never forgave him for marrying again and it was said he only married her for her money. On the Sabbath when Isaac visited his children, "she" was never allowed.

"She" had a store that sold penny candy, and pickles, rice, beans, flour and coffee, all in barrels. When my mother went there, "she" gave her candy which my mother remembers quite well—mint drops, cinnamon sticks, red licorice—but no matter how hard I press her, my mother cannot remember this woman's name.

When Isaac died on the Sabbath, "she" did not cry. Isaac lay dead in the back bedroom while "she" lit the candles for Friday night and served the Sabbath meal to her own children, for my mother's family never went to her house. And then when the sun went down on Saturday, "she" tore her sackcloth and mourned.

Women, my mother said when she told me this story, lived terrible lives. They were abused, but who would listen. They suffered, my mother said, but whom could they tell.

THOUGH THE FACES of travelers were different, the Chinese International Travel Services office seemed the same as it had a few days before—a sign I did not find encouraging. The Chinese bureaucrats were still shaking their heads, muttering, shouting *"Mali, mali,"* and exasperated tourists were waiting, pleading, slamming fists into counters as if in some orchestral syncopation. But I did as I had done before. I stood in line, voucher once again in hand. When I reached the front, perhaps an hour later, the same nervous bureaucrat I'd seen the week before shook his head. He passed my voucher from person to person. Everyone shook his or her head. Finally I was led into the maze of rooms in the back of the Travel Services, but still no one seemed to know where my ticket was. Every question was greeted with shakes of the head, shrugs of the shoulder, backs turned. Now I knew that I would never see Russia. I would never get on the train.

I left in utter despair, about to burst into tears, when a Chinese student accosted me. He had crooked, overlapping teeth and thick glasses. "Do you like Chinese food?" he spat. "Are you married? There are fifty states in the United States, including Alaska and Hawaii, and only twenty-nine provinces in China," repeating as a litany the lines all Chinese students who want to practice their English say.

It occurred to me that perhaps he could help, and so as a last-ditch effort I explained my problem to him. He listened intently, nodding from time to time. Then he grabbed me by the arm and dragged me inside. He was a man with a mission as he led me to the front of the line, shouting in Chinese in the same way the bureaucrats had been shouting. A man who was picking his nose stopped, looked up, stared at me. He shouted something back, then pointed to the door that I now knew led to that maze of corridors and stairs in the bowels of the Chinese International Travel Services.

I followed him as he raced up six flights—I counted them again. He led me into the office I had been in the other day. The man was still practicing his tai chi, the woman still reading a novel, as if this were some time warp from the previous week. He shouted at them. The woman shouted back. The man stopped doing his tai chi. The shouting went on for a moment, then it became more polite. The man who was doing tai chi nodded, listened, then went off.

He was gone for a long time. The Chinese student kept telling me to be patient. "No way out," he said. "No way out." I began to pace. "You must be patient," he told me. "You've got an altitude [sic] problem," he said. I tried to sit and make conversation with him. "I want to go to America and study," he said. "I want to eat pizza and watch American TV." The thought of this only sank me into deeper despair.

"There are other things to do in America," I said.

"Like what. Tell me and I'll do them."

"You can drive around the countryside. You can go to the beach. There are many museums." I sounded like a Sunday school teacher, but he hung on to my every word, not because what I was saying was interesting, but because he was trying to translate. "You can visit the Washington Monument. Visit the Statue of Liberty." I was beginning to grow homesick and had almost forgotten what I was doing there when suddenly the clerk returned, a green-and-pink ticket flapping like a captured bird in his hand. "Here," he said. "Your ticket."

I stared, reading, "Peking-Moskau via Erhlien." I thanked him. I thanked the woman reading the novel, I found myself walking out of the room kowtowing, like some forgiven erring scholar.

Outside, I thanked the student profusely. "Oh, no thanks," he said over and over, beaming through his crooked teeth. "My pleasure. No thanks."

Then on a whim I offered to take him to lunch. "Maybe we can find a pizza," I blurted, but then I saw that I had made a mistake. Somehow I had insulted him. "Oh, no. No need." His pride was injured. He walked away from me now backward. "I go back to work. You are welcome."

"You can practice your English—" I called to him, but he was gone.

IN THE THIRTEENTH CENTURY, having easily traversed the Great Wall and conquered the North China plain, the invaders from the north decided to build a great city. On the site of the old Ch'in city of Chung-tu, the great Mongol leader Kublai Khan spread out the parameters of his palace which would be its centerpiece. The Mongols would call it Da Du and the Chinese Ta-Tu (Great Capital). Later, after the Mings threw the Mongols out, it would come to be known as Peiping, Northern Peace.

It was here that Kublai Khan built the great palace for himself which Marco Polo describes in his writings. Marco Polo tells of thick walls stretching a mile on each side, whitewashed and fortified. Of a game park between the outer and inner walls where white harts and musk deer roamed, ponds where the animals drank, paths where the Khan might walk. There was the Green Mound where the Great Khan had hundreds of evergreens planted and the mound covered with lapis lazuli. He speaks of walls bedecked with pictures of dragons and birds and horsemen, of a dining room that could seat six thousand, of a roof ablaze in scarlet, gold, blue and green, varnished like crystal.

And then Marco Polo talks of inner chambers, passageways leading to private apartments where the great stashes of gold and silver were kept, as well as the ladies and concubines. Yet he writes of these rooms only from hearsay. Even under the Mongols these rooms were impenetrable. No one was allowed.

Then in the fifteenth century the Mings threw off the Mongols and transferred their capital from Nanking to the improbable place of Ta-Tu which soon was called Peiping. On the site of what had once been the palaces of Kublai Khan, the Ming ruler, Yung Lo, set his palaces. From that day until the early part of this century, imperial China was ruled from within the walls of the Ming Palace, which most people refer to as the Forbidden City.

The palace was built according to the laws of geomancy, enabling the power of the Emperor to radiate out in the four directions as if he were himself the sun. Yet within its thick walls the rulers of China reigned in virtual isolation, true to the contradiction that is its name, for how can a "city" be "forbidden"? Hardly anyone penetrated the moat and the four concentric walls that enclosed the Emperor. If he left the palace grounds to venture to the Summer Palace, it was by night in a covered palanquin.

From its cloistered corridors under the Mings to the virtual prison it became for the last Emperor of China, the boy ruler P'u-i, who was abruptly hurled overnight from the only home he had ever known out into the world, almost no one saw the emperors of China except for their eunuchs, which came to number some seventy thousand, their concubines and immediate family. From within the walls the emperors of China controlled one of the greatest countries on earth, isolated, protected, and alone. And then at the end of the civil war between Mao Tse-tung and Chiang Kai-shek, after Mao proclaimed victory on October 1, 1949, the gates of the Forbidden City were thrown open for all to see.

I walked through the Wu Men Gate, the Meridian Gate, into the entrance to the Tzu Chin Ch'eng, the "Purple Forbidden City," which was once considered to be the heart of the capital, the empire, indeed the world, where, according to ancient Chinese texts, "earth and sky meet, the four seasons merge, wind and rain are gathered, and yin and yang are in harmony."

It was called the Purple City, purple referring not to a color, but perhaps to the polestar, indicating that the Emperor was the central body around which everything on earth evolved. Confucius himself allegedly wrote, "He who exercises government by means of his virtue may be compared to the north polestar, which keeps its place and all stars turn toward it."

Inside this Forbidden City, as if within some chiropractic holistic view of the self, the Chinese envisioned themselves in balance with the world. I needed only set foot within the once sacroscant walls to feel its sense of balance. According to legend, when Yung Lo first arrived at his future capital a famous astrologer handed him a sealed envelope containing a plan for rebuilding the city according to strict geomantic principles, with every major structure representing a part of the body of Lo Cha, a mythological figure. Indeed, passing through the city feels as if one is moving through a symmetrical, balanced human form.

I walked the Imperial Way, across the Canal of the River of Golden Water, toward the Hall of Supreme Harmony, across the marbled terrace and down the steps toward the Hall of Complete Harmony and the Hall of Preserving Harmony. Recalling the cruel and unharmonious history of this country from its first ruler Qin to the Cultural Revolution, the names seemed like wishful thinking. But to the Chinese this was the center of their universe, the place where balance was supposedly kept. Along this axis from the Emperor's throne his divinity and benevolence were extended to all the reaches of the realm. Just as the God of Heaven dwelled in the Purple protected enclosure, so the Son of Heaven dwelled in the Purple Forbidden City.

Chinese tourists gazed impassively at the throne of their Emperor. Some held their children up to see. There was not the crush I had grown accustomed to in the streets of the cities of China. It was more awe and disbelief. This was very un-Chinese to me. But this was the first time I'd experienced the Chinese in the face of authority. So rooted is it in their culture that this city is closed for only the Emperor, his eunuchs and concubines to see, that they moved through it as if they expected to be ousted at any moment.

I found myself stunned before the expanse of walls, courtyards, terraces reaching more than half a mile, whose marble was carried from the Burmese border on the backs of elephants. The main buildings existed on the central axis with the lesser buildings laid out asymmetrically around them. At the far end were the Palace of Heavenly Purity where the Emperor lived and the Palace of Earthly Tranquillity where his Empress had her chambers.

I walked among the pagoda-like structures with their red tile roofs with the steep pitch, jutting edges and upturned corners. Gazed into the faces of carved stone owls and dragons representing the imperial virtues, and at the fantastic carved creatures poised at the edges of roof gutters to drink.

Yet I was perhaps more captured by the space, the open expanses, than by the buildings themselves. For here I could imagine the Emperor being carried up the Imperial Way in his palanquin by his bearers. Or making his traditional New Year's Day appearance.

I continued through the open promenades into a maze of alleys, sequestered walks, private passageways. I came upon a Chinese couple secretly kissing at a secluded fountain. They saw me and turned away. Yet I was struck by the impersonalness of it all. There was no sense of the people who had ruled here. No trace of Kublai Khan, or Yung Lo or Ch'ien-lung. The past seemed obliterated. Each dynasty had made way for the next. Each ruler was hemmed in by the mandates of his office and by his own debaucheries. It felt as if no one had ever lived here, yet here the Son of Heaven dwelled, never leaving the walls of the Purple Forbidden City. He existed without a single view of the city of Peking or of the people over which he ruled, such was his isolation.

I sought the more secluded paths as I made my way from palace to palace, through corridors, across terraces, down steps leading to fountains where concubines had played the lute, into apartments where eunuchs had served their aging consorts, into the bedrooms of princes, the throne rooms where the emperors of China had bestowed their grace or handed out their punishments in this now vast museum. I thought less of the art objects before me—the golden lions, the ancient scrolls, the gilded furnishings, the jade figurines and silver vessels—than I thought of the intrigues, the passions, the cruelties and loves.

I moved somewhat uneasily through the sacrosanct walls as if I could overhear a plot being hatched, a conspiracy unfolding. I recalled the stories of the hapless concubine who had pleaded for her emperor in the midst of a coup, only to find her own self hurled into the depths of a putrid well. The story of the suspecting general, asked to guard the palace in the Emperor's absence, who had castrated himself, hoarding his testicles in a safe place so he might meet his accusers with his grim innocence. Now all this history, from the Kublai Khan to the present, was stored in this rather sterile museum that the Purple City had become.

As I crossed bridges, moving from palace to palace, the words of Coleridge came back to me, a poem I had not read since college. "In Xanadu did Kubla Khan/A stately pleasure-dome decree: Where Alph, the sacred river, ran/ Through caverns measureless to man/Down to a sunless sea." While Xanadu was really Shang-tu, the summer palace of Kublai Khan, the poem seemed applicable here. And as the poem had come to Coleridge in a dream, so the words came back to me: "A savage place! as holy and enchanted/ As e'er beneath a waning moon was haunted/By woman wailing for her demon-lover!"

Sitting on the steps between the Palace of Heavenly Purity and the Palace of Earthly Tranquillity, I stared at the ring on my finger. Ten days before, I had stood at another sacrosanct place, the Jokhang Temple in Tibet, the seat of Tibetan Buddhism. With my companion I had visited the temple. On the outside, monks in red robes, heads shaved, lay prostrate on the ground, praying, groveling. Inside, the temple was lit with candles sitting in red glass, casting a reddish light. The whole temple seemed to be bathed in a warm glow and the smell of incense was intoxicating and sweet.

We had walked among the monks praying to the Buddha of the Yellow Sect, the Buddha of the Red Sect, the Buddha of the Past, the Buddha of the Future. Some looked at us tentatively, some with fear, for we had a Chinese escort with us. But I managed to separate myself from this escort for I saw how uncomfortable the Tibetans were with his presence and then they looked more relaxed, smiling, and I moved through the temple feeling transported, wanting to kneel, myself, in that fetal-like yogic posture called "pose of a child," but containing myself from doing so.

Outside the Jokhang Temple a flock of women gathered. Tibetan women draped in turquoise jewelry and brightly woven cloth. They pushed beads, amulets, earrings, baubles, necklaces and rings in my face. They were laughing as I began to barter with them. One woman caught my attention. She had jet-black hair pulled back, revealing her clear, glowing, burnished skin. She had playful dark eyes and a turquoise pendant dangling down her forehead, a red-and-blue shawl tied across her shoulders. She seemed to be about my age.

I examined what was extended. An amulet with a dancing woman inside, a long strand of coral beads, another amulet with an emblem that seemed to represent the sun. For one, she indicated with her fingers thirty yuan. I shook my head, held up all my fingers, twice. "Twenty," I said. We made a deal. We did this several times until I had made my purchases for the day.

My companion, who had gone off to buy small buddhas, returned and we thanked the women, waving good-bye. I had not walked far when the woman with the playful eyes came back to me. She opened my hand and put a blue turquoise ring in it. I shook my head. She thrust the ring onto my ring finger, smiling knowingly at me and my companion. "No," I said, shaking my finger. I felt his hand touching my shoulder. She pointed to the ring, then to the both of us. But she put her hand firmly around mine, closing my hand into a fist, then she squeezed it, pushing my hand and the ring it wore away from her. She smiled, as I tried once more to refuse what I now understood to be a gift. She put her fingers to her lips to shush me.

Now I sat alone on the steps of the sterile Imperial Palace, thinking how different this felt from where I'd been ten days before. No one had come to sell me her wares, to barter with me playfully. No one had put a caring hand on my shoulder. Here I imagined myself engulfed in some palace intrigue, some unfortunate liaison. I was a concubine whose time had come. Or perhaps an aging eunuch in the service of some idle consort, without prospects, knowing I would live out my days loveless and alone. For a moment I thought I could pick up the strains of a lute, but it was just the wind whipping around the palaces. I thought of the wailing woman crying for her demon-lover. If I listened, I could hear her cry.

A PEKING DUCK DINNER in an old Chinese restaurant was advertised for tourists in my hotel and, wishing to celebrate my imminent departure for Russia, I signed up to go. I had brought one traveling dress and one pair of heels with me for such occasions and I dug these out of my duffel. The dress, which had been buried for several weeks now, was wrinkled but it would do. I hung it up in the bathroom while I showered. The steam made it look better. I combed my hair, put on a little makeup and then slipped into the dress.

It was a snug-fitting dress that zipped up the back and while I did not feel I had gained weight, it seemed a little tighter than usual. I was thinking about this as I began to zip it up the back. Distracted perhaps for a moment, I let the zipper snag. It was about midway up my back in an awkward place, and I tried again but it would not budge. I tried to pull it up, then down, then up again. I tried to move the fabric aside and force it, but it was stuck. I tried to take it off my shoulders and shimmy out, but I was immobilized there, like a madwoman in a straitjacket as I turned this way and that, determined to be free.

I thought I would remain caught there forever. Whom could I call for help? Would the woman at the front desk understand my plea? Whom would she send to rescue me? The thought of this made me more determined. Like the Chinese acrobat who worked his way through the loops, I willed my body small and managed to crawl out of the dress that had entrapped me. I caught the bus to the restaurant just as it was pulling away.

The entrance to the restaurant was a courtyard across a small fish pond, and we tourists made our way inside. Our hostess, dressed in a traditional Chinese gown, greeted us. The restaurant was in a pagoda-like design with a drop roof and the raised corners. We were seated at a large circular table and we introduced ourselves. Our group was an eclectic one. An English human rights activist sat to my left and a body builder from Chicago to my right. Across from me was a man from New Zealand flanked by his two dowdy daughters. The man from New Zealand loved Reagan and wanted to discuss him with me during the meal.

I turned to the body builder from Chicago, who wore a Zen symbol around his neck. He was huge and his shoulder mashed against mine. "I'm from Chicago," I told him; "I grew up there." He had been traveling in Asia for over a year. "I can't wait to get back and eat Gino's pizza and coconut cream pie and Cap'n Crunch with bananas," he blurted. I wished I could introduce him to the Chinese man who had helped me procure my rail ticket. I turned to the West German psychologist who immediately began to speak of his trip down the Yangtze and the several bodies he'd seen floating there, "all puffed up and blue."

A waitress brought in our first course. Sesame chicken feet (only the skins) and marinated sea slugs. I tried to pass, but the offerings were automatically placed on my plate. A nice Jewish couple from Santa Cruz sipped the wine happily, saying it tasted "just like Manischewitz." The body builder from Chicago was talking about his Zazen training, how the monks come and hit you. A woman and her husband to my left kept shaking their heads. He was a chemist and she a Chinese scholar. She kept shouting orders to the waitress in what sounded like pig Latin and had the waitress running around in a frazzle. She said the Chinese call her Purple Horse. She was very proud of this, but she was a very large, ruddy-looking woman and I could see how the name applied.

The English human rights advocate turned to me and began speaking, for reasons I do not understand, about disastrous human practices such as sharia, the Islamic practice of hand amputation, and the Tibetan habit of chopping up their dead and feeding them to the vultures. As the duck was brought in the Englishman said, "You know, it became such a tourist attraction that they had to stop it. The monks got so angry that they were chasing the tourists around with people's guts."

"I'm sick of Asia," the man from New Zealand said. "Give me America any day. America with Ronald Reagan, that is," looking at me for some agreement, but I was moving the sesame chicken feet around on my plate. Purple Horse kept shouting in Chinese for more sauce, more rice. Whenever she bellowed, the staff went into a flurry.

In the evening when I returned to the hotel, Wong was waiting in the lobby, a guitar resting between his knees. He had come to say good-bye. I had a gift for him, because he had been so helpful in arranging our trip. It was a wool blanket I had purchased at the friendship store, where Chinese cannot shop, knowing that blankets were very dear in China and winters could be cold. "Oh, no," Wong said, "I cannot accept this."

"But you must."

"Oh, I cannot. I cannot. I have neglected and abandoned you. I have not spent much time with you. I was preoccupied with many things. No, I cannot accept."

"But you must. Send it to your wife. For your little boy."

He seemed more tolerant of this idea, but remained mired in unnecessary guilt over his neglect of me. "Next time I will spend more time with you. I will show you more of my country. I will accompany you to Hungzao."

"That would be lovely. I would enjoy that," thrusting the blanket into his hands.

"I thank you for my wife and family. I thank you for my son."

"It has been my pleasure."

"I consider you my friend," he said. "I will do anything I can to help you."

"I consider you my friend, as well."

Finally he took the blanket. Then he opened his guitar case. "I wanted to sing you a song. For your departure," he said. And he sat down and with a thick Chinese accent and a rather tinny sound to his guitar, Wong sang for me. He sang many verses, and I applauded tearfully when he was done.

The next day, my last day in China, I rented a bicycle. When I went for coffee in the morning, I had spotted a small bicycle shop off Jianguomenwai Avenue and people bringing bicycles in for repair and rental. Unable to communicate a single word, I pantomimed again with my hands. I held out money. The man took it and I was off.

First I rode through residential streets to test my skill

before entering the throng on Jianguomenwai. Women doing their wash held up babies, who waved at me. Men squatted by the side of the road, smoking, spitting. I rode past people's houses, their gardens, their laundry. People shouted as I went the wrong way down a one-way street. I rode on like a deaf-mute until I crashed into a man with a bike loaded down with live ducks. He cursed me under his breath, the ducks squawking.

Now I crossed over to Jianguomenwai Avenue, joining the crowd riding in the direction of Tiananmen Square. I joined the steady stream of the men and women in their navy blue suits, their Mao jackets, others in shirt sleeves, girls in cotton dresses. I rode past the Beijing Hotel until I came to the square and there I rode out of the mass that carried me along and paused beneath the huge poster of Mao, founder of Chinese communism, hero of their revolution, author of their darkest hour.

I pulled up against a wall and stopped. I watched as toddlers ran, their faces covered in red gauze, couples held hands. Old people, perched on canes, sat in the shade. It all seemed so peaceful this warm June day as if nothing could go wrong here. It was hard to remember that this was the same people who in the 1950s set out to destroy their birds who were eating too much grain. For a period of twenty-four hours, the Chinese beat tin cans and blew whistles so that the startled flocks would find no place to rest, and millions dropped from the sky, dead of heart failure.

It had seemed when I read this the way a perfect metaphor in a poem feels, just right, summing everything up. But now I was not sure. I had seen the streets of China pulsing with life, carts laden with live chickens, eel cutters ripping the spines out of live eels. In the streets I had eaten boiled eggs, ices, watched children race, sparklers in hand. And I had peered into the eyes of men in Wuhan in a dormitory of straw mats with their eyes bulging like fish I'd once seen whose tank water had boiled.

I had also peered into the remnants of the cruel history of this land. The prison at Chungking where the defeated Kuomintang as they were leaving burned two hundred prisoners alive. And I had sipped tea, listening quietly to the tales of the Cultural Revolution. I could not help but feel ignorant as I stood beneath this poster of Mao, this entrance to the Forbidden City, in Tiananmen Square; there on June 3, 1986, China's fate seemed as inscrutable as the faces riding before me.

Suddenly the wind picked up. The sky darkened. As I gazed to the north, I saw coming toward me a thick yellow cloud like pudding. I had never seen anything like this and it frightened me. People began scurrying, seeking a wall, a corner to protect them. Bikers hurled their bicycles down. They covered their faces. Some pulled their coats and sweaters over their heads.

It was the yellow loess dust from the Gobi, a storm of dust which worsens each year as the desert grows closer and the evil of the North approaches. Before I knew what to do, it was striking my eyes, my face, my throat. Blinded, I groped for cover, but I was caught in the middle of the great Tiananmen Square. I staggered toward a wall and there beneath a tree found some shelter from the wind. Others huddled beneath branches, faces hidden in their hands. I pulled my sweater over my head and waited, still as a statue, until the dust storm passed.

Then suddenly the dust was gone, as quickly as it had come. I got back on my bicycle and rode once again with the throng that, it seemed, had never stopped moving.

Across the Gobi

TRAIN TRAVEL for me is the fictive mode. Trains are the stuff of stories, inside and out. From windows I have seen lovers embrace, workers pause from their travail. Women gaze longingly at the passing train; men stare with thwarted dreams in their eyes. Escapist children try to leap aboard. Narratives, like frames of film, pass by.

On the inside I have had encounters as well. I've met people who have become briefly, for the length of the ride, a lover or friend. A strange and sudden intimacy seems possible here. On the Puno-Cuzco Express through the Urubamba Valley of Peru I met a man I thought I would follow across the Andes. On the night train from Chungking a woman stayed up half the night telling me the story of her life. On an Italian train I met a woman who pleaded with me to go to Bulgaria with her, saying she knew it was where I needed to be. I've been invited off trains into homes, into beds, asked to walk into people's lives, all I am sure because people know a train traveler will never leave the train.

My life even as a little girl was intimately tied to trains, with those fast-moving machines that raced across the Midwestern plains. When I was five, my parents concocted a train journey to Idaho, a family vacation at Sun Valley. My father was not with us on that ride. He would be joining us later, flying in after a meeting, coming for a short spell, his vacation time always being trimmed like lean meat.

So it was my mother, brother, and myself in our tiny compartment, my mother a frazzled woman, alone with these children on a long train ride, lonely I think, but dedicated, as mothers were then, to us. She didn't get angry about the toothpaste flushed down the toilet, the small suitcase that kept falling on her head. She wore lipstick and a blue dress and high heels to dine in the dining car and secured our water glasses with glove-covered hands as the heartland sped by. My mother's agenda was London, Paris, Rome, maybe Hong Kong, but we were en route to Boise, Idaho.

So I escaped and sat, hour after hour, beneath a glass dome, staring at the light over the cornfields. I sat—a dreamy, somewhat forlorn child of five whose father had too much work to do, whose mother was left with the unwelcome task of ushering us to a place of horses and duck ponds—watching the stars coming on like city lights, until my mother retrieved me back into the warm womb of our cramped compartment. Here I kept my eyes open, peering into the night at the passing towns, at the dark expanse of prairie, through a turned-up corner of the window shade as the world as I knew it receded and we moved into the West.

In the morning before daybreak I made my way, still in my night clothes, back to the domed car, to await the rising sun. Slowly it came as the train sped, never changing its pace, and the light opened on the plain. There before me suddenly stood the white peaks of mountains. I had never seen a mountain before and these shimmered—their glacial caps sheathed in sunlight—against the endless blue sky and the flat, green Midwestern plain from which they rose. There on that Union Pacific Railroad, carrying these reluctant travelers to our indeterminate destination, the mountains came upon me as my first truly complete surprise—the way the remarkable events of life have come upon me since.

As the train hurtled to those mountains, even my mother, as she came wearily to find me and try to coax me back to our compartment, paused for a moment in awe.

In the high-ceilinged, dark-wood waiting room for the Trans-Siberian Express, Chinese Muslims, the women with veils over their heads, sat on sacks of bulgur and rice. European students studied their travel guides or slept on their duffel bags. Eastern European diplomats in dark navy suits and shirts with frayed collars milled close to the doors. The noises were those of train travel. Announcements in Chinese blared overhead through static speakers. Anxious travelers—bound for Ulan Bator, Moscow, Warsaw, Bucharest, Belgrade, Berlin, London, and some even for Mecca—checked their watches or bid their good-byes, though there was none of the frenzy I'd seen at the Chinese International Travel Services office.

I sat on my duffel and went through my papers as well. My ticket, Mongolian transit visa, Soviet visa. Everything seemed in order as I leaned into my duffel, once again suddenly overcome with fatigue as if I had sunk there never to rise again. But suddenly the doors to the waiting room were opened and a surge went through the travelers as we headed like an obedient flock for the door.

I moved slowly from the rear, dragging my duffel behind until I passed through the doors onto the platform. There it stood. An army-green train with perhaps a dozen or so cars, circa 1950, "Peking-Moskau" on its side, Chinese porters in red caps standing at each car, ready to show us to our cars. I stood amazed and thrilled.

I made my way to carriage number 3 where a very tall, very un-Chinese-looking porter, who would take care of our car for the entire ride to Moscow and who spoke enough English and French to make brief conversation possible, took my duffel out of my hand. He led me into the first compartment on that car. Dropping my duffel on the lower berth, he wished me a pleasant journey.

I stared at the lace curtains, the small lamp, the writing table with lace tablecloth, the chair, the small sofa that would convert into a bed. On the advice of a friend I had purchased a deluxe ticket, as opposed to first-class. First-class consisted of a hard bed and four people in the compartment. Deluxe was a soft bed and two people in the compartment. For six days, at a cost of two hundred dollars, I knew I had made the right choice.

I tossed my duffel overhead, pulling out just what I'd need for the day—the copy of *Anna Karenina* I'd planned to reread, my journal, some snacks, and a toothbrush. Then I inspected the compartment more closely. The sofa felt relatively comfortable and I thought that it would make an adequate bed. I opened the door to the semiprivate bath which consisted of a hose shower and a sink, so that at least I'd be able to bathe instead of taking what I'd come prepared for—Wash n' Dri sponge baths.

I sat down at the small table by the window. Travelers scurried outside. Porters helped them with their bags. My porter brought me a pot of tea and said that the samovar was always hot.

I breathed a sigh and settled in. I was opening my journal when Cecilia arrived. She sported a full pack and a loud Liverpool accent. "So here we are. We're roomies. Isn't this great!" She dumped her pack on the floor, hurled a few things onto the top bunk. She was large, a dishwater blonde with square features and a boisterous voice. In a matter of moments I learned that Cecilia was English, living in Singapore with her second husband and her two children, having marital problems, and also, she hinted, an affair. "Going to London," she said. "I needed a break."

I predicted rather accurately that Cecilia would not stop talking for the entire six days and that I'd learn more than I ever cared to know about her, her private life, her feelings for the royal family, her politics, and that if I wanted to think or rest I'd have to work my way around her, which did not seem very easy in an eight-by-six-foot room.

I got up to stretch and Cecilia took the seat at the table by the window, facing the direction in which the train was traveling. There she planted herself for the rest of the trip where she'd sit with her tea, her rock 'n' roll tapes, and the snacks she'd eat all day long, never seeming to have a meal.

I left the compartment and stared out the window. Soon there came a whistle, a brief announcement in Russian and Chinese. The wife of a Yugoslav diplomat who had the compartment next to ours stared out the window as well. When she heard the announcement she turned to me and said in English, "Now we are leaving." She gave me the only smile I would see on her face the entire trip. Suddenly the whistle came again, piercing and more insistent this time, and in a matter of moments I felt the tug of wheels, the power of engines as the journey began.

I found a jump seat at the window. I pulled it down and sat there for a long time. I watched as the residential streets of Beijing drifted away; the stream of bicycles receded, then disappeared. Rice paddies came into view. Farmers in broad-brimmed straw hats bent, legs in upside-down V's, planting in the sodden fields. Oxen pulled plows across the yellow-earth fields. I was oblivious to the other travelers, all with noses pressed to the glass, until someone shouted, "the Wall, the Wall." There it was, snaking across the mountains, crumbling here and there, careening down a ridge, only to rise again; the Great Wall of China wended its way like a mythological beast, fortified and useless against the ostensible fears. Then slowly it diminished until it was only a thin line, like a crack in the earth. And then it was gone.

I GUARD my grandmother's naturalization papers in a vault back home. But I made a copy which I carry with me on this trip and these I hold in my hand as we leave the Wall behind. In the same vault I keep her wedding ring, which I am intended someday to wear. It sits wrapped in tissue with its beveled edge, its interweaving pattern that could be leaves or pebbles on a beach; I often stare at it, trying to decide. How this ring came to me is somewhat by default. My only other female cousin, Marianne—who in childhood was like a sister to me, but now, for various reasons which have little to do with us but rather with family feuds, we do not speak—was married before my grandmother died in 1973. That is how the ring came to be mine.

Often when I go to the vault, I slip it on. It is odd how it is a perfect fit. Sometimes I want to wear it when I leave the vault, but always I put it back in its tissue, locking it away, believing that the right time will come.

I cannot look at the ring or at the papers that I keep there without thinking of a picture I have of my grandmother, an aging bride at twenty-two. In 1904 she was robust, austere. In the picture she is unsmiling, something rare for her, and there is already a middle-aged thickening around her waist.

I do not believe she wanted to marry. She wanted to be a dancer, she told me once, twirling around the room, and dance with the Bolshoi. Never mind that the Bolshoi only came into existence after her family had fled or that Jewish girls could not be dancers then. Or that her petite, buxom frame was not what one traditionally associates with Russian ballerinas. My grandmother wanted to dance her way around the world.

Instead she married a redheaded man with a fiery temper and a sad, complex history, named Zimberoff, though the "e" was dropped when a sign painter couldn't fit all the letters over my grandfather's saloon door. At twenty-one my grandmother was an aging bride. Her marriage was an arranged one of convenience, though over the years affection would grow between them. He would bring her flowers, usually to make up for his erratic outbursts such as hurling plates or slamming his fist into a wall. They produced three redheaded, fiery children, my mother being one. My grandmother was widowed suddenly at forty-five and would live more years than that before she died, but she never married again. When he died, my grandmother—who had held parties on Friday night and sewn and lit fires on Saturday—suddenly kept the Sabbath. For reasons no one ever understood (guilt, my mother said), my grandmother began to pray. But she didn't seem to mind her solitude, even when blindness made her doubly alone.

My grandmother was a lady. In her later years, even into her nineties when she was crippled with arthritis and could barely see, my grandmother would get dressed up and take the bus to Marshall Field's whenever there was a sale on pistachios. She wore white gloves and a veil. Hardened bus drivers would descend from their buses to help her board. Often they refused to budge until "the lady" was given a seat.

People said Lena had psychic powers. She was said to predict births, calamities, deaths. The day of my grandfather's death a picture of Little Bo Peep he had hung on the wall collapsed. It was a picture the family hated, for Little Bo Peep had foreshortened arms and played a banjo. My grandparents had fought over it. At lunch my grandmother looked at the wall. "The picture," she said, "the picture," moments before it fell. When her husband died that evening, my grandmother said she knew.

I believe she knew what was happening to me without my telling her. Though the family guarded secrets from her for years (she never knew for instance that two entire families of relations hadn't spoken for years, except when they sat at her table), I felt she knew everything there was to know about me. Even though she is long dead, I feel this is still true.

When she married, she became a citizen of the United States. Her naturalization papers declare that Morris Zimberoff (my grandfather) is no longer under the sovereignty of the Czar of Russia. Only on the back of the document does my grandmother's name appear. She was his chattel, my mother explained. In those days, she told me, a woman belonged legally to her husband and all legal matters were in his name.

There are family members who can tell me more of the things I long to know but many, even as I try to research, won't answer my letters or return my calls. We have been split apart by personal rifts, contested wills, assorted griefs. My father's nephew and my mother's nephew went into an ill-fated business venture years ago. My father had to settle their differences in court. People stopped speaking. People who grew up in the same house will not say hello in synagogue. Only Bessie, in Brooklyn who will tell me what she knows. But Bessie is almost ninety and what she knows is mainly grief. She tends to repeat herself as she complains of the way the family treated her father, my grandmother's uncle.

"They ignored us," she said. "They never paid us any attention. Once, in 1933, my family went to the Chicago World's Fair. I remember your grandmother. She was beautiful then. She had a nice laugh. Your mother held my hand as we walked. Then we didn't hear from them again. There was a girl living in Boston who my niece tried to contact. She never called her back."

"I was the girl in Boston," I said. "I never got the message."

"That's what they all say," Bessie says with a sigh.

Before I left, I called or wrote everyone I could. No one answered my calls. Cousin Harvey, who keeps the family tree, didn't respond. Now I travel with what is left of my past, my grandmother's naturalization papers in my hand.

I think of the dinners at my grandmother's house when forty or fifty people would eat steaming bowls of soup, roasted chickens, specially baked breads. Now the only keeper of these recipes is my grandmother's failing, alcoholic maid. I always think I will call to get these recipes. That I will learn to bake those sweet meats, those sugary

rolls. I imagine for myself a household full of guests, relations now reconciled. The people who inhabit my world,
both living and dead, are ghosts.

When holidays come around I go to films, buy tickets for
shows. Sometimes I go to synagogue for memorial services,
wondering what I am remembering, for whom it is I
mourn.

THE DINING CAR looked more like a Chinese laundry
than a restaurant—noisy, frenzied, boiling hot. Warm Chinese beer was being handed out and I grabbed one from a
passing tray as everyone else seemed to do. The car was
packed and I saw no seats, but then Pierre, the French saxophone player I'd met at the Mongolian Embassy, waved
from across the room, pointing to half a seat. "So," he said,
putting an arm around my shoulder, "you made it." He was
sitting at a boisterous table of European travelers—Swiss,
French, German and Dutch. They were all speaking assorted European languages, though French seemed pre-
dominant. When I joined them they switched to English
but I told them French or German was all right.

A small fan blew overhead, the kind a secretary might put
on her desk, but the heat continued to rise. Everyone was
sweating. Plates of delicious fried meats, sautéed vegetables,
rice, were being passed. "Open the window," Pierre
shouted in French. Someone who spoke broken Chinese
shouted the same thing. The soaking waitress ignored our
pleas. Someone opened a window and the cook went wild,
screaming in Chinese, slamming it shut. "Dust," he yelled
which someone translated, "dust." We drank our warm beer
and ate hot food as we baked in the sun.

The heat did not let up and felt close to a hundred and twenty at times. None of the Chinese porters would permit windows to be open. "The desert," our porter explained to me. But finally in our car protests were mounting. At last he let us open the windows in our individual compartments if we kept the doors shut. Cecilia had gone to the dining room to sit, for I don't believe she actually ever dined, and left me alone at the open window, dust blowing in my face.

The landscape had altered. From the farmlands and rice paddies we moved into a mountainous, more arid terrain as we crossed the Northern Chinese province of Inner Mongolia. Though we had yet to reach the desert, a scrub grassland reached to the horizon with occasional sheep grazing. I sat as the day shifted to evening and the heat subsided.

At eight-forty that evening we reached the outpost of Erhlien, the border town between Inner and Outer Mongolia. It was the gateway to Russia, Mongolia being a Soviet protectorate. The station was old-fashioned, like something out of the American West—a small, wood-slat structure. Chinese border guards came onto the train. After checking our passports and visas, they told us we could leave the train.

I stood on the platform, breathing the cool evening air. It was unclear how long our stop was, but to my surprise and almost fear, suddenly they took the train away. I watched as it receded, disappearing behind us. The Chinese Muslim men smiled benignly, but the Europeans seemed dismayed. Then I recalled the words of a friend who'd taken this trip before. "At the borders," he'd told me, "they take the trains away." They have to change the wheels because the track has a different grade, which in part makes international hijacking impossible across Asia and Europe. Also they take the train away because each country has its own dining car and now for Mongolia the new car must be attached.

I was happy to leave the train and walk in the cool night air. It was a lovely night now and a full moon shone overhead. All the travelers went into the station house, but I walked the platform. Chinese Muslim men strolled, but their women were nowhere in sight. In fact the Chinese Muslim women would never leave the train. They would not be seen in public. Instead they remained in their compartments, facing Mecca, eating from the giant sacks of food they had brought and cooking on small portable stoves in their compartments. I always knew where East was and roughly the time of day because the Muslim women would be facing East at specific times.

I went into the station where a small postal service was open. I bought stamps and began to write postcards from the border of Inner and Outer Mongolia, to many people seemingly the most remote place on earth, though in fact it was fairly accessible. I bought a bag of stewed apricots and a warm orange soda from a small stand. I sat in the station on a wooden bench, writing cards while border guards patrolled around me and a bolero of bullfighting music played incongruously on the overhead speakers.

On the platform an hour or so later, I ran into the Chinese Muslims I'd sat next to on the floor of the Chinese International Travel Services office. We greeted one another like long-lost friends. They laughed, happy to see me, and pointed to my pen which remained in my hand. One made a sweeping motion as if to wipe sweat off his brow, indicating how hot they had been. Then they pointed to the yellow moon over Mongolia, clasped their hands as if in blessing, and smiled.

At about midnight the train returned with new wheels and a Mongolian dining car and we crossed into the People's Republic of Mongolia. The temperature had dropped considerably and it was actually cool. I grabbed a sweater from my compartment. Then after perhaps half a mile the train stopped and Mongolian passport officials boarded. They had wide bronze faces, reminiscent of the indigenous peoples of America. Some theories of human migration say that these ancient Central Asian peoples crossed the Bering Strait and were the first inhabitants of the Western Hemisphere, the people from whom all the Native Americans descended.

But now their being part of the police state was clear. The train was thoroughly searched. Beneath bunks, overhead racks, suitcases were moved aside to search for contraband. Then, at 1 A.M., they left and we entered Mongolia.

I found I could not sleep so I wandered to the darkened new dining car, which, with arching windows, scalloped seats, red curtains, looked more like a mosque than a dining car. Pierre was sitting with two Dutch girls. The Mongolian dining crew—a man and his wife—were already setting up for breakfast. They worked noiselessly in the background.

Pierre ordered a bottle of Mongolian vodka and poured drinks all around. The man, who wore a small, brightly colored skullcap, and the woman, with a scarf around her head, both with sharp Mongolian features, wide, flat faces, brought glasses out and joined us. They raised their glasses and we raised ours. Then we sat in the darkened car, watching the beginnings of a moonlit Gobi rush by, drinking Mongolian vodka into the night.

MONGOLIA, the homeland of Genghis Khan and his grandson, the great ruler Kublai Khan, is a land of towering snow-capped peaks and forests with rivers, streams and lakes. But it is hemmed in by a wall of mountains in the east, the west, and the north that prevents precipitation, and the Gobi Desert, to the south, is the result. Suitable for neither a pastoral nor an agricultural economy, it is almost lifeless. Its heat is unbearable in the summer. Piercing winds and snow make it miserable in winter. Only a few humans and sturdy animals can survive this inhospitable land.

In the morning, just after five, I woke in a cold and dusty compartment. By my breath alone, I could tell that the terrain had changed. Bending back the shade, I peered at half a million miles of golden sand. As if in some time warp, two men in motorcycles raced across the dunes. But then camels and yurts—those large, round nomad tents, the same color as the desert, in which the wandering traces of the warrior race still dwell—appeared. They were infrequent but they were there, camels blending into the sand, the round yurts in which Mongolians had been living for millennia.

It was not long before sand filled the air of the train, covering our pillows, our belongings. A fine golden dust seemed to settle on everything. The porter would not permit any windows to be opened as the heat of the day grew and we baked like prisoners of a sauna. Cecilia could not bear it and she staggered to the dining car where she would remain for the morning. I munched on a breakfast of melba toast, sardines, V-8, transfixed by the emptiness beyond, longing to get off the train. I imagined a horse awaiting me. I fantasized my yurt, a caravan, me munching on yak meat. I had a desire to flee across the great Gobi flat. I pondered the life I'd left behind—no job, one cat, good friends, devoted family, a questionable companion who it seemed was always on my mind. It would all be there, I reasoned, when I returned.

In the thirteenth century Genghis Khan, whose original name was Temuchin, which means "ironworker," unified groups of nomadic tribes that roamed the Gobi Desert and began one of history's most remarkable military conquests. His father, the chief of a small tribe, was poisoned by an enemy and at the age of thirteen Temuchin became the leader. According to *The Secret History of the Mongols,* a Mongolian epic written in the mid-1200s, Temuchin and his family lived a harsh, miserable life as herders of a few head of livestock, digging roots for food.

But soon Temuchin began to attract followers. He built an army using rigorous training and discipline, and eventually created a superb fighting force. He ensured that his troops were well equipped and he appointed officers on the basis of achievement, not family connections. In this way he made his officers loyal to him. Temuchin used his army to extend his power and by 1206 he was ruler of all Mongolia. That year an assembly of Mongolian chieftains proclaimed him Genghis Khan, a name which means "limitless strength."

In 1211, with 100,000 fearless horsemen, Genghis Khan penetrated the Great Wall of China and conquered a million people. Drafting thousands of Chinese engineers and technicians, he then swept through Central Asia into Persia, through the mountains of the Caucasus and into the Russian steppe. Mongol cruelty on these campaigns was legendary. They were said to carry baskets on the sides of their horses into which they put the children they stole, which they would then sell into slavery in the markets of Turkey. Once they executed resisting Russian boyars by placing a platform on top of their captives and then proceeded to have a banquet on it, crushing them to death.

Whatever the truth of these unsavory tales, neither Russia nor China would ever be the same again after the two hundred years of Mongol rule, beginning in the thirteenth century. Genghis Khan established, and his grandson Kublai Khan consolidated and ruled, the greatest empire the world has ever known. It stretched from Korea to western Russia across its northern latitudes, from Burma to Iraq on the south, and from the Arctic Circle to Canton. The Mongol armies, the Golden Horde, swept from the Ch'in capital of China to Hungary and Poland.

In their conquests they razed once beautiful cities, burned churches that contained great works of art, destroyed libraries that contained all the literature up to that period. They killed and enslaved mercilessly. They abducted women and smashed sick children into trees. Yet their empire, which stretched from the Pacific to Poland, brought Europe and Asia into contact for the first time, helping to unify the vast country that was then the unknown territories of Russia and paving the way for modern-day foreign and economic policy.

With the death of Kublai Khan in 1294 came struggles for succession. The empire dwindled back into tribal conflict, wandering bands. However, invasions of the Tatars, successors to the Mongolians, continued to ravage Russia into the fifteenth and sixteenth centuries. As late as 1571 the Crimean Tatars raided Moscow, killing as many as 200,000 people, carrying off another 100,000 into slavery.

Then in 1691 the Manchus conquered Mongolia, reducing the Mongols to serfdom and poverty for two hundred years until 1911 when Mongolia declared itself an independent state. However, Mongolia's independence would be short-lived. Neither China nor Russia would ever forget the havoc Mongolian rule wreaked on their countries. Mongolia would become a political pawn in the hands of its neighbors until finally, earlier in this century, it became a Soviet protectorate, which it remains today. Now it is a country of collective farmers and herders working on Soviet-style planned farms, and of civil servants. Outer Mongolia is thought of only for its remoteness. It is not a place travelers think of with interest. But for a time, the Mongols ruled the world.

□   □   □   □

At midday we pulled into Ulan Bator. Located some nine hundred miles from Beijing and a staggering three thousand seven hundred more miles from Moscow, this capital of Mongolia looks like a Moslem city, bespeckled with mosques and houses with scalloped windows, domed roofs, and arching doorways. Yet plunked down in the middle of these, like the legs of storybook giants, were Soviet-style apartment complexes on the outskirts, government buildings at the center. Despite what I'd heard about the train being locked in Ulan Bator, we were free to descend.

On the platform, to my surprise, Soviet police—blond, enormous in knee-high leather boots, with tight-fitting green uniforms—patrolled while russet-skinned, broad-faced Mongolian women dusted the tracks with colorful green or purple feather dusters. Some of the women wore hats or white scarves tied around their heads. Their dresses were dark. Dirty aprons were gathered around their waists. On the fringes of one of the world's great deserts, scarred with hundreds of miles of sand-laden track, this feather dusting seemed rather futile and I found myself amused at what appeared to be some Soviet-contrived scheme to ensure full employment.

I wanted to take a picture of the women, who were oblivious to me and intent upon their work. But when I raised my camera a Soviet guard materialized, out of nowhere it seemed. He put a finger across his face. *Nyet,* he said. I put my camera down. I crossed to the small station house. On the other side there was a small park. Pigeons fluttered. A Mongolian child in a kind of Chinese suit, trapped between two cultures, toddled. I was about to enter the park to sit for a moment in the shade when another guard emerged with the same practiced finger across his face and slowly I backed away, toward the train.

I ran into Pierre. He had purchased a small loaf of bread from a stand near the train. "Lunch," he smiled, holding it aloft. With his Swiss Army knife, he cut into the bread. Dead beetles lay inside.

Some passengers were leaving the train at Ulan Bator where they'd stay about a week, until the next train arrived. I watched as they lugged their duffels, happy to be getting off. A beaming father and son waved good-bye. A bevy of European students offered tiny salutes. Other passengers sat on duffels, bleary-eyed, waiting to board.

I wanted to be among those who were leaving. At that moment I decided I had planned this trip all wrong. As a traveler who had always followed her impulses, I had gone wherever the bus would carry me, but this trip had clipped my wings. Soviet travel must be preplanned, prepaid. You can't just get off the train on a whim and show up next week. But now I felt encaged by my journey, and I wanted to leave.

Standing on the platform as the whistle to board came, I rationalized. My journey had a purpose, a destination, a place I longed to be. Next time I'll make all the stops. I'll do it differently now that I know how. Still, I felt like a Chinese Muslim woman, a captive of the train.

My mood was gloomy as I returned to our compartment and found Cecilia and her newly found friend Janet munching on biscuits and tea. Janet was also English and thinking about moving to South Africa, a place Cecilia had lived. "You know," Cecilia said, "the Africans are like little children. Of course they should rule, everyone knows that. But they need to learn how. You have to teach them everything."

"Oh," I said, sitting down, "I imagine, like most people, they could learn quickly."

"We had a woman working for us once and every day we had to show her again and again how to put the dishwasher on."

"I never get those things right either," I said.

"Well, they can't just take over the country," Janet blurted. "That's obvious."

"Now, I'm against apartheid, just like everyone is," Cecilia said, "But you can't just take it away like that."

I shrugged. "Why not? We freed the slaves like that, not that blacks have fared very well in my country, but for other reasons. . . ."

"Well, in South Africa they are little children and you have to teach them over and over again" Then Cecilia leaned toward Janet, "You know I've never told anyone about this before, but . . ."

I grabbed a book and journal and headed for the dining car, the only place on the train to escape to. It was fairly empty, it being after lunch, and I took a seat by the window, feeling suddenly old, stodgy, trapped in an itinerary, something I'd avoided all my life. But then as we started to roll I could feel the movement of the train, the motion of the wheels. We passed a village with a giant sign of a hammer and sickle, and Lenin's face carved into a hill. A small herd of camels grazed at its slope. A Soviet lorry bounced across the dunes. Now I pressed my face back to the glass, thinking of what might await me, and how, if nothing else, there was the motion of this train to carry me along.

Pierre came into the dining car and joined me for a late lunch which the chef reluctantly prepared. We ordered kefir, sourdough bread, Mongolian borcht, a cabbage stew with some kind of broth and to my surprise it was all delicious.

"So," he said, finishing his soup, "tell me, what's your story?"

"My story?" I laughed.

"Sure," he said. "Everybody on this train's got a story. I think yours might be more interesting than some."

I told him I was traveling on a magazine assignment—which was partially true—to find my childhood home which was thirty miles from Chernobyl and that all in all it seemed like an ill-fated trip.

At the word "Chernobyl" he shook his head. Then he paused. "That's not the real story."

I laughed, knowing he was right. "Well, tell me yours first and then maybe I'll know what to say."

"All right. I have three daughters. Twins by one woman and another by a second woman." He was smiling. Obviously he had delivered this information before. "And the girls are all the same age."

My eyes widened. "Do they know about each other?"

"Oh, we're all great friends. The kids all play together. I baby-sit for them all the time, except since I've been away."

"For two months . . ." I reminded him.

"I needed a break," he said. "Now you tell me. What is it? Are you running away? Is it a secret you carry? Unrequited love?"

"All the above," I said. "You choose."

"Is there somebody in your life?"

I thought about where he would be right now. Perhaps on the tennis court or with friends eating Chinese food. This was the longest we had ever been out of touch. I have no memory of not speaking with him for more than two days. "Yes," I said softly, "there is somebody in my life."

"So what's wrong?" he asked.

"Nothing's wrong," I said. "I wish he were here, that's all." A wave of homesickness came over me. Perhaps a letter would be waiting in Moscow. Perhaps I would have some word.

Pierre pursed his lips. "So why isn't he?"

"He had other things to do," I said.

Gathering up my books, I told him I was going back to my compartment. I needed to rest. When I returned, saying I was tired, Cecilia and Janet got ready to leave. It was a rhythm we established. Except for sleeping, we were hardly in the compartment at the same time if we could help it. I settled down, my door open, with a book I had been meaning to read. An anthology of Soviet writers. I had not been reading for long when the wife of the Yugoslav diplomat, whose compartment was near ours, came into my room. "We are approaching the Soviet Union," she told me. "I'd tear the cover off that book if I were you."

I turned the book over; Aleksandr Solzhenitsyn stared me in the face. I opened the book and skimmed the contents. Pasternak, Mandelstam, Solzhenitsyn and others—exiles, dissidents, or dead in Stalin's labor camps. I looked back to say something to the diplomat's wife, but she was gone. I couldn't bear to tear the cover off the book. Instead I read for a while, then hid it on a shelf above the bathroom, hoping they wouldn't look there.

Digging into my pack, I pulled out *Anna Karenina* and a Rachmaninoff tape which I put in my cassette. These, I assumed, would offend no one.

I fell asleep and dreamed troubling dreams. I dreamed that I am on the Trans-Siberian Express with my mother and my companion. There has been a flood and the train is forced to stop. My mother, assuming it will be a long wait, wanders off in the Siberian forest. My companion lectures two attractive women on global matters. My mother is lost in the dark woods and the train is about to leave. I plead with the engineers, with the conductors, but they will not wait. My companion says it is her fault for wandering off. I say it is her fault for marrying you.

The meaning of the dream was rather obvious and I woke distraught. I was shivering and the landscape had shifted again. We were in grasslands now, rolling foothills approaching the Siberian woods, the forest primeval. But for now buttercups and bluebells graced the rises. The Gobi was gone and it was as if spring had come while I slept. But now we faced—and were unprepared for—the freezing Siberian nights, which even in June would be icy cold. But despite the cold and the disturbing dreams an excitement came over me, for Russia lay not that far ahead.

Why did I care for a land I've never seen, for a country I knew only through stories? What had made me determine, despite the odds, to go on with this journey alone?

All my life I've listened to stories. As a little girl, the only way I ever got to sleep was by listening to the stories my father made up: "The Brook and the Bridge," "The Lady and the Pumpkin," "The Littlest Snowflake." Stories which to this day forty years later I can recite by rote. My girlhood was dull in suburban Illinois. Only gossip and tall tales kept us going. Superstition abounded. The evil eye was everywhere, transported by my grandmother who spit into the air or shouted insults to keep it away.

My grandparents grew up in the land where their spirits dwelled. They grew up with their own place myths. My family's life, though I am now far removed from its history, has been one of exile and banishment. They brought nothing with them from the old country except what they could carry and a few memories and tales.

But my life has not been that way. I do not live in the place where my spirits dwell. I have to make this up as I go along. My gods and demons, my nurturers and detractors, the pranksters and mischief-makers, the goblins and good faeries, the witches and caretakers, the ones who see us through and the ones who disrupt our lives, I do not live in the land where they dwell. I am orphaned, disenfranchised, removed. A *desdichada,* a Jew, a lost one, searching for my clan. I have not been able to find my mate, my place. Like most Americans I dwell far removed from the source—in deserts where no one knows where we've come from, in cities where no one cares. Like the ghost of a restless soul, it seems I must search until I find what I am looking for—community, family, the place to belong.

Meanwhile I dream. Joseph Campbell has written that in the absence of myths, we dream. If myth is our collective dream, then the dream is our potent individual wish. The emphasis on dreams in modern Western thinking reflects our alienation, our singleness, our non-communal lives.

We live alone. Our families are elsewhere. We wander from city to city, from man to man. I have never bought sheets for myself. I sleep on those I left home with at eighteen. Like so many Americans at night, with no one to talk to, I dream and I tell those dreams to the few friends I think might understand.

At eleven o'clock, with little fanfare and no time for musing, we reached the border with the Soviet Union. Suddenly I heard the sound of clomping boots on top of the train. Loud, stomping noises. Voices shouted in Russian. Doors and compartments were opened, then slammed shut. Without being told to, the Eastern Europeans had already left their compartments and stood with rehearsed indifference in the corridors of the train. It was 1986, just at the beginning of glasnost, and while change had begun, it would be slow.

I climbed to the shelf above the bathroom and ripped the cover from the book of Soviet writers. Then I dropped two packages of Marlboros which I'd brought for such an occasion onto my bunk.

Guards came into the compartment. Half were Mongolian. The others were large, blond Russians. I had planned to hand them the cigarettes, but they motioned for us to leave. This had not happened before. From the corridor I listened to the sound of beds being lifted, suitcases pulled down. The wife of the Yugoslav diplomat looked at me askance.

Suddenly they left, as quickly as they had come, and we were told we could exit the train where a small money exchange was open and we were to purchase rubles which we would need from now on in the Soviet dining car which would soon be attached. I fumbled through my things, about to leave, when one of the blond Russian guards returned. He shut the door behind him. I had no idea what he wanted to do. He leaned forward and I thought he was going to kiss me. Instead he pointed to the cigarettes, which I gave him. Then he pointed to my Walkman, which I did not want to give him.

Instead I slipped it onto his head and turned on Rachmaninoff's First Piano Concerto with Van Cliburn playing. He closed his eyes and swayed back and forth like an agitated elephant, swooning in another world. Then he hesitated, returning the Walkman to me. I was grateful for this. I took the tape out and slipped it into his hands. Rachmaninoff, I said. Pressing it to his heart, he smiled. "Thank you," he whispered and the next thing I knew he was gone.

At the money exchange, I ran into Pierre. "Meet me in the dining car for a drink," he said, his breath forming a cloud in the cold Siberian night air. It was 1 A.M. when they brought the train back with its new wheels and dining car and he waved to me as he leaped on, his car separated from mine by the dining car.

As the train crossed into Siberia, beneath floodlights and a freezing black night I tried to make my way to the dining car. But the door was locked. I pounded and pounded, for I was accustomed to being able to pass through whenever I wanted. From its forbidding darkness, moments later, the door was flung open.

A huge, walleyed old Russian peasant in a soiled apron sat in complete darkness, a bucket of potatoes at his feet which he was peeling. *"Nyet,"* he said. He was vintage Dostoyevsky, I determined, and had simply walked out of one of those novels that had held me spellbound in my youth. *"Nyet,"* he repeated, slamming the door in my face. It was late and who was I to argue. I left the lonely potato peeler with his wandering eye to his darkness as the train zipped, faster it seemed than ever before.

I went back to my bunk, cold as could be. I could see my

breath inside. Cecilia snored beneath the layers she had put on and I dug into my duffel for a flannel shirt and an extra sweater, which I would wear all night for several nights to come. But I did not care. I felt something remarkable lay ahead, like the surprise Fabergé always put inside the great imperial Easter eggs—a peacock sitting on a golden tree, a horse-drawn coronation coach, a gliding swan, the face of child, a rock crystal carved into a frosty design. Or perhaps a miniature twelve-car train that could pull, made to work by a tiny key concealed within the magical egg. I lay awake all night, thinking of what surprises lay ahead as the train carried me into the ancestral homeland, the first of my kin to return.

Mother Russia

IN EARLY TIMES the men of Novgorod marched into the remote lands beyond the Urals again and again, never to return. The legend grew that only Alexander the Great had ever succeeded in crossing the "Iron Rock," as the Urals were called. It was said that he forded an icy sea until he came to a land with inhabitants who ate carrion, corpses, and all kinds of filth. The people of Novgorod called this race the "Yugrians," which meant the "impure," for they were warlike, heathen and vile. If guests came, it was said that they carved up their children and served them on a plate. When one of their tribe died, there was no burial. There was a feast instead.

So Alexander prayed to God to free the world from such monsters. God heard his prayer and bade a great rock to close before these impure tribes. He left one single copper gate in the great rock and this gate he locked and bolted, to be opened only on Judgment Day. Behind this gate, sealed with a lock from heaven, lay a land of ice and snow, a rugged terrain of primordial forests and pathless bogs, the place of abandonment and exile that we have come to know as Siberia. Perhaps derived from a word referring to the ancient Huns or Savirs or perhaps from a Mongol word, *Sibir*, meaning the sleeping land, bounded on the north by the Arctic, the east by the Pacific, the south by Mongolia and China, Siberia is all the land east of the Urals, the Asiatic dominions of the Russian Empire.

For centuries the world beyond the iron gate of the Urals was shrouded in mystery and superstition, until in the early sixteenth century an ambitious and clever man named Anika Stroganov, along with his sons, began sending out expeditions across the mountains to bring back the fur of an ani-

mal called a sable, distant cousin to the mink. The sable is
found nowhere else on earth, except for the Russian
steppes. The fur of this creature was believed by one foreign
diplomat to be the Golden Fleece that the Argonauts had
searched for. Just as the conquest of the American West—a
more romanticized and slower process—began with gold,
so the conquest of Siberia began with fur.

Besides fur, Anika and his sons discovered salt, precious
to Moscow, and a land fertile for growing corn. He told
the Czar he believed precious minerals would be found in
the mountains near Perm. He spoke to him of gold.

The Czar Ivan granted Anika and his sons a twenty-year
lease over five and a half million acres. With a faulty map
and a lease to land the Czar did not own, the Stroganovs
set out to explore and consolidate the Siberian terrain.
Here they found a land of salmon- and pike-swollen rivers,
of luxurious furs—beaver, ermine, black fox, and sable—of
mushrooms from which entire fortunes would be made, of
forests so dense and sinister even the bravest could become
disoriented there.

In order to consolidate their territory, the Stroganovs
put together a reserve of men who had had their falling out
with the laws of Moscow. They were vagabonds, robbers,
escaped peasants and condemned murderers, the very riffraff
the Czar had specifically forbidden in his lease to the Stroganovs. They called themselves Cossacks, these first Russian
citizens of Siberia. Forming a kind of Robin Hood band
under their leader, Yermak Timofeyev—a former pirate with
a price on his head—the Cossacks patrolled the lower Don
and became the conquerors of Siberia.

In 1580, armed with flintlocks and harquebuses, they
used boats and rafts to launch successful attacks against the
native peoples—the Voguls, the Ostyaks and Tatars, to
name a few—who were armed with only bows, arrows and
swords. They made war against the Siberian Khan,
Kuchum, who retreated to his capital at Kashlyk. There

Kuchum was defeated in October 1582, though he managed to escape. The Czar rewarded Yermak with a suit of golden armor, reinforcements, and a pardon for his past misdeeds and those of his men. But in 1584, the same year when Ivan the Terrible died, Kuchum returned, surprising Yermak, who slept in his suit of gold, on an island in the Irtysh River. According to legend, Yermak, who tried to swim to safety, drowned under the weight of his armor. To this day local inhabitants say that on the shortest night of the year they can see a golden arm rising from the waters, but if they reach for it, it disappears.

Under Yermak, Russia came to control its Asiatic frontiers. Under Peter the Great, exploration was carried further. Peter sent Bering off to explore the easternmost recesses of the land. Peter opened mines in the Urals for the mining of semiprecious stones. The unification of East and West, begun with the Mongol conquests, was completed under Peter the Great. By the seventeenth century Russia had consolidated its hold over that vast Asian land mass.

If, as it has been said, anatomy is destiny, then geography must be history. The land from the North China plain to the Urals was once mainly steppes, open and flat. Russians had already witnessed two centuries of darkness when the Mongols, united under Genghis Khan, swept without obstacle across the Russian land. Historically the Russians would always dread another sweeping attack from the east. Given their history with the Mongols, it made sense that Russia would want to consolidate itself to the east, hence the conquest of Siberia became essential to Russia's national security as well as to its economic policy. To this day if any two themes have marked Russian foreign policy they are Russia's isolation from Europe, as witnessed by its failure to report Chernobyl to its western neighbors, and an almost paranoid fear of invasion from the east, hence the strategic importance of keeping Mongolia a Soviet protectorate.

Stretching five thousand miles from the Caspian Sea to

the river Amur, Siberia's five million square miles presents (among other things) the largest expanse of pastureland in the world. Its steppes, or grasslands, seem to go on forever. Combined with the taiga and the other less dense and forbidding forests—about nineteen hundred million acres of forest—this territory is six times larger than the whole of Europe, not including Russia. All this made Siberia—a land so rich in sable that women fetching water could practically kill them with sticks—more and more desirable to Moscow.

The climate, however, is foreboding and renowned for its grimness. The peculiar climate of Siberia comes from the structure of its surface, unprotected from the keen cold air that descends from the polar tundra. Separated on the south from Central Asia by a barrier of snow-clad mountains, the Hindu Kush and the Himalayas, and essentially landlocked without much benefit from ocean currents, Siberia is shut off from mild winds from the south. It is dry, cold, windless, relentless, at least six months of the year. Its ground has been found to be frozen as deep as sixteen hundred feet and even in summer it never warms. This unyielding land proved itself to be rich in minerals and ores. For centuries men would be sent to Siberia for the most minor of crimes to work as slave labor in the mines or, later, to build the railroad upon which I was traveling. In the nineteenth century alone a million men were banished to Siberia. But it is the climate that has given Siberia its true reputation—as the place of desolation, of exile, of gulags. The place where you send people to punish them.

I woke to an icy compartment, frost covering the window. Cecilia seemed to have achieved some hibernating state and for hours she did not budge. I lay beneath all the layers of clothing I had—flannel shirts, warm socks, two pairs of pants—freezing under the thin blankets as the train whipped across the frigid Siberian plain.

All my life I had imagined this terrain, a country as much

within me as without, a landscape that seemed almost of my own making. I could not look at this land and not think about its history. And I could not think of its history without thinking of my own. We crossed frozen ground, ice-trimmed lakes. Peering through the open shade, I saw a world outside that seemed no different from the one I carried within. Cold, hungry, empty, and vast. We passed a little cemetery—each grave safely ensconced in a fence of its own, separating dead from dead. Even the Siberian dead were alone. A terrible longing seemed to come from the land itself.

Outside, a thick mist rose off the lake. Stocky railway workers in small villages, mainly women with picks or shovels in hand, red scarves around their heads, waved. Siberia was settled quickly mainly to protect the eastern frontier. Its boomtowns attest to this fact. Wood-slat structures, the kind you might find in the gold rush ghost towns of the California hills or on the set of a grade-B Hollywood western, lined the track. Functional, and barely that, they looked slipshod, thrown together, not much protection from the penetrating cold. Occasionally we came to a town of gingerbread houses, their scalloped trim painted in bright yellow or green, but most of the houses were drab, and when we left them behind to plunge once again into the dense poplar forests and fields of wildflowers, I was relieved.

The fatigue I'd experienced at various stages of this journey returned and I lay in bed for a long time, finding neither the strength nor the will to rise. Diagnosing it as travel fatigue, I decided a shower would make me feel better, but still I could not bring myself to get up. At last, forcing myself from beneath the thin army-ration blankets, I peeled the layers off and went into our small bathroom. Perhaps feeling Spartan, a delinquent member of some polar bear club, I made myself bathe beneath the hand-held hose which drained into a hole on the wooden floor, for the first time since I'd gotten on the train. I bathed what parts of me I could bear in water that was only slightly warmer than the air in which I stood. The dust of the Gobi swirled down the floor drain. Layers of dirt rushed off my skin. Drying quickly, I put my clothes back on and returned under the covers.

Crawling back into bed, I watched the Siberian landscape pass by. I contemplated the vastness of this land. Two and a half times the size of the United States, the Soviet Union reaches halfway around the world and is one sixth the entire land surface of the earth. My own rail journey, totaling some 4,600 miles from Beijing to Moscow, would cover only a fraction of its breadth. My vision obscured by the thick forest in which I found myself, I could only imagine the thousands of miles of tundra—those treeless northern plains where the ground is frozen solid all year round,—or the sweeping steppes to the south, with their endless miles of unobstructed grasslands. Even in the spring in which I journeyed, it seemed to be a miserable stretch of wintry tracks, broken only by abundant rivers and a few glacial lakes.

I do not know how long I lay there that morning, reading, sleeping, thinking about the land. Cecilia hadn't budged either. It was beginning to occur to me that she had died in her sleep when I heard her stir. Then I made my way toward the dining car.

Dimitri had been a waiter on the Russian dining car of the Trans-Siberian Express for fifteen years. He wore a black bow tie, a white shirt, a trimmed black mustache, and had a portly belly. He reminded me of a Viennese waiter who'd once served me an eclair at the Plaza Hotel. A kind of lethargy had seemed to settle over the train and the dining car was empty except for me. I had noticed as I made my way to the dining car that fewer noses were pressed to the glass. Cabin doors were shut. With a great flourish, Dimitri invited me to sit down.

The cook, who wore a gigantic plastic bag that stood straight up on her head—she would wear it for the entire trip—and the disgruntled dining car manager, her husband, it turned out, who was doing the books, didn't want me there. Breakfast was over. Lunch hadn't begun. A sharp exchange took place among them all. Igor, the old potato peeler who'd stopped my passage the night before, now stared dumbly among them all, looking more like a retarded child than the ominous figure he posed in the night. At last I spoke and they turned to me in silence and awe. I was Russian, I told them in a halting college Russian, one hundred percent. "My name is Marushka," I said, telling them my grandmother's pet name for me.

Dimitri was overjoyed. "A Russian! Yes, you have Russian eyes," he told me. A Russian face, he shaped his hands into a flower. The cook and her husband agreed. And later, when the cook and her husband had their backs turned, Dimitri indicated by making sweeping cups with his hands that I had Russian breasts as well.

He handed me a new menu which included chicken Kiev, beef Stroganoff, blintzes. "Oh, I'll have blintzes," I told him, already tasting those rolled pancakes stuffed with jam and smothered in sour cream.

Dimitri held his hands together and tilted his head. "*Nyet,* I'm sorry. We don't have them."

"Oh." It was almost noon and I was getting hungry. "Then I'll try the mushrooms and Stroganoff."

He tilted his head the other way, twisting his hands as if to plead with me. "I'm sorry . . ."

I put the menu down, smiling. "What would you recommend?"

Breathing a sigh of relief, "Oh, the cabbage is very good. And there is beef borscht, but perhaps you'll want that for supper." He made his recommendations as he would each day, and I would no longer embarrass him by ordering what was listed but unavailable on the menu. I ordered a breakfast of fried eggs, kefir, sweet cabbage, and bread with cheese and butter. Dimitri brought me a cup of sweetened tea. The cook rose with great ceremony to fry my eggs.

Dimitri asked politely after my husband as he served me and I told him I was traveling alone. He looked saddened, then he smiled. He had a son he adored, but his wife, he told me, waving his hand back and forth, was so-so. "Sometimes it is better," he gave me a reassuring pat, "to be traveling on your own."

As I ate, I stared out the window. We had reached the fringes of Lake Baikal, the great Siberian recreational lake near the city of Irkutsk. It was spring and along the edge of the lake wildflowers were in bloom, but outside there was a cold gray mist. People in boots fished along the pebbly shore or huddled before driftwood fires outside the shacks where the fishermen lived. I rubbed the frost off my windowpane so I could see.

As we made our way around the lake, women in babushkas, stoking the fires in front of log cabins and clapboard houses or pausing from their housework, waved as they shivered in doorways. I thought I could see my grandmother from the train. A lump of sugar resting in her mouth. She waves a feather duster, seeming to scold the wind. Her long skirt rises as if she can fly. The babushka flaps around her head. Sweetness fills my own mouth as I sip my tea and feel a presence float through the dining car. It is a freezing morning as I think of my grandmother, a little girl in the Ukraine.

I come from the Midwest, from the most suburban place on earth. I grew up with all the modern conveniences, 31 Flavors, the same set of friends. Streets were paved, the trees lush and green. Danger never crossed my mind. I have no memory of a night of fear. But my grandmother came

from this strange foreign place of mud-lined streets, Cossacks and pogroms. Her early years were years of hiding and
flight.

I never really knew her until I was in my teens and I never
became friends with her until the winter I was eighteen and
had embarked upon my first journey without parental su-
pervision—to Florida for spring break, hardly a momentous
trip, but I was on my own and I tried to forget that my
grandmother was there for the winter. Miami Beach proved
boring. The boys were dumb, the weather lousy. I called
my grandmother one day and she offered to show me
around.

She took me to a place where flamingos stood on one
leg, where alligators could eat out of your hand. She took
me to Wolfie's where we ate Dagwood sandwiches and
strawberry egg creams. At night she cooked me chickens
and stews. I gave up my hotel room and moved onto her
floor. And it was there that I began to understand how she
had lived a life different from mine, grasped the details of
how her mother had put her in a grave in the ground. That
she had been raised with the fear of kidnapping and rape.
When she was twelve, she said good-bye to everything she
knew.

She lived only five more years after that visit, but every
time I saw her she told me more. What she could not remember I'm sure she made up, just to keep me at her side.
When I was twenty-three and she was ninety-two, I took
her to the hospital. For some time she had complained of
pain. What was the date of your last period, the intern
asked, and my grandmother doubled over with laughter.
Before World War II, she replied.

For weeks she lingered and I went back to New York.
Then one day my mother phoned and said I should come.
For five days I sat beside my grandmother as she lay in a
coma. Finally I told my mother I had to go. There was
school. I had things to do. On the way to the airport, on

an impulse, I told my father I wanted to see her one more time, and he detoured for the hospital.

She sat up in bed, yellow ribbons in her hair that the nurse who'd come to care for her had tied in bows. She looked like a schoolgirl, her long silver tresses bound with the bows from plants that had been sent. I clasped her hand. The skin was soft like doeskin. The flesh felt as if it could slip off into my hand. It will be fine, I told her. I'm going back to school. I'll get my Ph.D. I'll marry a nice man. Smiling, she clasped my hand, blessing me.

She died as my plane rose. When I got to New York, I called home. Then I turned around and flew back. The nurse had told my mother she'd seen this happen before. That a person in a coma will wake up to say good-bye.

ON MAY 14, 1891, the Czar Alexander III wrote to his son Nicholas—the future and final Czar of Russia—who was traveling back from the Far East:

Your Imperial Highness!
Having given the order to build a continuous line of railway across Siberia, which is to unite the rich Siberian provinces with the railway system of the Interior, I entrust to you to declare My will, upon your entering the Russian dominions after your inspection of the foreign countries of the East. At the same time, I desire you to place the first stone at Vladivostok for the construction of the Ussuri line, forming part of the Siberian Railway, which is to be carried out at the cost of the State and under the direction of the Government. Your participation in the achievement of this work will be a

testimony to My ardent desire to facilitate
communications between Siberia and other countries of
the Empire, and to manifest My extreme anxiety to secure
the peaceful prosperity of this Country.

I remain your sincerely loving, ALEXANDER.

The question everyone was asking, however, was not why
Alexander wanted the railroad built, but rather why he had
waited so long. The Americans had completed the Union
Pacific in 1869 and the Canadians soon followed with 2,893
miles of track of the Canadian Pacific in 1886. But the Russians, a people often slow to accept change unless it is
thrust upon them at a revolutionary pace, had difficulty
with the notion of uniting their European and Asian parts.
Also there were economic factors such as fear of a decline in
the price of wheat as well as the value of land in Europe if
Siberia were opened.

And there were political concerns. Domestically, the construction of a railroad would serve to undercut the power of
independent nobles and help the Czar to consolidate his
industrial power. And abroad it was the age of imperialism.
Britain and the United States were in an expansionist period. Russia badly needed an ice-free port on its eastern
frontier and it needed a stronger foothold in Asia to keep
that port open. The best way to consolidate its political
hold in Asia was to unite the country. Alexander was beginning to realize that communication was the means to unite
Russia, and in that era it meant the building of a railway.

Though Vladivostok at the time was a miserable port, ice-
bound 110 days a year, whose main exports were sea cabbage, ginseng roots, mushrooms found on oak stumps and
lichen found on corn, it was Russia's best exit to the East.
And so it was here that on May 31, 1891, the future Czar
Nicholas I at his father's behest dug the first turf and cere-
moniously filled a wheelbarrow to signal the groundbreak-
ing for the Trans-Siberian Railroad.

Prior to the existence of the Trans-Siberian Railroad, travel was primitive to say the least. The only route across Siberia was the Trakt, or the Great Siberian Post Road as it was inappropriately called. Basically a trail of mud, dust or snow, depending upon the weather, the track was trudged by exiles and convicts, traversed only by sleighs. To this day there is no transcontinental Soviet highway.

An old Baedeker's gives this cheerless description of travel possibilities across Siberia, pre-railroad: "The Telega, or mail cart, is a four-wheeled conveyance without springs and somewhat resembling a rude edition of the American buckboard. As a rule no seats are provided except for the driver, the passengers sitting on their trunks, or on the hay or straw with which the bottom of the cart is littered. As the roads are bad, travelling is very rough and often painful . . ." Drivers were invariably drunk, often whipping the horses senseless. Frequent changes of horse and driver made travel terribly slow, not to mention the hazards of frost and snow. Imperial messengers from Peking to Irkutsk were an exception. They covered six thousand kilometers in sixteen days, traveling constantly at sixteen kilometers an hour, a speed possible only because they made over two hundred changes of horses and drivers.

For years people had been proposing to the Czar the idea of a Trans-Siberian Railroad. In 1857 an American, Perry McDonough Collins, proposed the first steam railway through Russia. Then an English engineer named Dull suggested a tramway drawn by wild Siberian horses between present-day Gorky and Perm. These along with other proposals were turned down.

At last when political pressures were mounting to consolidate the eastern frontier and facilitate communications across the country, when eastward expansion became inevitable, the Czar proclaimed on March 29, 1891, that a railway from the Urals to Vladivostok would be built.

The Trans-Siberian Railroad was not only intended to

link Russia to Siberia. It would also link Europe to the Pacific and eastern Asia. It would open a new path and fresh horizon not only to Russia, but also to world trade, the modern equivalent of the old Silk Route. The railroad would enable Russia to take part in the struggle for the Pacific and would open the markets of China and Japan to her merchants, increasing Russia's power in the Far East. It would even deepen ties between Russia and the United States. It would assure the Russian fleet of all the supplies it needed and the fleet could be significantly strengthened. In a word, the building of the railway was a way of making Russia a true power in the world.

The construction was to begin in five different locations, building only one track and using thin logs for purposes of efficiency, as all this work would soon have to be replaced. Like some old railroad joke, the problem was to make those places meet. The workers were a mix of Turks, Persians, Italians, Chinese, Koreans and Russians, not to mention convicts (some 12,000 of the 29,000 workers at the height of the building were convicts, offered reduced sentences for their work on the railroad). Stonemen, riveters and bridge builders were hired in winter when the rest of the crew departed.

Conditions were grim, to say the least. Bridge builders often lost their grip and were hurled onto the icy surface of the river below or drowned in the freezing waters. In summer, workers toiled amidst swamps of fever-spreading mosquitoes. Horses were wiped out by Siberian anthrax. Rivers rose to unbelievable heights, sometimes sending mountains of water crashing between the passes. One flood near Lake Baikal took out sixty miles of newly completed track. Bubonic plague, cholera, bandits and Manchurian tigers attacked the workers. The families of Chinese coolies working on the China line were given the "golden handshake"—the promise of compensation if their relative died working on the railroad—to keep their workers from fleeing for fear of almost certain death.

But in 1897 the first official train thundered down the track to Vladivostok at a speed of 16 kilometers per hour. In 1903, at a cost of some 250 million in U.S. dollars, the Trans-Siberian line—5,778 miles, making it the longest continuous track in the world—was completed and in 1916 the entire railroad with all its additional routings, including the China route, was finished.

IRKUTSK, a onetime Cossack fortress and gold-mining boomtown, was our first Siberian stop. Once again some of the travelers departed for good and I was left once more with the feeling that I was missing something, that I had planned this journey all wrong.

I wandered to a flower stand where a woman with translucent blue eyes and stark white hair was selling bouquets. "How is business?" I asked and she laughed. "Good when the train comes in." I bought a small bouquet. I told her she was very beautiful, which she was, and she laughed and said, "No, no, not beautiful at all." I told her again she was beautiful and said I wanted to take her picture. She laughed again, refusing with modesty. But when I raised my camera she began to pose. She turned playfully this way and that, like a model.

But suddenly a man ran up. He was shouting at both of us. He wore a dark jacket and trousers, a gray vest, and he had those middle-aged gray features I saw on so many Soviet men. "No pictures," he shouted. The flower lady, ashamed, hid her face as the man chased me back toward the train.

On the train platform I again tried to take a picture, this

time of the train itself. But a soldier stopped me. "No pictures." When I saw the military attaché from the U.S. Embassy who was on our train, he explained. The Russian train system is electric and vulnerable to sabotage. "They think pictures are a security risk," he laughed. "That's how backward they are."

No one on the train knew what time it was. Some people said the train traveled on Moscow time but operated on local time, if you can figure that out. But half the people were on Beijing time and one diplomat said he was on Tokyo time, which was the same for some reason as Ulan Bator time. Our Chinese porter changed his watch fifteen minutes every few hours or so but this was a system of his own devising.

The military attaché and his very nice wife, who needlepointed her way across Siberia, had a large piece of graph paper with some elaborate scheme that looked like a major military invasion but was really the way he figured out train time versus local time, and everyone turned to him for advice. It was the only occasion in my life when I found myself impressed with the efficiency of the U.S. military. But the dining car was on continuous service, so nobody really cared.

The car was packed now as I sat with the two Dutchmen and a woman from France. The men were bored students with a flare for espionage. They said that there was a KGB agent for every Westerner on the train. They pointed to the buxom middle-aged cook, stirring stew, and her hacking husband. KGB, they said. They pointed to roly-poly Dimitri. Definitely KGB, they said. They said that all conversations in hotel rooms are recorded. That each hotel has a room devoted to surveillance. Nothing escapes their eye.

A middle-aged Swedish man who had been traveling with his son in China for several weeks joined us and he asked about Chernobyl. Hardly anyone had dared bring it up directly on the train, as if there were some taboo, but he asked if we had any news.

"We've heard that thousands have died," one of the Dutch girls said.

"I don't think that's true," I said, recalling what little I knew, "but many will."

"Those poor people." The Swedish man shook his head forlornly. "I am afraid to go home. I am afraid of what it will be like there. I have heard that our crops are ruined."

When they left, I noticed that Dimitri's mood had turned very glum and I wondered if he had understood our conversation. I would spend the rest of the train ride watching Dimitri's moods go up and down, as if they were some kind of barometer of life on the train, but this time he seemed particularly saddened. I thought of the Chinese, whose depressions or elations were lost on me, but Dimitri wore his feelings on his sleeve, the way my mother always said I did.

I went back to my compartment and returned with the flowers I'd purchased from the flower lady in Irkutsk. These I gave to Dimitri who accepted them with such an effusion of thanks that it sent the cook almost tumbling out of her plastic hat and her husband gasped in deep, cigarette-tainted laughter.

Russian cars from the far reaches of Siberia, from the place where the train begins in Vladivostok, had been added to the train in Irkutsk, and for the first time Russian passengers were on board. They never came to the dining car, perhaps because they knew there was not much in the way of food, but remained enclosed in their compartments. Like the Chinese Muslims, they brought what they needed with them.

One of the drawbacks of the Trans-Siberian Express is that there is no lounge car where one can just sit and relax. You must either be in your compartment, in the corridor, or in the dining car. With no possibility for exercise except on our short stops, being constantly in the dining car was making me feel bloated and stuffed. I began to walk the train.

Each car could be distinguished by its smell. I could wander from car to car blindfolded and know who occupied the car. The Chinese Muslims smelled of grain and bulgur. The Chinese cars smelled of rancid oil and cooking rice. And the Russians smelled of onion and salted fish, of bodies festering. The Russians kept their cars closed, both in their compartments and in the corridors, and the air in them was fierce.

I began moving, pacing back and forth, up and down the corridors of the train. I greeted the Chinese Muslims and once their women invited me in. I sat on a sack of bulgur. The men explained (I assumed) how they'd met me weeks ago at the Chinese International Travel Services office, and the women laughed over our shared fates. And then there was nothing to say. We smiled dumbly at one another. They offered me a cup of tea which I sipped in a silence that grew more and more awkward for us all. Soon I slipped out, feeling faint from the enclosed air, and stood for a long time between cars, my face slapped by the wind of Siberia, breathing the fresh, bracing air.

On one of my pacings I met Sonya, a schoolteacher from Vladivostok, of Tatar descent. As I stood, nose pressed to the glass in the Russian car, the door to her compartment opened and she handed me some sweets. Her daughter, named Tina, had giant red bows in her hair, and a perfectly ironed and cleaned dress. They had already been on the train for four days, but they looked as if they had just walked out of the house, bathed, ironed, ready for school.

Sonya invited me in and I sat on the bed while Tina showed me her toys—a stuffed animal, a book. Sonya told me she taught second-grade reading. Her husband was an engineer. She opened for me a box of smoked and dried salmon. She told me how her husband had carved a hole in the ice and sat there for hours waiting for the fish.

Though I protested, Sonya insisted on giving me two fish. I held them in my hand. They were dessicated, flat, their eyes little dried-up beads. They were stiff in my hand. I thought of her husband sitting at the ice hole for hours, waiting for these salmon to take his line. Feeling honored but slightly embarrassed, I wandered between cars carrying these fish, wrapped in last week's *Pravda*. Thinking Dimitri might know what to do, I made my way to the dining car.

He was ecstatic with my find. "This is excellent fish," he said, "the finest." The cook came out of her kitchen to examine them. Even her disgruntled husband came over, pinched them, and nodded in assent. The whole staff was thrilled. "We must celebrate," Dimitri said and the cook and her husband agreed by looking away.

The car was virtually empty as Dimitri pulled out his personal stash of vodka, which was completely illegal, and poured balalaika cocktails (vodka straight up). He brought out a jar of caviar and a hunk of Russian rye. He showed me how to cut slices of the fish, which we munched on as we ate and drank. The fish was tough and salty, but both Dimitri and Cook said it was great.

We were laughing, Dimitri telling me stories about his life on the train, as Pierre came in, whistling the way he had when he left the Mongolian Embassy the first time I met him. The manager of the dining car, resuming his somber expression, told him to stop. Pierre sat down with us, picking up a slice of fish, and continued to whistle. The manager told him to stop. Dimitri got up quickly, cupping his hands in supplication, asking Pierre to stop.

"You know, the Russian conductor told me to stop whistling. Now this guy's telling me to stop whistling. What's wrong with whistling?" he shouted in French.

I suggested he be quiet.

The manager came over and said to him in English, "No whistling."

Pierre kept whistling. Now I told him to stop, but he kept on, defiantly. The manager of the dining car disappeared and returned with Victor, the short, compact, Russian conductor, who came back shouting. "Get out," he told Pierre. Pierre whistled in his face. "Get out," Victor said, "or I'll throw you out."

I got up and walked out. In my compartment I found Cecilia and Janet having tea and some kind of sandwich. "And so," I heard Janet say, "I told him it was her or me and he, of course, just stood there, not knowing what to say . . ." Cecilia was helping Janet restructure her life, which she appeared to be escaping via Budapest. I dug into my pack for some chocolate and headed toward the Russian cars.

I found Tina and Sonya stretched on their bunks, half asleep. I apologized, but they invited me in. I handed them the chocolate, thinking it was a paltry offering in return for the gift of remarkable fish in whose pursuit her husband had almost frozen. But they were as grateful as if I had handed them a winning ticket to the lottery.

Leaving Tina munching on a chocolate bar, I made my way back toward my car. It was dark now and the cold had settled back in, the kind to chill the bone. Pierre was standing between cars and I realized he was waiting for me. "You're crazy," I told him, thinking about the dining car scene.

"I don't like authority," he told me. "It makes me nervous."

"Well, you think you're going to change the world by whistling," wondering if perhaps this weren't as good a place as any to begin.

"I might," he said, "I just might."

I stood beside him, the night air in our faces, watching a now dim-lit Siberia zip by. He put his arm around my shoulder and pulled me to him. I tried to squirm away but he held me, his arm firmly around my shoulder. At first I felt awkward. I am in love with someone back home, I started to say, but we both knew this already. I wanted to get away, but I also just wanted to stand there. I didn't want anything more to happen. I just wanted to let myself rest against his arm. He seemed to be looking for the same thing for neither of us moved from the spot. We stood like that for a long time, his arm like a barricade holding back the world, as the cold breeze was bracing upon our faces.

At last I excused myself, slipping away with hardly a word, leaving Pierre standing alone between cars. The compartment was empty, Cecilia off somewhere with Janet, and now it was dark. The vodka had gone to my head. My mouth was dry with the salty taste of fish. Pulling up the shade, I collapsed on my bunk. Floodlights shone in, the train's whistle screams through my sleep. My dreams are a scramble of life—New York, California, Istanbul; old lovers, lost friends, strange places I've never been. I am on a wagon train, a ricksha, an L.A. bus, and suddenly I am dreaming my dream of winter, of snowy roads and twisting ravines, of Indian paths I followed as a child, the place I go back to in my waking and in my dream.

As we rush through the pine forests, the taiga of Siberia, frost on the panes, the air as cold inside as out, across a ground snowy in mid-June, it is as if all my dreams become this one dream, and it is my dream of return, of reconciliation, of home.

FARMLANDS raced by. Mile after mile of wheat, blowing in the wind. I sat, face pressed to the glass. It was the first real farmland we'd seen since we'd left Beijing and yet the sight was bittersweet. I could not look at these acres of grain and not think of Stalin's collectivization plan, carried out mostly in the Ukraine but also here. In a massive and brutal effort he appropriated the land, putting millions of resistant farmers to death who refused to give up their land, and created the low-producing state-sponsored Soviet farms. In protest, kulaks (the well-to-do farmers who profited from the labor of peasants) cut the throats of their livestock: sixteen million horses were killed, cattle were reduced forty-five percent. One hundred million goats and sheep, two thirds of the entire stock of the nation, were slaughtered. But the kulaks were rounded up and marched into the depths of Siberia. Two million of them were executed. Private property was finished. Grain shortages began. What was left of the farmers was a broken fragment; incentive was lost from these fields for decades. The Russians have been hungry ever since.

I was relieved by a knock at my door. Tina stood there, big red bows in place, a new dress once again perfectly pressed. "My mother would like you to have breakfast with us." I packed up a small bag of juice, crackers, sardines and fruit and followed her, legs shaky, through the cold corridors of the train.

Sonya had taken the train many times before and she came well prepared. Along with her fish, she had brought homemade breads, cheese, her own tea, a heating pot, and yogurt which, it seems, had no difficulty staying cold. She had made a small spread for us to which I added my contributions. She was thrilled with the sardines, amazed as I opened the can, watching the little oily bodies revealed. She picked one up by the tail, sniffing it, examining it with her round Tatar features. Like a pelican she dropped it down her throat and swallowed it. She clapped her hands and then she fed her daughter in the same way. "These are wonderful," Sonya said. I told her I had two dozen cans and was already beginning to tire of sardines (indeed, I have not looked at a sardine since), and I would give her in the course of the train ride half of my supply.

Sonya's family came from Kazan, the birthplace of Lenin, a fact of which she was very proud, though she'd rarely make mention of Stalin in any of our talks. This was her annual trip home. They were going for the summer, which they did every year, although it always made her sad because the summer in Vladivostok wasn't bad. "But we have no vacation in winter." It is nice in Kazan in winter, she told me, but very cold in Vladivostok. They would stay with her family until August. Her husband would join her in July when he had his holiday. "I am a teacher, you know. I get a longer holiday."

"I am a teacher too," I told her, which was from time to time the case. I had made a decision not to tell many people I was a writer, something I'd been warned not to do.

"You teach children?"

"I teach at the university."

"Oh," she looked a bit ashamed. "You must be smart."

"You must be patient," I said. We both laughed.

Tina clung to her mother, beaming at me. She was radiant, like an advertisement for a healthy child, and I envied Sonya traveling with her daughter by her side. Slowly we munched our food. The yogurt she gave me was quite good, though the bread was beginning to turn stale. I chewed it slowly.

"So what do you think of all the changes in Russia?" I asked her. "What do you think of Gorbachev?"

"Oh," she smiled, clapping her hands together. "Gorbachev is wonderful. He is very good. A fine leader, a hero. Like Kennedy," she said, trying to give me a cultural reference.

"But is he helping the Russian people?" I asked. "Is life better for you?"

"Oh, you'll see. He will do great things. Many changes

will come. Already he has made many changes. He is a new Peter the Great. A new Lenin," she said, beaming. "Jobs are easier. There is more food. We have more freedom. Our relations are better abroad." Sonya said this with the same sweet smile she said everything.

"How do you have more freedom?"

"The newspapers are freer to print what they think. People are freer to travel abroad."

"And Gorbachev, is he a good man?"

"Oh, he is a very good man. He has recognized the mistakes of Stalin and is trying to correct them. He is a man dedicated to change. He will make my country great again."

Suddenly, despite agreeing with much of what she said, I had the sense that Sonya, the teacher, had been well taught. I could not help but feel that what she was saying to me—the generalizations, the platitudes—she had learned by rote. There was something missing and I had the sudden sense that I was speaking to one of those people in *Invasion of the Body Snatchers,* the great science-fiction allegory about the McCarthy era, people whose individuality has been snatched up by extraterrestrials in the shape of giant pods.

I was happy when Tina changed the subject. She handed me some hard candy and said I must come to Kazan or even Vladivostok, to visit them. I told her I would like that very much. "And bring your little girl," Tina said, grinning at me a hardy red-cheeked smile. My harsh thoughts melted now. I'd made no mention of a little girl, but I promised Tina I would.

Dullness had settled over the train. The cold and almost five days of perpetual motion had sapped our strength. The dining car was empty more and more, in part because there was very little food, and the kitchen staff had begun a card game out of tedium, one they had been playing for years. The rules seemed vague and difficult to discern. At first I thought it had to do with colored suits, then it seemed it was about sequence. The cook tried to explain the rules to me. She showed me half a dozen times what a good hand was, when I could ask for another card, but it made no sense to me. Nobody seemed to care. They dealt me in.

Dimitri sat next to me, directing my hand. The cook smiled. Igor, the potato peeler, his walleye wandering every which way, held his hand, but he was more like a statue, never making a move. Dimitri told me to ignore him. "He's a nice fellow," Dimitri said, "just dumb." I kept thinking that now the cook would take off her hat, but it remained upright, eight inches high, like a creampuff on her head. She began talking about her life. "Fifteen years on the train, fifteen married years," she grunted, nodding at her husband, who was concentrating on his cards. "Try making love in one of those compartments," she said with a laugh. "Try making love with him . . ." She didn't complete her thought but her husband was rotund, huge in fact around the waist, and I could see her problem.

"We have children," she said, "two grown children. But since they were seven years old, we hardly see them. My mother takes care of them. We are home for a few days, then we turn around."

"It's a good living," her husband said. The cook sneered, shuffling her cards around.

Dimitri, I could tell, was growing depressed. "I've been at this for fifteen years too. I started when I was twenty. My boy is ten. I see him for a few days, then turn around. I always bring him something, a trinket, some small thing." He handed me a small carved wooden boat from Vladivostok. "I'll give this to him when I see him tomorrow." His eyes seemed to brighten at this thought. "But then we turn around and go back out again. Two weeks out, three, maybe four days home."

"Do you ever get off the train? Do you ever get to visit? Irkutsk? Perm?" I thought of how much I had wanted to get off and stay at various points.

Dimitri shrugged. "In fifteen years, I've never visited a single stop. I've never gotten off." He put a card down for me. Igor suddenly rose, tossing in his hand. His hulking form banged the table. "There," Dimitri said, "you won."

A lone jogger ran along a sodden street, dressed in a state-of-the-art running suit as we pulled into Novosibirsk—the seat of the Academgorodox Complex, an important scientific center. The future of Siberia supposedly lies here, but it was a dreary place to be. We pulled into a station lined with freight trains. Giant impersonal tenement-style houses lined the tracks. A light drizzle fell. Almost no one left the train.

I went back to the compartment and, finding it deserted, lay down on my bunk, exhausted from doing nothing. I was growing more and more tired, it seemed, by the day. The motion of the train felt within me as I lay, rocking inside of me. Overhead, Chinese music played. It had played for days, those high screeching voices, and I hadn't really heard it until now. I took out a tape of balalaika music and put it in my Walkman. The music filled my head as I lay stretched out, dreaming of troikas, vodka, snowball fights. I imagine a bonfire, someone lifts me into his arms, sweeping me away.

Later I woke to late afternoon sun pouring in. Suddenly it was a beautiful spring day outside, sixty-five degrees. We made an unscheduled stop in the middle of a small woods to check the brake pressure. It was unclear how long we'd be delayed.

Off to the side of the track in a dense grove of blue-green pines a pond shimmered in the late afternoon light. Blue-bells and buttercups danced along its banks. Ducks skirted the surface of the pond. I stood between cars, scanning the platform. Like an animal set free, I escaped from the train. I jumped down and raced into the Siberian woods. Redolent pine filled the air. I stood for a moment at the edge of the pond, giant spruce around me, breathing in deeply the pure air.

Then suddenly I bent down, plunging my fists into the dark Russian soil. Now I touched the ground for the first time. I held dark earth between my fingers. I rested on this earth, felt its coolness as I dug into the ground beneath me. This was Mother Russia, I thought to myself. To the Slavs, all the destinies of living things were linked—people, plants, animals. They reveled in the cycles of nature—birth, death, rebirth. While they worshipped the cross, their true symbol, their Easter gift, was the egg, giver of life. The earth and the notion of Eternal Motherhood was the Russian ideal. The Virgin was not worshipped for her purity, but for her motherhood. In Russian iconography she is almost always portrayed with child. When Russia was under Tatar rule and Kiev under constant attack, it made sense that the notion of the Russian land grew not merely as a territory, but from its pagan origins as a motherland.

Now I had touched Russian soil. I thought of my own mother and grandmother. How far away I was from someone who would hold me. I let my body sink to the earth. If my journey stopped here, it would have been accomplished. If this was the end, I would have arrived. I thought I'd just close my eyes and the train would leave. I could sleep here. I could lay here forever. I wouldn't be responsible. I'd done nothing wrong. I'd stay for a while and someone would find me. They'd get me to Moscow. Eventually.

The porters started shouting, for others had also run away. But I lay on the sodden green earth, not merely thrilled to be touching land like a drunken sailor after months at sea, but rather to touching my homeland for the first time.

So this is what a prisoner set free must feel, I thought, never having imagined it before. My thoughts turned dark as I contemplated those who had been exiled here. Dostoyevsky, Mandelstam, Solzhenitsyn. Others, less prominent, who were sent, never to return. Suddenly, for a moment, I thought I understood. All I wanted to do was breathe the air, feel the ground. I never wanted to go anywhere else again. Yet this was a land of contradictory impulses—of good and evil, light and dark. Dostoyevsky wrote, "Perhaps the Almighty had to send me to Siberia to teach me something." But what was my lesson? I wondered as I clung to the earth. What was I to learn?

The train whistle sounded. I was aware of scrambling, shouting, people rushing aboard. I heard Pierre. "What are you doing? You're crazy. Get on board." My tall Chinese porter was signaling the chief engineer, motioning for him to wait. The porter ran to me and I was impressed by his stride. I rose suddenly and ran in the direction of the train. He caught me by the arm and I was amazed at his strength as he hoisted me on board.

After Dimitri served me sadly a bowl of thin borscht and stale cheese which he called dinner, with a shrug, I wandered back in the direction of Pierre's car. As I approached, I heard lively music being played. In the corridor of Pierre's car, a young man from Switzerland was playing the accordion, churning it with great Alpine songs. The Dutch girls and Pierre and other Europeans were all clapping wildly. But the Chinese in the car were disgruntled and wanted to sleep, though it was only eight o'clock. They began shouting and complaining. At last the porter asked everyone to leave.

"Let's go to another car," the Swiss man said.

And Pierre shouted, leading the way, "Let's go see the Russians."

We arrived like carolers on a winter's night, the round, mustached Swiss man and his entourage into the sealed compartments of the Russian car. Most of the doors and all of the windows were shut tight. The air, as usual, was stifling. An old Russian man peered out his door slightly to see what the commotion was and the Swiss man pointed to his accordion. "Do you mind?" he asked in French, "if I play?"

The old man nodded his assent, but shut his door. Soon all the doors were shut. We looked at each other, uncertain as to what this meant. But the Swiss, a bold fellow with a big belly, didn't seem to care. He picked up his accordion and began to grind. He played Swiss mountain music as if it were truly in his blood. He played fiercely and soon we heard clapping from within the compartments. Slowly doors opened. People peered out, children seeped into the corridors, smiling.

Pierre grabbed me by the shoulders and we began to dance. We twirled up and down the corridor. The Dutch girls began to twirl as well. Soon almost all the compartments were open. Husbands danced with their wives. Old men, raising their legs high, danced together. Children spun in the aisles. Suddenly another door opened and there was Cook, without her plastic bag on her head, in a nightdress, poking her husband until she gave up and just stood there clapping her hands over her head. The aisle was full of us, spinning in circles, strangers on a train, within the confines of the little space we had.

Suddenly Victor, the conductor, appeared. He screamed at the top of his lungs. He screamed maniacally and it occurred to me that he was crazed. The Russians backed into their compartments, quickly shutting their doors. The accordion stopped. We all stopped. The Swiss man, dumbfounded and broken in spirit, put his accordion back in its case as Victor disappeared as quickly as he'd come. Subdued, we made our way back to our cars. But as we left, we heard whispers. A door opening slightly. An old man bowing. Voices whispered thank you as we headed back to our end of the train.

□   □   □   □

Later that night, just as I was getting into bed, there was a knock at our door. Victor stood there, not in his conductor's uniform but in a blue flannel shirt and jeans. Cecilia peered down from her bunk, frowning. I was in my pajamas. "What do you want?" I said, thinking I knew full well. He made some gestures my way. Cupping his hand to his mouth, he invited me for a drink. "Where?" I asked. "The dining car is closed," I said. Then he stepped toward me and I put my hand to his chest, pushing him slightly away. He pointed to my Walkman and asked to listen to my tapes. I folded my hands beneath my head like a pillow, indicating I was going to sleep. After he was gone, I locked the door. "What did he want?" Cecilia asked, indignant and suddenly on my side. "He wanted to listen to music," I told her. She shook her head and went to sleep.

ON A BRILLIANT spring morning we crossed the Urals, penetrating the iron rock, through the copper gate that was intended to be bolted shut until Judgment Day. After five days and a distance of some four thousand miles, we left behind the would-be cannibals, wild Cossacks, and the frozen, sleeping land and crossed the spiritual border between Asia and Europe. I felt a sadness as well as relief as we left the East. We had traversed the barrier, leaving behind the land of Russia's great mineral reserves and much of her myth and superstition, and made our way into Europe. I gazed at the mountains as we passed through and thought how this could be Switzerland or my first train ride through the Rockies.

We reached a nondescript outpost—a freight yard surrounded by government housing. The slipshod clapboard houses of eastern Siberia wouldn't be seen again. The log cabins with old women stoking fires, the hefty railworkers digging by the side of the road, all this was gone, and I found I missed it.

The industrial North rose outside, a gray, smoky blotch on the landscape. Huge chimneys of refineries spewed smoke. The miles of housing complexes, all the same, monotonously flowed by. We passed not far from Gorky where an ailing Sakharov still languished, the phone call from Gorbachev that would free him from exile still six months away.

I stared out the window, thinking of what lay ahead. Several more weeks of solitary travel, uncertainty about Chernobyl and my visit to the Ukraine, doubts about returning home. I thought of my companion who was by now in New York and suddenly I was seized with the urge to call him. We had not spoken in a few weeks and now, as the possibility was soon to be before me, my urgency seemed difficult to bear. I was like some schoolgirl in class, longing to see her boyfriend, anxious for the bell to ring. But thousands of miles, cultures, and other things stood between us. A world of differences. An emotional wall.

I thought of how we had met. En route to a faculty meeting, I'd asked an older man tying up his bicycle where the meeting was. He'd shown me inside. Then I sat down beside a friend. "You see that man, the one you came in with," my friend said, pointing to the man who'd been tying up his bicycle, the one with whom I would spend the next several years of my life, "that's the man who changed my life. Who changed the way I see the world."

Later that afternoon as I stood on the platform, going to New York, he was there as well. We rode the train into the city. We rode the subway. "Are you following me home?" I asked. His wife, from whom he was estranged, and sons lived around the corner from me. The first time we had dinner together, he made me laugh. It was what I will always remember because I had not laughed in a long time and he told me stories that had me doubled up with laughter.

It was a difficult time for me when I met him. My work wasn't going well. There was no one in my life. Nothing seemed to be right. When I told him that I felt alone, he listened to me as intently as anyone ever had. And when I told him I was going to apply to law school he shook his head. "I think," he said, "your destiny lies elsewhere."

It was not long after we met that I accompanied my mother to Paris where a gypsy in a ragged fur coat pulled me into an alleyway. Turning my palm over in her filthy hands, she said, "You are falling in love with a married man. He is older than you. He will leave his wife. You will be happy for the rest of your life."

I wandered into the dining car where Igor lumbered past, like a huge ox, bumping into me. For the first time I saw him smile, a benign, foolish smile. "He likes women," Dimitri said.

Everyone was packing, preparing to depart. Pierre had tossed a few things into his rucksack. He was filthy, looking as if he hadn't bathed in weeks. But then it occurred to me we all looked filthy. Greasy hair, dirty clothes. We stank and looked disheveled, but I had not thought about this on the mirrorless, virtually showerless train for days. Touching my own hair, I recalled that I hadn't washed it in a week.

I went to Sonya and Tina's compartment with half a dozen cans of sardines as a going-away present. They were thrilled to have them. Sonya gave me her address in Vladivostok and told me when I next took the train, I must take it from Vladivostok and I must come and stay with them and go ice fishing with her husband, which I assured her I would do.

I packed up my few things and then went to the dining car, which was closed for service but the card game was going on. The four of them sat like a portrait by a Soviet social realist painter. "Life on the Train," I'd call it. Cook in her hat, her husband in his apron, Dimitri in his bow tie, and Igor in a filthy smock, eye rolling around in his head, faces all buried in a hand of incomprehensible cards.

They dealt me in. And suddenly I seemed to know how to play. I was making good plays, raising bets. I knew when to ask for a card and when to back down. Even Igor looked at me, amazed.

Then Cook put down her cards and, with great ceremony as if she were about to abdicate a throne, removed her white plastic hat. "Moscow," Dimitri said, as if this were the signal. Outside were suburbs, housing complexes, small houses with little gardens, children playing in the street. Dogs, women with groceries in their arms. Everyday life. Billboards appeared, reminding me of how I'd always felt that the theme of Soviet literature once struck me in college as "boy meets tractor." A man and a woman toiling in the fields. "Peace Through Co-Operatives." A woman smiles, stoking a furnace, a child crawls in the background. "The Party Provides." Then suburbia receded and tenements, monolithic brick buildings, block after block in the Stalinist neoclassical style, rose, gray against a gray sky.

Cook took a beautiful enameled comb from her pocket and began to comb her rather dry, brittle hair. The handle of the comb was etched in luminous colors. Flowers in interweaving patterns. I touched it admiringly.

Now there was a scramble to leave. Everything had to be done quickly. Dimitri kissed me on both cheeks, tears in his eyes, and said, "You must ride my train again." As I made my way to the door, waving good-bye, Cook intercepted me. I thought she might scold me for something—her face looked very severe—but instead she pressed the comb into my hand. I tried to hand it back to her, but she wrapped my fingers around it firmly. "For Marushka," she said.

Moscow

ACCORDING TO LEGEND, when the cathedral known today as St. Basil's was completed, Ivan the Terrible had the architects blinded so that they could never repeat their marvels anywhere else in the world. Though the legend is without basis in historic fact, this conglomerate of churches, consisting of eight cupolas and eleven multicolored domes, is one of the unique architectural splendors of the world, the crowning glory of Red Square, of Russia itself.

Two hours after my train arrived, I walked across the street from my hotel to Red Square where I stood incredulous in front of St. Basil's. It was late afternoon and the Square was almost empty. A few soldiers patroled as I ambled for the first time in six days on somewhat shaky legs, like a newborn colt.

Despite what many Americans think, the "red" of Red Square does not refer to the political persuasion of the Kremlin nor to the color the flagstones take on at dusk, but rather to Old Slavonic, in which the word "red" was synonymous with "beauty." Before the revolution Red Square was not the vacant, forbidding place it seemed as I crossed, but rather it was a bustling marketplace where bears on leashes performed and gypsies whirled. Traveling in large bands, colorfully dressed minstrels and jesters played, encouraging people to join them with songs and dance.

Here in the marketplace you could buy fish or cabbage, silks and religious icons. Stands overflowed with plums and cherries, red currants and apricots. Onions and garlic, a staple of the Russian diet, were sold in abundance as were the furs Russians needed for their warm winter hats and coats—sables and foxes, beaver and silver mink. You could trade with trappers from the innermost reaches of Siberia or with spice merchants from Turkestan. Or sample the many varieties of vodka flavored with gooseberries, blackberries, or lemon-lime. And when your shopping was done, you joined your friends at the various taverns called *kabaki* that lined the square.

But now at dusk I traversed the near-empty, austere seat of the Soviet regime. Even the endless queue before Lenin's tomb along the Kremlin Wall was gone. But at the end of the square, rising in its whimsical, magnificent and mysterious way as it had for centuries, was St. Basil's. Its curlicue onion domes in brilliant shades of blue, red, green and yellow (whose shape may have been practical, as it was more suited to heavy snow—or poetic, to catch the prayers of the holy and send them up to heaven) captured the light of the setting sun as I paused before what seemed more fantasy than real.

In 1552 Ivan, who was not yet called the Terrible, ordered his architects Barma and Postnik to build a great church. It was to be named the Cathedral of the Intercession, in celebration of the feast day that came on October 1, 1552, when Ivan's troops conquered Kazan, one of the last Mongol fortresses. Ivan was young then. He was victorious and in love. His first son had been born on that day, the same son Ivan would bludgeon to death twenty-eight years later in a rage, then mourn the rest of his days. But when he commissioned this church, it was a happy time in his life and the cathedral seems to reflect it.

He ordered a church to be built in the shape of the eight-pointed star of the Virgin, surrounded by a cluster of chapels of different heights and colors, all of this on the site of an old, existing church. It was begun in 1555 and consecrated in 1560. The architects managed to incorporate the features of Russian wooden churches into masonry. To this day their work stands, though it was added to in the sixteenth and seventeenth centuries, as one of the most unique pieces of architecture in the world. Whether its architects were blinded or not, no church like it has ever been built before or since.

The Cathedral of the Intercession popularly came to be called St. Basil's, after a holy fool whose bones lie consecrated in the cemetery of the existing church, and St. Basil's is the name we know it by today. Basil the Blessed was said to be one of the holy fools who dared to stand up to the Czar, renowned for his cruelty, and criticize him for his actions. With long white beard and perhaps dragging chains, Basil remonstrated with the Czar and instead of executing him, Ivan listened. It was, however, not uncommon in the Middle Ages for a ruler to listen to an inspired individual who bore the stigma of madness. Perhaps it was this precedent Nicholas and Alexandra followed shortly after the turn of the present century when listening to the demoniac Rasputin who brought about their ruin.

It is here in Red Square that Byzantium meets bureaucracy and the two sides of Russia stand face-to-face. Somewhere between the onion domes of St. Basil's and the towering brick walls and crenellated medieval towers of the Kremlin, the real Russia lies. During the Mongol invasions, Russia had sought help from Europe, only to be met with indifference. Once it had thrown off the Mongol yoke, Russia continued to look with fear toward Asia and distrust toward Europe, a pattern which persists to this day, and which has marked Russia's centuries of isolation.

After standing awestruck before St. Basil's, I strolled back toward my hotel. Head down and oblivious, I wandered, deep in thought. This was a history I thought I understood. This was a place I felt I knew something about. Yet now that I had arrived, I realized I had no idea how to begin. Also I found myself faced with what I had been avoiding thinking about for a few weeks—my intention to journey south to Kiev and to reach the outlying districts of the Ukraine. The reality of how East meets West was brought home to me. And Russia's isolation was made all the more poignant when I thought of how it was so slow to inform Europe about Chernobyl.

It had been almost two weeks since the information officer at the U.S. Embassy in Beijing had given me a copy of *Time* magazine and I had been staggered by what I'd learned. Although it was still some weeks away, the thought of my actual departure for the Ukraine loomed and I found myself frightened more by what remained unknown than by what I had already read. Radiation has no smell or taste, no palpable traces. It is just there, in the air, the water, the food. I had been told by the journalist in New York that the half-life of radiation from an accident such as Chernobyl was short. I would arrive almost two months after the accident. But was that short enough? Eventually I would have to find someone who could inform me of what the present situation was.

Reflecting on what my next move would be, I became aware of shouting, loud noises around me. I looked up and saw people pointing. I turned and saw that the large gates of the Kremlin had opened and a cavalcade of official-looking motorcars with police escort were careening straight at me. A man along the side motioned for me to jump in his direction and I shot toward him just as cars passed where I had been standing. It occurred to me that they would have run me over if I had not jumped out of the way. Later, in fact, I learned that this was true. The pedestrian has no right of way. It was my obligation to step aside or be run over. Outside of border guards, this was my first encounter with the state, and the feeling was not a pleasant one. I walked with my head up, looking both ways, more cautious now as I crossed Red Square.

When I returned to my hotel room—a small, dark room with a tiny, hard, narrow bed about the shape and consistency of the Ry-Krisp I'd brought with me—the phone was ringing. Since I knew no one in Moscow, this seemed odd, but when I picked up the phone I heard someone say my name. Then I recalled that a friend of my mother's had a nephew who worked in Moscow at the embassy. Ted Cavendar welcomed me and said, "There's a dinner and screening of *Out of Africa* at the ambassador's tonight. Can you shower and change your clothes? We'll pick you up in an hour." I had seen this movie once and I smiled at the irony of seeing it again, for it seemed somehow suited to my present circumstances. I said I'd be downstairs.

The shower was a hose I held over my head and the tub was the size of a large sink. I had to squat in a very awkward position in order to bathe, but the water was hot and it was the first time I'd washed completely in days. I crammed myself in, feeling a bit like Gulliver in the land of the Lilliputians, and sat there for a long time, letting the water pour over my head, wondering if I'd be able to rise again. Then I dried myself with towels the size of washcloths. Then I took out the dress that had gotten stuck in the back in Beijing and carefully pulled up the zipper. Only hours after I'd left the Trans-Siberian railroad behind, I walked out into the June night air of Moscow in high heels and a dress.

Spaso House is located on a residential street in Moscow that could be a side street of Washington, D.C. At the entranceway stood two beleaguered carved wooden Indians with dazed looks in their eyes, trading-post vintage, out of place and startlingly inappropriate beneath the Great Seal of the United States. I passed through these sentinels abashed. Suddenly I was ushered into the giant marble hall of the ambassador's residence where, greeted by a well-dressed crowd and waiters in tuxedos passing trays of caviar, marinated mushrooms, smoked salmon on pumpernickel and deviled eggs, I felt not unlike Cinderella, my life momentarily transformed from what I had known.

The guests included the elite of Moscow, "the real bigwigs," Ted whispered with proper diplomatic panache as he told me, between introductions, who took bribes, who was old-guard, who would be a fine journalist if only he told the truth, and other variations on the Moscow scandal sheet. "See that guy," he'd say. "He's really on the take. He's got two dachas and drives a Volvo . . . Vladimir, how nice to see you . . ." I was whisked from person to person, with quick introductions. Diplomats and correspondents, members of the Soviet film industry ("where changes are happening at an amazing pace," Ted whispered). He grabbed two vodkas on the rocks off a passing tray and handed me one. "The finest Russian vodka you'll ever drink," he said. Photographers, artists, business people all flitted from person to person, moving like flocks of birds as some new dignitary entered the room.

Ted introduced me as an American writer "of some note." But my real claim to fame seemed to be that I had just gotten off the Trans-Siberian Express. One extremely tall man who looked like Abraham Lincoln got down on his knees and kissed my hand as Ted told him the news that I had just arrived via Beijing. Others looked at me as if I had returned from the moon. "Mongolia," one elderly statesman muttered as he walked away. "You've just crossed Mongolia."

Ted left me in the hands of the scientific attaché to the United States Embassy. "What are you doing here?"

"Here?" I said, pointing to the room around me, wondering myself what I was doing there.

"No, in the Soviet Union—what brings you here?"

"Oh, I am traveling. I am planning to travel to the villages my family came from."

"Oh, where's that?"

"Around Gomel, Nezhin and Chernigov."

"Oh, really, that's interesting," he said, sucking his cheeks in, then clearing his throat. "I don't think anybody's going there these days."

"Well, I thought if I got to Kiev, I could perhaps get a driver to take me north."

He shook his head, indicating he would not do that. "I don't think you can. I think the roads are blocked."

"Well, then Kiev, I'd settle for Kiev, and the outskirts. The suburbs. Do you think it's all right to go to Kiev?" I did not mention to him that my itinerary had me scheduled to be in Kiev for a week.

"Oh, sure, you can go for a day or two." He spoke cheerfully now as if this seemed like a fine thing to do. "Are you planning on having children?" he grinned as Ted caught me by the arm, dragging me once again away.

He handed me over to Bertrand, the agricultural attaché, a large blond man who looked as if he belonged on a farm in Minnesota, speaking Norwegian. Bertrand was eating a cucumber. "I hope you don't mind my asking," I said, "but do you feel safe eating that cucumber?"

"Cucumbers and tomatoes come from Bulgaria," he said nonchalantly, immediately grasping my meaning. "The wind didn't blow that way. But I wouldn't touch a sugar beet. I wrote an article—unclassified document, mind you —and as a joke I said that the Soviets will be harvesting two-thousand-pound sugar beets soon. Apparently some commodities brokers—you know those guys who don't know a tea leaf from a turnip—they took me seriously. The bottom fell out of several products. I got a reprimand—an official reprimand, mind you—from Washington. Nobody in this business can take a joke."

"What won't you eat?"

"Oh, leafy vegetables, milk products. Beef in about six weeks. But this stuff," he munched again, "it's all right."

"Where did you study agriculture?" I found myself feeling a bit weak from the train ride and the vodka, and I felt like changing the subject.

"Cornell. I studied all kinds of things there."

"Like what?"

"Oh, like camel management." I laughed but he checked me. "No, it's a serious subject. No joke in some parts of the world. Camels, you know, they've got this umbrella-like hair that keeps them cool during the day and warm at night, kind of like the old bubble hairstyle." He reached up and fluffed my hair. "Another thing about camels. They won't walk in circles the way oxen will. That's a big problem in parts of the world where you can only have camels. So if you want them to turn a grindstone, you've got to blindfold them. Once in India, I saw this camel turning a grindstone with a bra around its eyes. I took a picture and sent it to Maidenform. . . ."

Someone announced that *Out of Africa* was about to begin and I managed to sneak away. I had paused at the hors d'oeuvre table once more for Russian rye and caviar when someone leaned against my arm. "I understand," a man in a thick Russian accent said to me, "that you are thinking about going to Kiev." I kept leaning into the table, not looking at his face, but I saw the blue sleeve of his jacket as he reached for something. "Don't go," he said. "It isn't safe." Then he pulled himself up and walked away.

All through the movie, I thought about what the man who came up to me at the hors d'oeuvre table had said. I squirmed in my chair, uncomfortable in my dress, trying to find him in the darkened room. When the movie ended, the doors to the main hall opened and a buffet, a city block long, was revealed. Giant serving casseroles of beef Stroganoff, chicken Kiev, blinis with caviar and sour cream, mushrooms in cream sauce—all the food promised and dreamed of on the Trans-Siberian Express but never served—simmered over blue flames. A dessert table of fresh strawberries, charlottes russes, Black Forest cake, floating meringues appeared bedecked for kings. I gathered food as if this were my last meal, which for a time it actually would be. Off in a corner, plate in hand, I stood alone, devouring.

Ted caught me and dragged me over to an American

correspondent for ABC. ("You should meet this guy," he said.) "Did you cover Chernobyl?" I asked him as I tried to balance my plate and a glass of champagne.

He had a nice youthful grin, a blond mustache. "Sure, I covered it." He paused, smiling at me. "From Moscow."

"You didn't go to Kiev?"

"Are you kidding? My cameraman said he'd quit before he'd go near the place."

"And the network didn't insist."

"You know," he said, "I've been in lots of war zones. Nicaragua, Lebanon. But I don't know a correspondent who'll go near the Ukraine."

I was growing despondent. "I planned this journey . . ." I told him, "around going to the villages my family came from. Near Kiev. I could just take a day's drive."

He leaned forward. "I wouldn't touch it. We don't know half the story. The Soviets haven't been exactly forthcoming." He turned to walk away. "I know someone who can help you. Talk to Nicholas Daniloff. He's the correspondent with *U.S. News & World Report*. He knows everything and he's a good guy."

Once again I stood alone and was beginning to feel overwhelmed by the vodka, the food, the sudden array of people and problems thrust upon me. It was too jarring a change from the solitude of the train and I felt myself reeling. I was about to leave when through the crowd I spotted the blue suit, the shoulders and back of the head that had walked away before the film began. I moved near him and did what I would find myself doing a great deal in the Soviet Union. I whispered. "May I speak with you?" I said.

He had a handsome face and sharp blue eyes. He took me by the elbow and led me into a corner. "I was told you are trying to get to a town north of Kiev." He dropped his voice and I had to lean very close to him to listen. "When the reactor was on fire, the people from the town came out to watch it burn. No one did a thing. There was no evacuation plan. When the people were told the water was bad, they boiled it. The government told us nothing." I looked into his face. He was handsome, perhaps in his early thirties, but there was something sad and aging about him. Later I was told he had been trying to leave the country for years.

"Who told you about me?"

He ignored my question. "They let the children stand and watch the fire. They let people go about their business. Those children and people will probably all die. They didn't want to admit anything was wrong. You can say something about all of this. You don't have to stay here. You don't need any contacts. The other journalists can't write the truth because they'll lose their contacts and won't have anything to say or they'll be asked to leave, but you don't ever have to come back here again." He turned to go, then spoke to me again. "But be careful. What you write and who you write about can be identified. People can burn here. There are people who will dig salt for the rest of their lives because of what some journalist has said."

That night I slept badly. The bed was too small and I could not move. Every time I turned, the sheets engulfed me like a cocoon. And a weakness was once again in my limbs, a dizziness. Perhaps it was the vodka I drank or perhaps the movement of the train had entered me. The walls seemed to be closing in. I felt trapped with noplace to go. I had become a prisoner, somehow, of this journey. All night long I seemed to rock. When I dreamed, it was of the train and its motion. Or I was crossing the Gobi, wild horses chasing me. In one dream I leaped from the train onto a horse. Without saddle or bridle I rode across the Gobi, a renegade on a wild horse.

I turned and fell out of bed. Lying on the floor, tangled in sheets, I felt humiliated as if I were being watched, the vestiges of Stalin's system. I pictured the surveillance people in hysterics. I thought I was going to be sick and made my way to the bathroom. As I turned on the light, a giant water beetle raced to its hole in the wall. "The room is bugged." I laughed at my own tasteless joke. Then I staggered back to bed.

IN HIS ESSAY "A Room and a Half," Joseph Brodsky wrote that the Russians have more difficulty accepting the breaking of ties than anyone else. The Russians, he says, are a very grounded people. For them a house, a village, a country are all forever. Their sense of permanence is deeper; their feelings of loss also run deeper.

I have contemplated how it was just by chance that my family was thrust upon the Midwestern soil. Wrenched from their native land, the Jewish "pale" of the Ukraine where Jews had lived for centuries, my family would count itself among the lucky, the ones who got away. They could have gone anywhere, because after leaving Russia, nowhere would really be home—home now being a random, arbitrary place.

In an odd, hardly dramatic way, I felt I understood. I myself was thrust out into the world, unprepared, at the age of eighteen, not by politics, but by societal mandate when my parents drove me from the safety of the Midwest to a college in Boston where I was to spend the next four years. My parents drove from Chicago via Canada because they wanted to see Niagara Falls. At the Canadian border, I was so small, huddled in the back seat with the luggage and bags of clothes, that the customs official didn't see me, and

I was left with the sense that my own parents were kidnapping me, forcing me away.

I never wanted to leave, yet I was never to return. At times I tried. Once a year or so when I am gloomy, my parents say why don't you come home? At times the possibility draws me near, but I try to envision this for myself. Lunches at the Country Kitchen with high school friends. Gossip about who will divorce, who will remarry. Girlhood squabbles repeating themselves well into adulthood, over and over again. Sundays spent with my family, watching a football game. Chicago winters, the wind off the lake. Or summers, baseball at Wrigley Field. It is a reality that is incomprehensible to me.

I am caught in this web between a desire for permanence and a deep sense of loss. It is as if my dark Russian soul, plunked down in the Midwest, has been exiled, banished, relegated to another place. I thought that by coming to Russia, by traveling to the country my grandmother called home, I would somehow find an answer. I would recognize what I had been looking for all along.

Once I intended to write a doctoral dissertation on the migratory patterns of Midwestern versus Southern writers. I thought how Midwestern writers—Twain, Cather, Dreiser, Wilder, Hemingway, Fitzgerald, Nathanael West— wrote about the Midwest from either coast, whereas Southern writers—Faulkner, Welty, O'Connor—stayed put. My theory is this. The South is an interesting place to be. Strange things can happen in the bayou, under the ginkgo tree. But the Midwest, with its flat, unrippled surface and its child's dream of innocence and balance, is a good place to remember. As a friend once said, "It's a good place to be *from.*" For the South is murky and the Midwest is clear. It is boring, but it is kind, as opposed to the South which is always interesting but can be, I am told, compelling and cruel. The Midwestern writer, by and large, is a nostalgic one; his vision is innocent; his longing is for home. As

Fitzgerald wrote in *Gatsby,* the Midwest never told him a lie.

For years I have thought of buying a house on the East Coast. I squirreled away money for a down payment and there it sits. Sometimes I call a realtor who takes me on a tour where I peer into empty rooms, touch peeling paint. I stare into dusty mirrors. Always there is something wrong. The rooms are too spacious or too small. The house needs too much work. There's noise from the street. Or it's too quiet somewhere. In the end I don't buy. I'll wait. The market will go down. The realtors keep calling, but after a while, they stop. Eventually they catch on.

I used to think that none of the houses were what I was looking for, that none of them was right. But the truth is, all the houses were probably fine. I just didn't want to live anywhere. I had already had a home in Illinois which I spy upon when I go there. A strange man lives there now, married to a woman half his age, and a flagpole pierces the lawn.

I didn't want to live with someone else's memories. I didn't want to live in rooms imbued with others' hopes and dreams. I wanted whatever foolish loves and pointless disappointments to be mine. What is it, I ask, that makes me want to go back time and again, that will not allow another place to become home? I go there like a ghost. Or a criminal who must return to the scene of the crime. Like Raskolnikov I am plagued with the need to return, gripped with guilt. But I am an amnesiac. I cannot remember any wrongdoing. I have no idea what the punishment will be.

THE LINE around the crenellated red brick wall of the Kremlin to see the embalmed father of the Russian revolution snaked some five city blocks. It was replete with the requisite schoolchildren, workers, Soviet tourists. Foreigners, I was told, were quickly ushered to the front of the line, but so far no one had recognized me as a foreigner for which I was both grateful, for I was passing as Russian, and regretful as the heat of the day and my own fatigue were mounting. The estimated wait was three hours, but I had been standing still for forty-five minutes so I didn't feel hopeful. Ahead of me a flock of schoolchildren—from Social Studies I, I assumed—giggled, whispered, and moved restlessly in line while their somewhat endearing schoolmarm, a stocky, solid older woman, scolded them half-heartedly.

The Kremlin is the heart of Russia, troubled and tormented perhaps, like the dark Russian soul, but a heart nonetheless, and from here the lifeblood of Russia pulses. At the beginning of the twelfth century when the Mongols swept through Asia, they established a stronghold on the Eurasian plain where the great culture of Kiev thrived and here they remained for years, managing to turn the brilliant and rich civilization on the banks of the Dnieper into a wasteland. All who could fled north, into the forests. When the Tatar reign ended, a sizable population settled in the land between the Volga and the Oka rivers. They only needed to be united. This was accomplished by a small fortress, or *kreml,* on a hillock on the banks of the Moskva River called Moscow. The word Kremlin derives from the word *kreml,* a word we associate with Moscow but actually most Russian cities had their own central fortified kremlin. A view of the Kremlin from the banks of the Moskva River makes it easy to understand why this hill, protected by the river, played such a strategic role in the middle of these vast plains. It was here that the reconquest began and Moscow grew supreme.

With the fall of Kiev and the move in 1326 of the Metropolitan of the Russian Orthodox Church from his seat in the city of Vladimir to Moscow, Moscow became "the holy city," the third Rome. But the princes of Moscow were different from those of Kiev, who looked to the west. Moscow looked east, placating the Great Khan and turning Russia further and further from Europe. It would only be under Peter the Great who, impatient with the provincialism of the Moscow capital, built his capital in Leningrad that Russian eyes once again turned to the west. But the leaders of the Russian revolution would return Moscow back to its supreme place and to a Russia that had turned its back, once more, on the West.

Enhanced by the presence of the church, Moscow grew rapidly. By the fifteenth century the frontier settlement had reached a population of 100,000. It grew in circles (a look at the map of Moscow as well as its subway map reveals its concentric building), walled city within walled city, with many fabulous churches and wooden structures (most of which would be burned to the ground during Moscow's many conflagrations, including the spectacular burning of Moscow which forced Napoleon to retreat).

The walls of the Kremlin, which have loomed for centuries impregnable, wrapped in mystery and intrigue, were built by Italian architects in the fifteenth century. Within these walls judgments were handed down, tortures performed. Agonizing screams echoed from its towers. Czars were born, rose and fell. Revolts were quashed, liaisons conducted in its secret passageways.

In all probability the construction of the Kremlin walls

was supervised by Aristotle Fioravante, the great Italian architect who had been chosen by Czar Ivan III to build the Cathedral of the Assumption (also known as the Cathedral of the Dormition). A true Renaissance man, Fioravante was also an engineer, metal founder, expert on hydraulics and fortifications. Indeed, the Czar was so happy with his work that when Fioravante asked if he could go home, Ivan simply refused him permission. Fioravante died in Moscow, greatly honored but a prisoner of the Czar.

The brick walls of the Kremlin are twelve to eighteen feet thick. They are lined with passages and storage spaces, twenty towers, and five crimson-colored doors. The great walls of the Kremlin, combined with the ideal location of the raised hillock protected by the Moskva River, made the city virtually impenetrable. The Kremlin with its series of forts, armories, cathedrals, palaces, and convent was at its height during the sixteenth and seventeenth centuries. The splendor of this small city was legend. Cupolas rose in brilliant gold. Gold, silver and colored tiles gleamed from the walls.

Within its walls dwelled the czar and his entourage. Here was also the Terem, or female quarters, that gilded cage where the czarina and her ladies languished in tedious seclusion—a vestige from the time of Mongol rule when the women needed to be protected in that way—passing their days at religious ceremonies and embroidery.

In the Terem the czarina and the women who surrounded her spent their days preening, painting themselves, dressing, decking themselves in ermine and silver fox, in gold cloth in rooms replete with Persian rugs, jewels, ivory combs, mirrors, but with no one from the outside world to admire them. Their solitude was broken only by the occasional ball or at dusk as they stole through the secret tunnels that connected the churches, palaces and convents, but they never went beyond those walls, oblivious even to the marketplace of Red Square, just a few feet away from them and ablaze with life.

Few penetrated the Kremlin's walls. Few ever gained admittance to the upper echelons of its power. In modern times not much has changed. The government remains more or less absolute or at least centralized here in Moscow (some say it is the only way to rule Russia, as with China). The seat of government is now the Presidium, but essentially much of what happens behind the Kremlin walls, though they were opened to the public in 1958, remains cloaked in secrecy. If the Kremlin reflects anything about Russia, it reflects its consistency. Only recently glasnost has begun to cast some light into this darkness, but until now within the less than twelve acres that contain its museums, theaters, palaces, cathedrals, and houses of government from which all of Russia is ruled, the isolation has been complete.

Behind me an aging couple, arms looped, stood motionless as statues. I assumed from their dress and their patience that they had traveled across half their country for a glimpse at their revolution's hero. The woman in front of me clutched at her two children as if she were dragging them to safety. Dressed in a suit of gray gabardine, sweat dripping down the corners of her face, she turned to me. "It's very hot," she said. She was a robust, stocky woman. The children—a boy and a girl about a year apart who reflected their mother's robustness as well as her unseasonal dress—gazed at her with such adoration I could only assume they were desperate to persuade her to take them to the zoo or the circus. "Yes," I said, not wanting to think about it, "it is very hot."

"Oh, you are not from here. Where are you from?"

"America," I said, "New York."

"Oh, New York. New York." She pointed to me and then aroused the other drowsing members of our contingent who woke for a moment to absorb this fact. Even the old couple appeared visibly moved. "New York," I heard one of them whisper. "America" was echoed up and down the line.

"And you?" I asked the woman.

She smiled halfheartedly, then looked over her shoulder. "Kiev," she whispered as if this were a taint, something she could not say out loud. Then she began speaking quickly, long involuted Slavic sentences whose sense I lost before they began. She kept taking her children's hands, holding them up in the air. Tears came to her eyes. The old couple behind me had turned away, afraid, it seemed to hear her diatribe. But slowly I began to make sense out of what she was telling me. Chernobyl. They had been evacuated. But she was frightened for her children. She was afraid because they had drunk the water, breathed the air. They had marched in the May Day parade.

I explained to her as best I could that I was supposed to go to Kiev in a few weeks time. *"Nyet,"* she waved a finger in my face. "Don't go," she said. "It's not safe. No one is there."

Then she turned her back on me, and would not look at me again though I could see the rivulets of sweat coursing down her brow as she gathered her children to her. I stood there another hour until I thought I would faint, and the line had barely moved.

I pondered whether I really wanted to see Lenin, thinking how in truth the dead do not interest me. I have never been the kind of person to visit mausoleums, tombs, people resting in state. Perhaps it is my Jewish heritage. If I were Irish, maybe I'd love a good wake. The Jews pray for the living, even in their prayer for the dead. I thought with grimness about the wake for my Italian landlord, as his relatives from Calabria kissed his green face while a Chinese priest recited the Lord's Prayer in an incomprehensible Mandarin accent.

I made some gesture to the old people behind me, the

American equivalent of hold my place, because for some reason I was embarrassed to abandon the line. They nodded as I bid them good-bye. They knew I would not be back.

I headed over to the state emporium, GUM department store, thinking I would buy something to eat. Designed in 1888, along the lines of an Eastern souk, the building was intended to house the shops of different proprietors, over a thousand shops in all. In 1953 it was replanned, though the original design retained. Arranged along three tiers with wrought-iron railings and balustraded bridges, GUM claims to have over eighty-five million shoppers a year.

The lines to buy food were long and I had no strength for another line, so I slumped along the rim of the fountain that forms the centerpiece to the shopping center. Above me from the cross bridges Soviets peered down, some with the broad, flat faces that betrayed their ethnic heritage and the fact that they were from "out of town." At the fountain it was cool, almost peaceful. Toddlers played at my feet, dipping hands into the water. Lovers and hopefuls tossed coins. A rosy-faced child splashed water on me with glee while his ashamed parents scolded and uttered endless apologies.

The faces of the two children in front of me in the line to see Lenin would haunt me. Years later I'd watch a newscast of the victims of Chernobyl, children who had acquired leukemia. I had stared at pictures of hospital beds, rows of them lined with dying children, and searched for the faces of the children whose anxious mother had clutched them as if they were bundles she might lose.

Wondering now if I would indeed go on to Kiev, I wandered Gorky Street in search of food. (I had yet to discover the cafeteria at the Intourist Hotel around the corner which would provide me with breakfast and lunch for the rest of my time in Moscow.) At last in the very late afternoon I made my way back to my hotel to see if I could get a late lunch. There was an hour wait, which didn't seem so

terrible, so I sat until I at last pleaded with the maître d'
that I was starving and he sat me begrudgingly at a table
with a few Russians and an American film distributor from
Arkansas.

The distributor was perhaps fifty and he arranged for
films in the U.S.S.R. "Boy," he said, "I just love doing
business with the Soviets. Been doing it for years. Nicest
people to do business with. Honest, easy to get along
with." He didn't speak a word of Russian though he'd been
coming there for some time. "They all speak English," he
said.

He had a nice, fatherly way about him. A roundish, red
face, a puffy body, the kind of person you think you can
entrust your life's story to. I told him a relatively small
amount of mine. Just the surface, none of the facts. He
didn't pry but listened to whatever I said about my travels,
the purpose of my journey. "Boy, a woman traveling in this
country alone," he smacked his lips. "Don't see that every
day." Our orders of borscht and beef Stroganoff were slow
in coming. But the vodka was not. He told me about his
daughters back in Little Rock with his loving wife, Lor-
raine. Then he asked me hesitantly about my personal life.
"There's someone back home," I said, trying to remember
just who and where that someone was. "I think we'll get
married soon."

That evening I took a stroll through Red Square, pausing
before the moon rising above St. Basil's. The air was cool
and fresh and I felt my body starting to relax. Then I went
back to my room, opened the window wide and collapsed
on the bed. I drifted into that kind of deep sleep that only
comes a few times a year, when your fatigue is great and
your conscience for a moment at least is at peace.

I was in the deepest sleep of all when in the middle of the
night the phone rang, the man from Arkansas on the other
end. "I'm sorry," he said, "did I wake you? You seemed kind

of tense when I saw you this afternoon," he said, "I thought maybe you could use a back rub."

I thought how much I would love a back rub. "I don't think so."

"I don't mean anything strange by it."

"No thank you," I said, slamming the receiver down.

It would be hours before I could get back to sleep. I found myself sitting up, thinking about the person I didn't want to think about, the one I'd left behind. I didn't want to think about him because I harbored the hope that my life with him might turn around. I hadn't really faced the reality of our future together. That he was too old and had been married too many times, traveled too much and probably was seeing other women was lost on me. I was blindly in love with the person I believed understood me better than anyone had.

Even looking back now, it is not a love I can completely understand, but it seemed as if he saw through barriers, as if he knew how to go past the boundaries of self and reach inside. Never mind that after the first three months together, I already felt he was slipping away. Always on a plane, a tennis court, a conference. There were always reasons, excuses and now, I assume, lies why he could not be there.

I struggled for his time. For hours and days. We would spend months planning vacations, personal calendars opened. For a family trip to Florida, I'd beg for a week. He'd say four days. We'd settle on five, but then his ex-wife would call and one of the boys was being thrown out of school. The vacation we'd negotiated for so long dwindled down to three days.

Why was I so needy? I asked myself. Why couldn't I accept things as they were. You are the sea in which I swim, he'd say whenever I complained that I felt alone. If only you could relax, not be so dependent. Let go. If only I could be more confident, trusting, and self-assured. I was trapped and I knew it. Only his voice would soothe me. Only his reassuring words, like a drug, would assuage.

AT LEO TOLSTOY'S HOUSE they ask the visitors to put odd paper slippers over their shoes. Ahead of me a tour of widows shuffled, their feet sounding like sandpaper on the bleached wood floors of what was more like a country house than an urban dwelling. The wooden rocking chairs in the corner, sewing still on the table beside them, the calico curtains, the large park outside where stately linden trees grow all attest to this fact. I stayed behind in the dining room, letting the widows shuffle on, examining the everyday life Tolstoy lived in Moscow, a city he detested, this house that forged the deep division between him and his wife, a division that would drive them into embattled corners and the acrimonious marriage of their final years.

It was in October of 1882, at his wife Sofya's insistence, that the Tolstoy family moved to this house on Dolgo-Khamovnichesky Street (now called Leo Tolstoy Street). Tolstoy himself had no desire to leave his beloved Yasnaya Polyana, "Clear Glade," the house where he was born in 1828 one hundred and thirty miles south of Moscow. It was from Yasnaya Polyana that Tolstoy drew his strength. He loved the peaceful country life away from literary hubbub that tended to surround the man who had already written the great Russian epics and whose literary career, in a large sense, was behind him. He was moving into his spiritual phase where he ruminated for the last thirty years of his life.

It was at Yasnaya Polyana on a leather couch which Tolstoy kept in his study where Tolstoy himself and most of his thirteen children were birthed. It is there in the same glade that Tolstoy lies buried where as children he and his brother searched for the magic green stick which had inscribed upon it the secret to happiness for all mankind. At Yasnaya Polyana he walked among the linden trees, the birches and lilacs, paused beside his ponds, visited the 350 peasant families that lived on his land. He wrote *War and Peace* and *Anna Karenina* there. Yet Sofya, in part concerned for the education of her eight surviving children and in part feeling constrained by the country and longing to be near her friends and family, urged him, against his will, to buy this house in Moscow.

The house they bought was large, to accommodate their children. As I roamed from room to room, pausing to examine a book left open, a pair of spectacles on a desk, I thought how unhappy Tolstoy was here, how unhappy his family became. While his wife went to balls and social gatherings, he would slip out the back door to chop wood with the river men. How prophetic those words that open *Anna Karenina* became: "All happy families are alike, but an unhappy family is unhappy after its own fashion"—words written by a man who should know. Tolstoy fled back to Yasnaya Polyana whenever he could. He abhorred Moscow city life with a kind of Dickensian fervor, seeing here only a seething mass, the impoverished, the miserable. "Stench, stones, luxury, poverty, debauchery," was how he phrased it.

I shuffled upstairs, up a small, narrow stairwell. Pausing before the children's rooms with toys neatly lining the shelves, before the marital bed and the room where Tolstoy received the "dark souls"—those eccentrics who were his followers—I thought of what life was like for the Tolstoy family here. Tolstoy's own mother died when he was eighteen months old, his father when he was seven. Tolstoy was raised by devoted servants and when he was sixteen was sent away to board. For years he lived a life of gambling, debauchery, and indolence, dreaming of a great and pure love.

When he was thirty-four and she was eighteen, like Levin and Kitty in his masterpiece, *Anna Karenina,* Leo Tolstoy wedded Sofya Behrs. The first years of their marriage were a flowering of love and work and Tolstoy produced his masterpieces then. But he was a seeker, this orphan, who had looked for meaning in life first through freedom, then through love and marriage, through literature, and finally, in the phase that would drive them apart, through God.

In these benevolent rooms where children grew and in the park outside where they played, Sofya and Tolstoy drifted apart. She had borne him thirteen children, eight of whom survived. She had copied his work night after night, recopying *War and Peace* some seven times. Each morning when Tolstoy sat down to his desk he would find his fresh copies, which he would begin to edit anew. And yet on August 26, 1882, not long after they moved into this house, Sofya wrote in her journal, "It was twenty years ago when I was young and happy that I started writing the story of my love for Lyovochka in this book: there is virtually nothing but love in it in fact. Twenty years later here I am sitting up all night on my own, reading and mourning its loss. For the first time in my life, Lyovochka had run off to sleep alone in the study . . . Lord help me, I long to take my own life, my thoughts are so confused . . ."

I stopped at the study, recalling Sofya's words, thinking of the night he left her to sleep in his study. That night he would return to her, but he left her in small ways again and again over the next thirty years until at the age of eighty-two he wrote a note saying he was leaving her definitively, going on a pilgrimage from which he would not return. Sofya, reading his note, threw herself in a pond and would have died had one of her daughters not saved her. Tolstoy only got so far as Astapovo station where he lapsed into a coma, pen in hand, from which he never recovered.

The marriage that ended in this brutal way began as Tolstoy himself described, in *Anna Karenina,* the pure and great love of Kitty and Levin, a love that could only grow with time, unlike that of Anna and Vronsky, doomed to self-destruction. Tolstoy himself, the great visionary, never imagined his own marriage's bitter end.

I moved through rooms which showed no sign of acrimony and grief, rooms which only seemed to depict the simple joys of family life, of domestic harmony, not strife. I thought of my grandmother's house. My grandmother, Lena, had a back room with a cedar closet and this closet was filled with hats, boas, dresses from the turn of the century. She had a bronze elephant and an old sewing machine and dozens of bottles of perfume and creams. While my parents and other relatives sat downstairs in the parlor, my cousin Marianne and I dressed up, appearing in the parlor in boas and hats, perfumed like ladies of the night.

My grandmother's house with its foreign accents, smells, furnishings bore no resemblance to the antiseptic world of my own suburban life with its modern conveniences. Indeed, as I moved through the house of Leo Tolstoy, it was as if this was the house I had journeyed through all my life, as if I could close my eyes and smell my grandmother's sweet breads, her kasha, her savory fruit stews.

I thought of how much sadness dwelled within these walls. My own family was beset by strife, though I never quite saw it as a child. My father was a perfectionist; everything had to be done just right. My mother was a housewife who should have been a fashion designer. He wanted a spotless house, meals served on time. She wanted to be living in London or at least downtown Chicago. My father tried to teach my brother and me the proper way to do things, but children are notoriously imperfect. Nothing, it seemed, was ever done right. The napkin was never in our lap on time. The bread never broken before it was buttered.

Patience wasn't a strong point at home. Battles sent us fleeing into our rooms. Doors were slammed. My brother fled
to his television. I went to my books. My father was buried
behind newspapers; my mother took refuge in the sewing of
quilts. Here we fortified ourselves. We hid within the safety
of our walls.

My world was a made-up one. I invented roles for myself,
parts I played. Usually they evolved out of the pioneer past
of my little Illinois suburb. I was a woman in control of her
life. A mother on the prairie, a wife leading a wagon train, a
sister tending to an injured brother. In my dreams, along
the banks of Lake Michigan, in the ravines behind the
house, I was in charge. When I came home, I gave in to the
demands upon me. I practiced piano. I studied hard. I tried
to do everything right. Meanwhile I was seething inside. I
built strong walls around my world. No one came in. Nobody knew.

Then one day I exploded and what I'd built around me
came tumbling down. I shouted words my family never
knew I knew. I stomped out, barefoot, in the rain. I slept at
one friend's house, then in my boyfriend's arms. I shouted
again, but no one heard. How I could never be myself.
How there was a part of me I always had to hide. I set out
on journeys, wandering the world. I would find that part of
me I'd had to hide. Uncover what I'd lost, like buried treasure. And then I'd be able to tell my family and they would
understand.

Suddenly I felt stifled within the confines of the house. I
made my way down the back stairs where I deposited my
paper slippers and walked into the summer day. A large
enclosed park with rising linden trees, majestic, cool,
loomed to my right. Lifting the latch of the small gate, I
slipped inside Tolstoy's garden. Here Tolstoy walked and
pondered, searching for meaning in his life, for belief. Ev-

erything he had tried and succeeded had failed for him in some ultimate way.

A wave of despair overcame me as I walked among the lindens in Tolstoy's garden. Life seemed suddenly a series of compromises and trade-offs. Even the great ended up in disappointment. Earthly pleasures never satisfied his longing. Literature never satisfied his imaginings. The love and compassion Tolstoy sought, perhaps from the mother he never had, would never be found for him in his lifetime. His wife lived out her last days in misery, brokenhearted. Tolstoy, the man who preached peace, would spend his final hours in rage and isolation, dying alone in a train station.

I stretched out on a bench, linden trees arching overhead, the breeze cooling my body. I contemplated my own life, the man I loved who himself was a great student and lover of Tolstoy. Perhaps, I thought, history will prove things different. Perhaps, in my own case, it would all work out. I closed my eyes, content for the moment with the breeze overhead, Tolstoy's lindens waving above me. I folded my arms across my face and slept, a sleep that came over me as if I were floating.

A sharp banging awakened me. A guard with billy club and an army cap pounded on the bench. He spoke harshly. "You cannot be here," he said. "It is not allowed." Cruelly I was ordered out of the garden where I had found a moment's peace. But in truth I was shocked at myself. I am not given to falling asleep on park benches, let alone in the garden of a Russian icon. Now it seemed apparent that something was wrong. A parasite I'd picked up in China, a brain tumor, radiation sickness. Something was wrong with me. I found I could almost not stand. Like an old woman, her life behind her, I made my way to the gate where I briefly became entangled with the tour of widows before we went our separate ways.

□   □   □   □

I descended into the bowels of Moscow, deep into the underground, that remarkable feat of engineering which has become as popular as a tourist attraction as a mode of transport. Begun in the 1930s under Stalin, the first fourteen stations used more marble than all the palaces built by the Romanovs in three centuries. Although subsequent stations were built with less flourish and exuberance, the stations at the center of the city are veritable works of art with their colonnades, sculptures, paintings and mosaics glorifying the major events of Russian history.

I descended into a station less spectacular than those I had read of, but had yet to see, down a steep escalator taking me into a cavernous, well-illumined white station. It was Nikita Khrushchev who was responsible for the tunneling of the Moscow underground, which involved the work of five thousand engineers and sixty thousand workers. Often it was necessary to dig deep through solid earth and rock, hence the long escalators known for their breathtaking descent. It was in these tunnels that hundreds of thousands of Muscovites took refuge during the aerial bombardments of the Second World War.

Now the Muscovites milled, leafing through *Pravda*, chatting in a friendly way. Some looked anxiously at their watches. The train came and people rushed inside, as they would do anywhere in the world. I sat on a comfortable plastic seat in the well-lit, graffiti-less subway car contemplating my illness, for that was now what it appeared to be, and what I should do. Perhaps I should go to the embassy and ask to see a doctor, but that would cause a stir. Checking into a Soviet hospital seemed out of the question. I would wait until I got home.

We had reached the fourth stop. I almost missed it and a man had to thrust his body between the doors to let me out. I ascended on another great escalator, back into the light of day, and found myself in a tree-lined residential neighborhood that bore no resemblance to the heart of the inner city where my hotel was. Here was a park with prams lined up, children at play. Women sat on park benches, having lunch, talking with one another. Occasionally they shouted at a child. A line of old women snaked its way out of a bakery. Men smoked pipes, reading the newspaper.

I assumed the station was on the outskirts of Red Square so I began to walk back. I walked and walked, but the streets remained residential. The people were friendly, smiling at me. I walked for a long time and then stopped a man and asked if he knew where my hotel was. He frowned. Then I asked him where the Kremlin was. "Kremlin!" he exclaimed. He pointed in the direction I was going. As I turned to say thank you, he was shaking his head.

I walked for perhaps an hour, then collapsed on a bench. It was beginning to occur to me that I had taken the underground the wrong way—four stops in the opposite direction—and that I was perhaps miles from my hotel. Opening my map, I began to assess the damage. By the time I made my way to another underground station, I could be at the hotel. I walked on.

It was midafternoon now and I was famished. I found a bakery, but it had a very long line. I stood in the line for a while, but then moved on. I longed for a restaurant, a café, a deli, a bar. I wanted to sit at a table with a sandwich and a beer and watch people as they wandered by. But there was no free enterprise on the streets of Moscow. No signs, no places to pause, rest, have a bite.

Now hunger gripped me because I hadn't eaten since breakfast and then it was just coffee and a roll. But beyond food, I wanted people. I wanted to mingle. I thought how this country which had based its revolution on community and the notion of communal sharing had failed in this respect. Everything belonged to the State. The world around me presented itself in a muted gray. There were no colors, no goods, no neon, no store windows. Dwarfed trees stood daunted between buildings. Everywhere I looked there

were lines. The revolution that was based upon the selfless-
ness of man had somehow drifted into this drab despair.

All the stores had lines into the street and each store had
three lines—the one where you make your selections, the
one where you pay, the one where you pick up your purchase. The average Soviet housewife spends two hours a day
in lines. I found I had neither the patience nor the
strength. I pushed on until I came to a *kolkhoz* market, a
free enterprise market where individuals sell their own crops
—a kind of farmers' market. Here the lines were shorter,
though the cost high. I bought some small apples, a warm
bun, a bottle of soda. Pausing in a small park, I sat down to
eat. I ate as if I'd never eaten before in my life. I was amazed
at my hunger and my greed.

As I left the park, an old woman with gold and silver
teeth, a red babushka around her head, grabbed me by the
arm. She was asking directions, pointing in different ways.
It was the blind asking the blind. I told her I am not from
here. At first she laughed at her own foolishness. Then she
grew serious. Where? she asked, breathless, where? America, I said. Suddenly she took my arm and began to cry. She
sobbed, leaning toward me, whispering rapidly into my ear.

It occurred to me that she thought I spoke Russian flu-
ently, not the few words I could say to negotiate my way
down the street. She whispered rapidly into my ear, giving
me a message to take to someone she loves. Someone who
has gone away. A son, I imagine from the intensity of her
sobs. Or a daughter who has promised to send for her.
Please, she said over and over again, then whispering. She
took my hand, pressing it to her heart. Thank you, thank
you, she said, believing her message was safe with me. She
kissed my hand innumerable times, blessing me through her
gold and silver teeth. And then suddenly she was gone,
disappeared down the residential street. But what is the
message I am supposed to carry? I asked myself over and
over again. Whom is it for?

□   □   □   □

At eight-thirty that night I staggered into my hotel, exhausted, famished. I showered, put on my dress, and
headed down to the restaurant for dinner at nine o'clock. I
tried all the restaurants in my hotel—there were five of
them—and the wait was two hours minimum. There were
restaurants outside the hotel as well so I walked around the
corner, stopping at a few of these. In front of each restaurant was a long line. No one could say how long the wait
would be. The tourists seemed anxious and distraught.

I returned to my hotel. It was now about ten o'clock and
I was not feeling well. I asked again at one of the restaurants in my hotel and the waiter suggested I try room service. "Room service?" I said to myself. I had no idea there
was such a thing. He told me the key lady on my floor had
the menu. But the key lady on my floor had no menu and
she must call the waiter and half an hour later he arrived to
take my order. Without even looking at the menu, I evoked
Russian food. I ordered chicken Kiev. Then, recalling the
joke circulating around New York before I left—what has
feathers and glows in the dark—I changed my order to
beefsteak.

I went to my room and tried to place a call to New York.
I longed for my companion whom I had not seen in weeks.
It would be several more before we'd see one another again.
The operator said the call would take ten hours so I wrote
him a letter instead. I wrote until about eleven-thirty. Then
I went to the key lady, who called the kitchen. The kitchen
had forgotten my order. It would come right away. In the
meantime, I made myself a package of Eastern Mountain
beef Stroganoff which I cooked with a heating coil, the first
of many meals I would eat this way. I drank a shot of vodka
and went to bed.

At one in the morning there was a knock at my door.
"Room service, your dinner is here." I turned my face to
the wall, pretending to sleep.

□   □   □   □

In the morning I decided to ask Intourist if it would be possible to change my vouchers so that I would not go to Kiev. When traveling in the Soviet Union, it is all prepaid, prearranged. In order to make any changes one must deal with the government agency in charge of tourism, Intourist. I had not yet made up my mind that I would not go to Kiev, but I wanted to know if it would be possible.

At Intourist in each hotel nine or ten middle-aged and sometimes young women (I never encountered a man in this job) whose job it is to procure theater tickets, train tickets, excursions, museum visits and guides all sit in a row, formidable as a grand jury. I approached the woman in charge of travel vouchers. I asked if she spoke English. She nodded without speaking. "I would like to know if it is possible for me not to go to Kiev," I said politely, obsequious before her dour authority.

She was blond, perhaps my age, with severe features, a gray shirt. She gave me a cold stare. "Oh," she spoke indifferently, flipping through my vouchers. "You must go to Kiev. It is open for tourists."

"My embassy has a traveler's advisory against going into that area."

"Yes, I would not go." She spoke breathlessly, like Garbo. "Russians will not go, but you," now she smiled, "you must go."

THERE IS no phone book in Moscow. One was printed in 1914 and then again in 1930 and apparently a gigantic four-volume phone book was printed in 1972 that no one can afford and that is basically a collector's item. But a phone book, so you can look up somebody's number and reach them with anything resembling convenience, does not exist. To reach someone in the Soviet Union, you must have his number. And if you have his number, you and/or he or she can come under suspicion.

Through a contact, I managed to get the number of the man who warned me not to go to Kiev at the ambassador's a few nights before. I was told that this person would like to put me in touch with some other people. I will call him Ivan, although I am told I do not have to protect him because they have done everything that can be done to him, but still I feel I must change his name. Ivan has been forcibly separated from his wife, who is American. He has lost his profession. He has been declared a parasite. He cannot get a visa.

I am told other things. My phone is probably tapped. My room is wired. The maids work for the KGB. They will copy my address book if I leave it in my room. I am told that ten million people are KGB informers or work for the KGB in some capacity and that you cannot know whom to trust.

I phoned Ivan from my hotel room. He said he wanted me to meet some people, but he could not arrange it right away. "You must be patient in this country," he told me. "You must learn to wait." He wouldn't say anything more on the phone except this. "I know your itinerary. I will arrange something before you leave. You are not going to Kiev, are you?"

I went down to Intourist to see once again about making a change in my itinerary. A new woman sat at the voucher desk. She was older, with a blond bubble. Perhaps she will be more sympathetic, I thought. I handed her my voucher. "I am scheduled to go to Kiev, but I don't want to go." She looked at my voucher, then glared back at me. "Then you must leave the Soviet Union," she told me. "It is the only way."

THERE IS A PICTURE on my desk at home which I treasure. It is a picture of my family shortly after they had all arrived in the United States. They sit before a backdrop which in their lifetime they will never know—a farmhouse, a trellis, cherry blossoms, a picket fence. In the middle sits my great-grandfather Isaac with his long, dark beard, his blue eyes—my inheritance, I am told—and a stern, opaque face. My great-grandmother stands with her hand obediently on his shoulder, as if about to deliver an oration. Indeed, he seems no more than a podium, a prop upon which she rests. Around them are their children—the ones she buried alive. Dave and Harry with their long blond curls, Bunnie and Herman, older and not very attractive, Hannah, then my grandmother, Lena, a beauty about to turn ripe, and Eva, another beauty who would grow bitter with age, and Morris, the oldest. For me they have stopped at this moment before the fake backdrop, not long after they got off the boat.

In a drawer in my desk, I keep all my other photographs —the ones I intend to put in albums someday. Sometimes I even buy albums—smooth, tanned-leather books that I keep in a pile, empty, expectant for what I fear will never come. The ordering of my life. A chronology made clear. Though it is some plan I seek, it is what I seem to scrupulously avoid. I am sure I have spent more time thinking about putting the pictures into albums than the time it would ever take to do so. It has also taken me time to come to terms with this, in part because my orderly mother has all our photographs, over all the years, in stacked albums, our names and the years embossed in gold on the outside.

The truth is I want them to pile up. I like the way, in this drawer, time blurs over the years. I can reach in and retrieve myself at sixteen or thirty-three. I can find my grandmother, a young woman with small children, or older, eyes glassed over with glaucoma, squinting for the camera.

Moments are frozen here, beauty endures. My Russian family for me is forever in front of that picket fence. History has not yet altered our lives. I can pull out of the drawer pictures of me standing with people with whom I no longer speak. Others who are dead or in their decrepitude. I myself remain frozen in this time. I look into the mirror and sense that I am not the same person I was before, but I have found the means to rationalize. A good night's sleep, a dark rinse, a few pounds off, will restore me to my adolescent powers.

The picture on my desk and the muddle in my drawer make me feel secure. As if we will all, everyone we have ever loved, live on in one dazzling moment. I cannot envision dust gathering, my papers gone to waste. What I want is this blur, these moments standing still, frozen like the winters of my youth.

NICHOLAS DANILOFF lived in a tree-lined residential district in a railroad flat a bit on the outskirts of Moscow. When I reached him by phone and told him what I was trying to do, he suggested I come over. Daniloff was a pale, thin man with glasses, a studious type. He did not make small talk as he handed me an enormous map. *"Chernigov gibernia.* That's the district of Chernigov. Here is the area where you want to go," he told me, pointing in a circle around Chernigov, and for the first time I saw a detailed map of the Ukraine with all the little villages and towns.

Daniloff had been writing a book about a Russian relative of his and he understood the difficulties of doing research in the Soviet Union. "You need a special visa and with Chernobyl, you won't get it now. You need to learn more Russian. You need contacts here. You can't just go do whatever you want in this country." He made it quite clear that getting to the area my family came from on this trip would be impossible.

"And I would not go to Kiev now. There is nothing you can do. No one will take you out of the city and it probably is not safe."

"I thought if I could just see the outskirts. A few towns . . ."

He shook his head. "It is highly unlikely that you will be able to do this. You could go to Kiev and sit and try it, but in my opinion Kiev is not safe now."

"I've been trying to change my itinerary, but it doesn't seem to be working."

"Keep trying," he said. He spoke in a dry, straightforward manner and I believed him more than I had believed any of the others. Then he showed me around. I saw his research room, filled with newspapers and clippings like a small library, all neatly filed. He said he kept everything because he never knew when he would need it.

After about an hour, I thanked him and left. I had a ticket for the circus that night and his wife, as she saw me to the door, suggested I walk. "It isn't far," she assured me.

"Oh, but I'm so tired," I told her, thinking how true this was.

She laughed. "A woman your age shouldn't be so tired."

"You're right," I said, "but I am."

I headed out along the route she told me to take, but it seemed much longer than I had thought. I had to rest several times along the way. I paused at a place where I admired the view of the city, at about same spot where, three months later, Nicholas Daniloff would be arrested by the KGB for spying.

I arrived late at the new amphitheater for the Moscow circus and raced to my seat. Nearly collapsing, I looked up to see a panda riding a unicycle. Then an oriental woman appeared, balancing the bowls. A man made his body tiny as he moved through hoops. I had rushed to see the Shanghai acrobats, the same ones I'd seen in China, while the Moscow circus was on tour of the United States. I sank into my chair, awakened only by the house lights and the stampede of Muscovites hurrying home. I followed them into the Metro where the bright lights dazzled me and I managed to make my way without mishap this time back to Red Square.

In my hotel room, I waited. I wanted to meet with Ivan, the man I met at the United States Embassy who would take me to talk with some people. I also had been promised a meeting with the Russian poet Andrei Voznesensky. So I waited for the phone to ring. It was hot and there was no air conditioning so I lay naked on the skinny bed in tangled sheets, a hot, dusty breeze blowing in, and waited. My breasts felt distended, my belly large. This seemed like a foreign body to me, not the one I'd known.

I placed a call to my companion in New York and miraculously the call went through within an hour, but there was no answer. Instead, I heard his disembodied voice on the answering machine and wanted to leave a message, but the operator didn't understand. She cut off his voice in midsentence as I lingered over the words, the sound. It was the closest I'd come to him in weeks.

A new level of loneliness set in. I wrote an impassioned letter. I don't want to travel alone again, I told him. On a sheet of notepaper, I made a list of the guests I would invite

to our wedding. Then I tore the letter up and tossed it into
the trash.

The phone rang and it was Ivan. He told me that he was
trying to set up some appointments, but nothing could be
arranged now. If I returned to Moscow after my visit to
Leningrad instead of going to Kiev, he would have an ap-
pointment for me then. I told him that I had tried but
couldn't change my vouchers. "Keep trying," he said.

"You're the second person to say that to me," I told him
as we hung up.

Hunger grabbed me and I headed out the door. I had
discovered the Intourist cafeteria by now, thanks to the
man from Arkansas who told me about it when I ran into
him in the lobby, and I went there for lunch. I filled a plate
with stuffed cabbage, stewing meat, potatoes. I could not
imagine how I would ever eat so much food, but effortlessly
I did.

Returning to the hotel, I met the Intourist guide with a
covey of tourists she would take to penetrate the Kremlin
walls. This is not the way I like to see things, but I was told
that to see the Kremlin museum, this was the only way.

We walked to Cathedral Square, once the soul of Russia,
this place of numerous churches and palaces, now either
museums or government buildings. Dispassionately our
guide pointed from building to building, dome to dome.
She raised a limp wrist in the direction of the Cathedral of
the Assumption, built by the architect Fioravante, the one
who under Ivan III had died a much-lauded prisoner within
these very walls he had helped construct. She pointed to
the Great Palace where once sumptuous feasts were held
and seven hundred guests could be served on gold plates.
The Russian love of bigness seemed most prevalent here—
giant feasts; the biggest bell in the world, cracked, which
cannot be rung; the gigantic cannon with the largest caliber
on earth, its dark cavity pristine. The cannon has never
been fired.

We wandered through the Cathedrals of the Assumption
and the Annunciation, past the tombs of czars, pausing to
admire the splendors of imperial Russia—the mosaics, the
restored frescoes. In the Armory our guide, an ashen-faced
woman in her mid-forties who had probably been doing the
Kremlin tour all her life, pointed at a crown, a saber, a
portrait, a suit of armor. The remnants of Russia's historic
past, its lost art forms, of value now only for the tourists
they bring. The shadows of the czars who lived here seem
to flicker on the walls like a procession passing. Vasili the
Blind, Ivan the Great, Ivan the Terrible, Boris Godunov,
the False Dimitri. Even Peter the Great, whose energy
could not be contained by these walls, seemed to have left
his mark here if only by his absence.

We reached a hall of gowns and I grew weary of the
guide's indifference to us and to her task. She pointed to
gown after gown, passing over a creamy white satin and
ruby gown worn by Czarina Alexandra. "Excuse me," I
said, "but what about this dress?"

No one in our group had had the nerve yet to ask this
woman a thing and now the group paused, awaiting her
response. She looked at me with disdain, "It belonged to
the Romanov family," she said.

"When was it worn?" I asked.

"At a ball," she said, moving on.

I thought about all the things people won't talk about
here—the last of the Romanovs, and Stalin. It will be four
years before the Soviet press will speak frankly about
Chernobyl. It would take them forty to speak of the massacre of the Polish officers in Katyn woods. What if in America we couldn't discuss McCarthy, the Civil War, or Three
Mile Island? Perhaps we'd find our way around it as most
Soviets had. But the fact was, the guide was telling us what
she had been taught. It was the Party line. There was nothing more she would say.

I felt relieved when she let us go on the outskirts of the

Kremlin walls and we fluttered away like caged birds. It was now late afternoon and I decided to go to the Great Moscow swimming pool for a swim. Heading back to the hotel, I lay down for just a moment on the bed. I closed my eyes to rest them. A gentle breeze blew in. I felt myself floating as if through space. When I woke, it was dark and cooler now. I pulled the covers over my head and once again I slept.

In the morning I was determined to change my vouchers and headed straight for the Intourist desk. There was a new woman and I asked her what language she spoke. French, she told me. So in French I explained my problem and she stared at my voucher. "Oh, you can change," she told me, "but it will cost you twice what you have already paid."

The women, I knew, switched posts frequently, so I went to the Intourist Hotel for breakfast and a walk around Red Square. I contemplated for the last time a visit to Lenin, lying in state, but the line seemed longer than before, growing now that school had let out for the summer, and instead I wandered back to my hotel. Since I was departing tomorrow for Leningrad, this would be my last try.

A new woman had appeared at the Intourist desk, one I had never seen before. She had soft, gentle features and warm brown eyes. As always, I asked her if English were her language and she replied, "No, Spanish." This surprised me since so far no one had said they spoke Spanish. It also pleased me, since Spanish was my best foreign language and I knew Latin culture well. I thought to myself, standing there, what do Latin women care more about than anything in the world?

I turned to her and said, "I am going to have a baby and I am supposed to go to Kiev. I would like to change my vouchers."

She nodded, making it clear she understood. "Of course. No, you should not go." It was the first time anyone in an official capacity had revealed their human side. I leaned toward her across the counter between us. She glanced at my body, a questioning look in her eyes.

"Only a few weeks," I replied.

"I will be happy to change your vouchers. There will be no problem. There will be no charge." I watched as she flipped through my vouchers—the dream and destination of this trip now diverted by the tragic mishap of Chernobyl while perhaps another dream and another destination were unfolding.

"I would appreciate that," I said.

"Would you like to return to Moscow, then?"

"Yes, that would be fine."

And then I knew what perhaps I'd known all along. That I had been intending to travel to the place where the world's worst non-military nuclear disaster had occurred and that I was, by a quick calculation, six weeks pregnant.

"What is your name?" I asked.

"Natalia," she told me.

"Thank you, Natalia," I said.

I walked outside. It was a warm afternoon but there was a breeze in the air and I began a slow walk around Red Square, trying to absorb the conversation I'd just had, the facts of my life as they now stood. I was not going into the Ukraine, which was the purpose of my journey, and I was going to have a child, which was taking me by surprise. I felt thwarted, and yet at the same time I experienced a sense of completion. Still, I could not bear just to get on a plane as scheduled and fly home.

It occurred to me that it might be a long time before I'd be traveling on my own again. If I could not go to the Ukraine, I wanted to continue on and return to the West by rail. I wanted to complete this journey which had begun in Beijing by traveling overland to Berlin.

Natalia was still at her post when I returned. "Excuse me," I said, handing her all of my vouchers, my plane tickets, everything. "I am supposed to leave Russia in about two weeks by plane from Moscow after the visit to the Ukraine."

"Yes," Natalia said, shuffling through what I'd handed her.

"Well, I'd like to cancel my flight and take the train to Berlin. I'd like to buy a rail ticket."

She looked at me askance. "You will need transit visas. You'll need to change this airplane ticket. I'll have to check with the railroad. I don't know . . . Where will you stay in Berlin?"

I shrugged. "Somewhere. It doesn't matter." She looked at me, now somewhat amused. "Is it possible?"

"It will be difficult," Natalia said slowly, a smile crossing her face, "but it can be done."

Later that evening as I packed for Leningrad, the pieces were clear and suddenly I understood. I wasn't even sure how I had missed it for so long, but when one is traveling, time is sometimes forgotten. But there it was. Now as I thought back, reading through my journals, I knew that it was true. In fact I had dreamed my daughter before I had her. I had dreamed her on the Yangtze River boat ride where the dead bodies of pigs and cattle and humans drifted by. I dreamed her in a sweltering heat where the stench rose from Deck Class below. On the river the Chinese say is the river of life and death, I imagined my daughter and there I conceived her.

On that journey through China with my companion, I had met a young girl with copper-colored hair who liked to paint with watercolors to pass the time. Her name was Axelle and she was eleven years old. Her family, who lived in Fiji, traveled all over the world. I admired this family of intrepid travelers—each child wearing his own backpack—and I knew then that I wanted to have a child to journey with, to see the world. In the afternoon as our boat sailed down the muddy green river that seemed to ooze life and death, Axelle came to my room and we sat on the floor and painted. River gorges, farms, hamlets that lined the riverbank. We painted the sailboats and the sunsets we saw. We exchanged our paintings and promised to write.

That night in the hotel room in Moscow, eating yet one more can of sardines, I read over my journal and found this entry: "May 23, 1986. Arrived Wuhan, 6 P.M. Spent day painting and reading with Axelle. I long for a little girl— have a deep desire for a child, boy or girl, but a girl would be best. A child who will want to see the world."

For years I had wanted to try and have a child, but my medical history made the prospect dubious. Ten years before, I had doubled over in a Mexico City movie house. Thinking it was parasites that caused my pain, I went home and took some medicine for amoebas. Hours later an abscess on an ovary ruptured, sending disease coursing through my body. I lived on the outskirts of the city then and when I felt the pain, grueling now, which only hurt when I moved, I recalled the old cowboy westerns. How before you die it only hurts when you laugh. A surgeon's knife saved me, but a child was an unlikely goal. But in Tibet, perhaps in a moment of folly or great love, I'd told my companion I wanted to try.

Later one night in Wuhan we left the boat and entered the steamy furnace city of the Yangtze. The heat was visible, in undulating waves. The night was dark but the streets were illumined. Passing a boarding room, we stared in at men who lay miserable, solitary, broiling on straw mats in a concrete room. I walked with Axelle and her family, my companion at my side. Firecrackers went off in our faces, little boys ran shrieking off to the side. As we walked those sweat-drenched, stinking streets, where we sucked coconut ice and warded off the boys as they thrust sparklers in our faces, a coursing pain shot through my side. Yet it was not an unpleasant sensation. Rather on those stinking streets of the furnace town, on the banks of the river of life and death, it had been like a fire burning inside.

THE INTOURIST OFFICIAL was waiting for me in the lobby of the hotel to take me to the station for the train to Leningrad. He was a large, gray man with the same dour face I'd come to expect from Intourist. He said my name, then directed me to his car. A few moments later we were at the station and he was walking ahead toward the platform while I dragged my bag behind him. Though I had left many things with the concierge, because Natalia had arranged for me to return to the same hotel, my bag felt heavy and I kept thinking he would turn and see if I needed a hand, but he didn't. I scowled behind him as he passed car after car, moving farther and farther along the train.

Women with babushkas peered down. Young boys who looked like soldiers waved at friends on the platform. The train seemed quite full and I was glad. At last we reached a car. Then, turning around, he took my bag into the compartment and flung it on a seat. I followed and saw that I was sitting in the last seat in a completely empty car. He pointed, instructing me to sit. He did not seem like the kind of man to argue with, so I obeyed, feeling somewhat diminished. Then he left.

I sat for a long time and no one came. It occurred to me that perhaps foreigners were kept separate from the Russians on this train which was not the overnight tourist train to Leningrad. It also occurred to me that I was the only foreigner on the train and hence I would ride for some ten hours alone. I got up and looked into the compartment behind mine. It was full of Russians, laughing, passing bread and cheese among themselves. I felt as if there was a party going on in the next room and I was not permitted to attend. I thought I would just take my bag and go into the next compartment, which is what I decided to do, when people began to file into the car.

This railroad, ordered to be built by Nicholas I, has a mythical past. In a perhaps apocryphal story, it is said that the railroad has a curve near Leningrad because when the Czar indicated its route, he drew a line with a ruler between Moscow and Leningrad (then St. Petersburg) and the pencil slipped around his finger near the top. No one dared ask whether he meant the curve to be there. They just built it that way.

This was also the train where Anna Karenina met Vronsky that snowy night when her fate was sealed. Not unlike Anna Karenina on this very same train, her emotions shuttling between private passion and societal propriety, I contemplated my fate. As a young girl growing up on the banks of Lake Michigan I had made a pact with myself. If I ever got pregnant, which was a very dim possibility in my girlhood, I would fling myself off the bluff where I walked my dogs. This way I would not be a burden to myself or my family. I would hide my shame.

I had watched Sally Walters in her gym suit, her belly protruding more and more, until she was whisked away to a "private school" in New England and returned months later, trim and forever subdued. And I had seen what had happened when my neighbor and friend, Ginny Brown, got pregnant, and her father, a violent drunk who played cards with my father, tossed her out. I knew then that the bluff was the only viable option for me. But now, years later, I envisioned for myself a different scenario. I was no girl of sixteen. I had a companion with whom I had spent the last three years. I was almost forty with a career. I could take care of myself and I had someone to share my life with. My story would be different from theirs.

A pretty woman in a cotton shirtwaist came into our car. She was followed like a duck by a procession of small children, and then an old woman. Oddly they all took seats in different places. Couples came in. Then a fat woman and her two rather large sons crammed themselves beside me, one of the sons wrapping his legs around mine and going to sleep for the entire train ride.

The train started up and soon we left the station behind. As it snaked through the outskirts of Moscow, I peered forlornly at building after building of government housing. Then the government housing was gone and we were in the suburbs that were more bucolic. Small cottages surrounded by trees, old men working in their gardens. I stared out the window, the sun in my face, and watched then as the landscape alternated between farmlands and more industrial sites as it would for much of the journey.

Leo Tolstoy wrote in his novel *The Cossacks,* "It is always the case on a long journey that during the initial stages the imagination lingers behind on the place one has left, but with the first morning on the road it leaps forward to the end of the journey and there begins building castles in the sand." The gloom I had felt in Moscow was lifting. I was content to be moving ahead. And now I had devised a plan for myself. I would call my companion from Leningrad and tell him the news. We would plan our future. On a sheet of paper I remade the list of the guests who'd come to our August wedding.

The pretty woman in the cotton shirtwaist asked me a question I didn't understand. From my response she looked at me quizzically, then asked where I was from. America, I told her. *Amerikanska?* she replied. From New York, I said. New York, she replied, amazed as if I'd said another planet. Suddenly I became her property like a found dog and first she told her children, then an elderly couple who'd come on. Then she took me by the arm and paraded me up and down so that everyone knew that an American was in their car.

Clearly this had never happened to most of these people. They got up and looked at me as if I were a rare specimen in a zoo, something never dreamed of before. Others gave me small tokens. An old man handed me a pin of Lenin. Another a stick of gum. I had brought pencils with the Statue of Liberty perched where the eraser should be for such an occasion and I began handing them to the children, who took them with gleeful shrieks. The fat woman beside me kept trying to arouse her comatose son, but he shrugged her away and continued with his narcoleptic sleep.

After a while my novelty wore off and most of my fellow travelers went to sleep. I unwound my legs from the sleeping young man and made my way into the dining car. It was almost full and I realized that I was the only foreigner on the train. The old man who'd given me the Lenin pin was squeezed into a seat with some women and a young girl and he beckoned for me. American, he shouted so everyone turned; here, sit with me, pointing to a nonexistent space.

Somehow everyone made room. We introduced ourselves and the old man told the waiter, a handsome young blond Russian with a dark mustache and lovely dark eyes, to bring me tea and whatever else I wanted. You are from America, he said, his eyes widening. I smiled and the next thing I knew a plate of steaming kasha with melting butter sat before me and no one seemed to care that he had served me before the others or that he would never hand me a bill.

We told stories about ourselves over lunch. I told them of my journey and they were amazed. "Trans-Siberia," the woman with the young girl exclaimed. The little girl asked me where was my husband and my children and I thought about this for a moment. "They are at home," I told her. "They are waiting for me."

When they had all finished their meals, everyone got up, at once it seemed, waving good-bye, and I was left almost alone in the dining car. I was glad for the respite, thinking I'd have a little time to myself, when suddenly the waiter sat down.

"My name is Sasha," he said. I told him my name. "I want to visit America," he told me, "I've heard wonderful things. I like it here. It is my country. I have a good job. I meet interesting people, but . . ." he looked over his shoulder to see if anyone was listening. "Sometimes it is not enough. There are things . . ." again he looked to see if anyone was listening. I noticed an official-looking person counting receipts in the back and Sasha seemed uncomfortable in the presence of this person. "Difficult at times." Over the Soviet equivalent of Muzak someone sang in Russian, "We Shall Overcome."

I pointed to the speakers. "Martin Luther King," I said. He nodded and smiled. "Things are changing now, aren't they. With Gorbachev."

He shrugged. "Things happen slowly."

"How long have you worked for the railroad?"

He held up three fingers. "I am an engineer but for now I must do this," he shrugged, clearly not happy with his lot. "But eventually I will be an engineer. This is just my training period." But I noticed a sense of defeat in his voice, as if his training period would go on for a long time.

"What do you want to do when your training period is over?"

"Build bridges," he said proudly, "or perhaps hydraulic dams."

I had my phrase book with me and we kept flipping through it when we could not find a word. He came to the word "synagogue" and pointed, again looking behind him. I looked at him strangely. "Are you Jewish?" he asked. "Many Americans who come to Russia are Jewish."

I nodded.

"My mother," he said, "she is Jewish. So I am Jewish."
He took off his railroad pin and handed it to me. "Saturday
morning, be in front of your hotel. I will take you to synagogue." And I said I would.

Leningrad

IT HAS BEEN CALLED the Venice of the North, the Second Paris, Babylon of the Snows, North Palmyra—the age-old romance with Asia Minor transformed into the frozen Russian North. To Peter the Great, it was his window on the West. It is a dreamer's dream, this city built on bones. It was of Leningrad that Pushkin wrote in his epic poem *The Bronze Horseman*, "I love you, Peter's creation, I love your severe, graceful appearance, the transparent twilights and moonless gleam of your still night." Yet it is also of Leningrad that Mandelstam, awaiting the security police who would take him to his exile and death, wrote in a poem named after the city he so loved, "I returned to my city, familiar as tears . . . Petersburg! I have no wish to die . . . I still possess a list of addresses . . . I stay up all night, expecting dear guests."

Like a once great but troubled starlet, Leningrad has led a tormented past. For its beauty it has paid a high price. Its light possesses a dark side. Tens of thousands died building this city under Peter's relentless command. A million and a half died trying to defend it during the nine hundred days of its siege in World War II. To the Romanovs it was the capital of the world, the seat of their absolute power. To Lenin it was a sweatshop, ready for agitation and revolution. To Stalin in his paranoia, because it was the birthplace of the 1917 Revolution he feared the city might rise up against him. He consolidated the seat of his power more firmly in Moscow. Some feel that when he knew the Nazis were planning an assault on Leningrad, he turned his back.

If it was Moscow's fate to confront Napoleon, it was Leningrad's to face Hitler. If it was Moscow's fate to burn, it was Leningrad's to starve. Neither city was conquered and

both in their own way marked the defeat of the aggressor—
in part because the opposing armies could not withstand
the Russian winter. Yet Leningrad suffered almost beyond
belief in World War II. The packing crates of the Hermitage
Museum were used as coffins; children's sleds transported
the sick, the dead. When the shellings ceased, the blockade
was lifted, and the starvation of half its population over, the
renovation began. Its power depleted, Leningrad became a
living museum.

But for me, its potency remained. As the taxi hurtled
along Nevsky Prospect en route to my hotel, I was immediately captured, taken in. Perhaps it was the shock of arriving
at eleven o'clock at night and finding broad daylight, for it
was White Nights—that time of year in the North when,
because of the angle of the earth's axis, the sun never dips
very far below the horizon. Perhaps it was the whirl of
colors—the buildings of green and blue, pink and creamy
white that darted by. Or the austerity of its imperial structures bathed in Northern light and reflected in the waters of
the canals. Cold, expansive, indifferent. Leningrad, St. Petersburg, Petrograd, Sankt Piterburkh, or just Piter—Peter,
as its denizens like to call it—casts a spell that won't let go.

In this city of madmen and poets, its grip was visceral. I
myself would not have trouble in the trade-off between
beauty and bureaucracy, but Leningrad once had it all—the
power, the glory, the exquisite looks. Now only the façade
remains, though as splendid as any I'd ever seen; there was a
poignancy about this city which perhaps reflected my own
state of mind, a sadness I would be hard-pressed to name.

The lobby of my hotel was filled with the most beautiful
women I have ever seen, dozens of them who seemed to
have sprouted spontaneously out of the city itself. Women
dressed in silk of shiny mint and pale gray, electric blue and
soft violet. Women in shoulder pads and spiked heels with
exotic tresses of spun flax or the darkest Mediterranean

shade. Women who seemed to have materialized out of the pages of *Vogue*.

These were the women of Leningrad who emerged from their stale desk jobs or secretary pools every Friday night to service the Finnish men—often fat and jowly, with coarse ways and wads of money—who arrived like clockwork for the weekends. These modern-day Cinderellas transformed themselves into the beauties that they were. My hotel lobby appeared to be the ideal spot for this salient example of free enterprise which was taking place before my eyes.

I checked into the hotel, my room a quaint study of lace curtains and dark wood, a four-poster canopy bed tucked into an alcove. But I felt restless so I walked outside. I wanted to have a drink and be among people. There was a bar next door so I went in.

The bar was also filled with these same women who sat like mannequins, lips perfectly glossed, eyelashes thick as horse hair, curled to perfection, cheeks with just the right blush. They reminded me of actresses, when the call went out for a certain type, wearily awaiting their audition. Their dead eyes gazed at me as I entered their midst dressed in jeans, a bulky shirt. I thought about turning back, but it became a matter of pride. Instead I traversed the obstacle course set up by their legs which stretched across the room.

The reality of my pregnancy had not yet truly sunk in, so I ordered a drink. Vodka. After a few moments, a Finnish man sat down at my table and spoke to me in Russian. I glanced at my blue jeans, my bulky shirt. I felt the eyes in the room turn on me with icy stares. "I'm American," I said, wondering what had prompted him to select me out of all the possibilities in the room. "Oh, I thought you looked different, but I could use a little company that's different. These women, they're all lonely. You know what they want more than anything else, they want to talk."

"I can identify with that," I said.

"What're you doing in this place?"

"I wanted a drink," I said, "I wanted to get out."

"It can be taken wrong," he muttered. He was stout with thinning yellow hair. He wore a wedding ring.

"Are you here on business?"

He laughed, "Well, my wife thinks I am. A couple times a year I get over here, but," his hand swept the vapid faces of women, "it's getting a little tedious." He was a rather jovial if crass man. "But my wife, well, you know how it is. . . ."

Actually I didn't know and wanted to ask him more, but he took another line of discussion. "Let me tell you something," he spoke in a fatherly way. "You've got to be careful here. Oh, no one will hurt you, it's not like that, but in this city people will buy anything. They'll buy your jeans," he plucked at my leg. "Your shirts, your jewelry, but mainly they want dollars, so be careful with your money. But you can trade anything you've got. Sunglasses, lipstick." He slapped me on the leg, "Anything." I was enjoying his company and was sorry when he got up to leave, though clearly he did not just want to talk.

When he was gone, I looked around and saw that except for the bartender the room was filled with women. I was hungry to talk to a woman. I looked across for sympathetic eyes and found none. Just blank stares and suspicious looks. They must have been having a slow night, or business was generally bad. Whatever it was, they wanted to know what I was doing there, intruding upon their terrain. I sat nursing my vodka, staring into its cold glass.

At two in the morning I emerged from the bar into broad daylight. Knowing I would be unable sleep and with a long, sunny night ahead, I decided to go for a walk. I wandered to the small square near my hotel across from the Russian Museum and found myself before the statue of Pushkin. This was his city and he was their poet, the father of Russian literature. Descended from an Abyssinian prince named Hannibal, Pushkin was (and remains) Russia's most beloved

writer. A free spirit, he lived intensely, gambled compul-
sively, and died in a duel with a man with whom his wife
was probably in love, leaving generations of Russians to
mourn. For two days after he was shot Pushkin lingered,
his wounds turning gangrenous. After his death, the ordinary people of Russia filed past, dumbstruck at the premature death of their beloved poet.

As I sat beneath his statue, a disciple myself, the sun
shone still bright and the wisteria were in bloom. I
breathed in the nectar of lilacs. The air, fresh off the Gulf of
Finland, was redolent with the smell of jasmine. Sweetness
was everywhere. The park was not empty, nor were the
streets as the citizens of Leningrad ambled as they would
for two more weeks of White Nights, aimless and confused
as a disoriented migrating herd.

With no map, I set off thinking I'd make a loop, then
return along the wide boulevard of Nevsky Prospect in the
direction of the river. But it was not long before I left the
main street and was wandering down a side street lined with
canals, across a footbridge crowned with gold-winged grif-
fins, running my hands along the wrought iron, delicately
webbed.

The buildings of imperial Russia loomed before me,
painted in their shades of blue like robin's eggs, the pink of
Norwegian salmon, the soft yellow of cut wheat, the white
of fresh cream, all reflected in the brownish-green waters of
the canals. I cut through other side streets, crossed other
bridges, passing lime-green houses, others painted a muted
red. Though I kept thinking I would turn back, I found I
could not, for the colors and the night and the air kept me
moving along.

I walked until I stood on the cobbles of Palace Square
before the astonishing Winter Palace. With hundreds of
rooms, its blue-and-white façade shimmered like ice. It was
here on January 9, 1905, that Father Gapon led thousands
of peaceful demonstrators to petition the Czar for help for

their hardships and where they were met—men, women, children—with the gunfire of the imperial guards. Bloody Sunday, as the massacre came to be called, touched off the Revolution of 1905, and now in the middle of my first night in Leningrad I stared into its vastness and imagined the slaughter that had occurred, the dark side of all this beauty slowly revealed.

Continuing on, I reached the Neva where I paused before its wide, turbulent, exquisitely blue surface, and the stately, palatial buildings that lined its banks. Frozen solid for six months of the year, the Neva now flowed into the Gulf of Finland with a force that astounded. Along its banks in this strange, late-night splendor, I admired the handiwork of the architects and landscape architects Peter had commissioned from abroad—Trezzini, LeBlond.

I hugged the banks. Small fishing boats floated by. A barge in no hurry meandered past. Two lovers in light jackets sat on an old boat ramp, kissing with abandon as the river lapped at their feet. Gulls hovered overhead, then dived at their feet for crumbs they tossed them. It was here on the shores of this river that Russian literature came to be. All Russian writers, the saying goes, "came out of Gogol's 'Overcoat'." In Gogol's story that coat was ripped off a poor civil servant on the streets of Petersburg at the beginning of the nineteenth century. But it was Pushkin who immortalized the city he loved in his epic "The Bronze Horseman." Like the American frontier to the pioneers, Leningrad to the Russians was their window on the West. Their place to imagine, to dream, and perceive other worlds.

Now I found myself standing before that statue from which the great Russian epic draws its name, with Peter astride his rearing horse, symbol of Russia itself, trampling a serpent representing the forces that tried to oppose his reforms. Peter, to cite Pushkin again, "by whose fateful will the city was founded by the sea, stands here aloft at the very brink of a precipice having reared up Russia with his iron curb." I read the inscription, "To Peter the First from Catherine the Second 1782" and stood for a long time peering at the rising hooves of Peter's horse which I felt could easily trample me if it desired.

Then I turned back into the maze of winding side streets. I made my way along the murky canals, across arching bridges, down the narrow alleyways. I told myself I should go back to the hotel and sleep, but I was being sucked in, amazed at how easily I'd fallen into step with this city and its inhabitants. Like a Dostoyevskian hero, for this was his city as well, my emotions wound inside of me, a snail into itself, and I seemed to carry it all within, winding deeper and deeper, dragging it about.

I was like one obsessed, overcome, a fly in the radiant web. This was no linear, socially acceptable Tolstoyian world. There were no manners, no courtesies, no proprieties here. This seemed more like a city with a kind of perverse passion, a beautiful woman entrapped in vanity, the architectural equivalent of Narcissus: Leningrad staring at itself in its own canals, its beauty coming back to it over and over again.

I wandered its streets as one does through a museum, silently, with reverence. Or as you might after committing a crime, with stealth, yet feeling contemplative, planning your next move, your place to hide. I could imagine, as Pushkin had, the statue of Peter coming to life and stalking men along the ancient cobbles of this city. I walked as Raskolnikov might, plagued with guilt, or fearing you were about to meet your double—distracted, caught in your own thoughts. I saw how this could be a city to withstand a siege of nine hundred days, how it could withstand wars and progress and urban sprawl. It could just turn in on itself. It seemed I had walked into a Russian fairy tale and I could play any part—criminal, prostitute, destitute mother, coy mistress, woman alone—but not in some funky cardboard tourist attraction such as I'd done at the Ming tombs. This was all too real.

I have no idea how I came back to my hotel, but hours later I found myself there at about 6 A.M., the sun still in the place where it was when I left, but I was now exhausted, spent. The desk clerk gave me a perfunctory nod that was not without a sneer, for what was I doing out on those canals at this hour? A gloomy hooker, shoes off, slumped in a chair, did not move her legs as I made my way to the elevator and I had to step over her.

I crept into my room, bones aching, and pulled down the shade. The light from the day which would not end filtered in. Then I made my way through the velvet curtains that led to the small sleeping alcove. The bed was of dark wood, with a white lace canopy. Beside the bed was a small bedstand with a light, but I didn't even think to turn it on. Instead, I lay down for the first time on my narrow bed and pulled the canopy around it.

I lay in the small alcove, in the small room, and on that narrow bed enclosed in lace, I felt the small body contained within my own. We lay there together for the first time, one inside the other, inside the bed, inside the alcove, the room, like those Russian dolls I carried with me as gifts, each one smaller and smaller, tucked inside the other.

PETER THE GREAT stood at the delta where the Neva meets the Baltic, his soldiers behind him, miserable in the inhospitable swampland to which he had brought them, and declared that here he would build a great city by the sea. Here where the Neva divided into four branches, creating a marshy archipelago of islands, Peter would realize his dream of a city like Amsterdam with pristine, winding canals and tree-lined streets.

On May 16, 1703, on an island in the river that the Finns called the Isle of Hares, on land that he had only recently seized from Sweden, he cut into the ground. In Pushkin's words, Peter said, "Here a city shall be founded. Here we are destined by Nature to cut a window into Europe," and laid the first stone of what would become the fortress of Saints Peter and Paul.

Peter the Great was a giant, standing six foot seven, renowned for his Rabelaisian appetites for drink, lovemaking, smoking and bawdy humor, and for his dark side—his sudden rages, his cruel vengeance, his contradictory passions. In the very fortress where he laid his stone, he would have his own son by his first marriage beaten to death for treason. Even as he heaved his country out of the Middle Ages, he would have his Moscow *streltsy* (palace guards) who rose up against him flayed, then roasted over slow flames. Eventually their bodies would dangle all over Moscow.

From boyhood, Peter lived with a hatred of the Kremlin with its dark, secret corridors and its musty rooms that only served to remind him of the horror he had witnessed in the first *streltsy* revolt, when he had seen people he loved—mentors, relatives—stalked and cut to pieces as he trembled in his mother's arms. For the rest of his life the Kremlin with its looming walls was a prison to him. He needed to breathe. He dreamed of light, fresh air, open space, the sea.

As a man of gargantuan energies, Peter wanted Russia to be more like the West. He wanted Russia to turn away from its Byzantine and, Peter felt, barbaric Eastern ways. He cut the beards off his boyars, at times wielding the razor himself, and thrust women from the seclusion of the Terem unveiled into the world. He put them in dresses designed in France and chopped off the long sleeves of the boyars' caftans.

Peter didn't care about any resistance he met. He believed there was nothing he could not do. Indeed, in his life he is said to have mastered fourteen skills, including the sciences of gunnery and engineering, shipbuilding (which he learned in a Dutch shipyard where he went as incognito as a six-foot-seven-inch czar can go). He was an expert at papermaking, shoemaking, etching, engraving, leatherwork. He cobbled his own shoes, made his own furniture, built boats with his own hands. Once, as a present, he gave his beloved Catherine an ivory chandelier that he had crafted himself.

A man of vision, he created for Russia a modern army and—his true dream—a navy. He sent many young Russians to Europe to study navigation. At the delta of the Neva Peter knew he would put his ships. Ironically it was from this same harbor during the siege of Leningrad in World War II that the navy would fail the very city Peter had created it to protect.

Some say it was the curse of the bones upon which the city is built. For Peter spared no one. He rounded up tens of thousands of Swedish prisoners of war, peasants, workers and criminals from all over Russia, and forced them into swamps with freezing mud. Working bare-chested in the middle of winter, chest-deep in this muck, tens of thousands died. As many deserted. More were rounded up until in seven years Peter had his city. Then he needed people to live in it. So he simply invited his aristocracy to summer with him in his new city, which required that they build houses at their own expense. No one could refuse the Czar.

Until Peter, Russia had hardly known centralization. More like Italy before Garibaldi, it had never acted as a single entity. The forced labor and coercion exercised by Peter to get his project accomplished united Russia for the first time. It also set the stage for Russian totalitarianism, which has endured to the present. Peter instituted his system of meritocracy, in which all nobles and gentry would be tied to government service for life in fourteen ranks where you'd start at the bottom and work your way up, paving the way for the cumbersome and inefficient Russian bureaucracy that would follow.

But Peter wanted to pull Russia out of the Dark Ages at all costs. Some say it was vision; others that it was fool-hardiness that happened to work out. But the fact remains that Peter accomplished what he set out to do. He consecrated the spot on an island in the Gulf of Finland, stating that here he would build his paradise, his kingdom, and nobody believed him, but he did it.

No one knows how many died in this effort. A hundred thousand. A million. They came to dredge the swamps, hold back the sea, build the city of Peter the Great's dream, cursing him as they died. They died of malaria, influenza, colds and flu. They died in the floods that came as the Gulf of Finland swelled.

The city rests upon its dead, and one can only wonder that so much beauty came from so much death. The people of Leningrad do not forget this. Some told me they felt the dead stirring in the ground. Others believed that the nine-hundred-day siege was the payment due to those who died building the city. To this day it is standard practice for the brides of Leningrad to take their bouquets after their wedding service and place them on the mass grave at Piskarevsky Cemetery where hundreds of thousands who died during the siege are buried. That cemetery is bedecked in bridal bouquets: in the words of the Leningrad poet Olga Berggolts, "Let no one forget, let nothing be forgotten."

I WOKE LATE and wandered to the banks of the Neva where the same scene I'd witnessed the night before continued—lovers kissing, a gull diving for bits of bread—but now it appeared innocuous to me for while the light was the same as the night before, there was something, I was beginning to feel, about the light of White Nights that was not the same as that of the day. It was as if the world of those nights were lit in a way that uncovered the universe of antimatter, an unworld, a light that revealed what the naked eye could not see.

The banks descended to a boat ramp on the river, and I sat there, water lapping at my feet, catching the rays of the sun. Two boys sitting across from me worked a Rubik's Cube with some success, though also with indifference. They kept taking it apart, putting it back, over and over again. I watched as each time they were able to repeat the pattern and still manage to appear utterly bored.

I was hungry and had not had breakfast and felt faint. I had passed a restaurant on Nevsky Prospect and headed back that way. It was a lovely restaurant, painted an eggshell blue with lace curtains, with all the bustle of a restaurant anywhere in the world. Many Russians were already eating lunch. To my surprise I was seated with a family, a man, his wife, and their grown daughter. They glanced at me briefly, then continued to eat slowly, without speaking. I was handed a menu. When I opened it, I saw it was completely in Russian. Though I could read the alphabet, the words eluded me and I was befuddled.

I stared dumbly at the man and his family who looked at me. They were eating plates of creamy meat with potatoes and carrots. I wanted to say something, to explain my plight, but the few words of Russian I knew had left me. Somehow in China this hadn't bothered me as much, but I didn't want to call attention to myself by pulling out a phrase book or just pointing to the food my companions were cheerlessly eating. I looked for what might be familiar. Stroganoff, borscht, Kiev. But the letters all came to an incomprehensible blur and more than anything else I was afraid of bringing attention to myself.

I closed the menu, muttering some kind of apology to the people at my table, then to the maître d', who must have found me strange, and slipped out the door, feeling vanquished, some pathetic creature who'd risen out of the pages of Gogol himself.

Returning to the hotel, I got a can of sardines from the now dwindling supply, some crackers and juice and headed back to the Neva, where I munched crackers dipped in oily sardines under the sun. The lovers were gone. The boys with the Rubik's Cube had drifted away. Now I replaced the lovers as the gulls rose and dove above me, trying to get whatever crumbs I tossed them.

En route to the Peter and Paul fortress, I paused to see Russians in swimsuits, their flaccid bodies rippling, at the base of the fortress, bathing. I walked down to where they were and sat on the grass, dressed in shorts and a T-shirt. Handsome young men with stocky builds smiled at me as they tossed a beach ball between them. A huge woman, flopping on her belly like a beached whale, looked at me with disdain. The young men sat on either side of me. "French," one said. "Italian," the other.

"American," I replied.

They put their hands over their mouths. "American." By now I was accustomed to this response. "Where's your group?"

"I don't have a group."

They stared at one another. "No group?"

"No, I'm traveling alone."

They shook their heads, for this was inconceivable to them. "Do you want to go dancing?" one of them asked, leaping into the air and starting to do the Russian equivalent of the twist.

"Maybe," I said.

"Yes, come dancing with us. Tonight, under the stars." He put his arm around me.

The large woman shouted something that made them shrink away. "Or maybe tomorrow," they said, drifting away.

"Maybe tomorrow," I said, thinking that in fact I would like to go dancing with them, but now they had turned back to their game.

The Peter and Paul fortress stands along the banks of the Neva, its ramparts and bulwarks formidable, its golden spire piercing the sky like a lance. Here under its cathedral dome the later czars and czarinas of Russia lay buried in cold white sarcophagi adorned with simple gold crosses. Only at the tomb of Peter were a few flowers laid. The cathedral itself was designed by Peter's architect Domenico Trezzini who, more influenced by Dutch protestantism than Russian orthodoxy, made no attempt at russification of this austere cathedral where all the czars since Peter have been buried.

Descending into the dungeons, now a prime tourist attraction, I gazed into musty cells that had once held the likes of Bukharin, Gorky, even Dostoyevsky. Peter's own son Alexis was tortured to death in these dingy rooms. The dank coolness of the dungeons and the pressing need of tourists to gaze into their misery rankled my nerves and I ascended, crossing over swiftly to the park and promenade of arching oaks.

It was here that St. Petersburg was born. In 1703 from this small three-room wooden cabin, which has been preserved, Peter lived during the building of his city. In this log cabin where the Czar of all the Russias had to stoop in order to move from room to room, he watched his dream unfold. He was too busy to have a house built for him and throughout his life his personal needs and tastes would be simple. But from here he could see the river, the coming and going of his ships. He could watch the city rise out of the swamp and this was all he required.

I paused on a bench beneath the trees in the cool shade of a small promenade lined with benches and trees where some Russians sat too, mostly grandmothers with prams beside them, slumbering as their charges slept. I thought of the remarkable will that had made this city. Possibilities loomed around me.

I too closed my eyes and contemplated what it was to watch your dream unfold. Or the opposite, to watch it collapse. I pondered the things I had wanted in this world. What had I accomplished? Where had I failed? The roster came out about even, I decided in the end. But I knew that there was something I had to do now. I could delay it no longer.

Returning to the hotel, I placed a call with the key keeper, asking if I could please reach the States. I gave her his number. She said they'd call me when they had my party on the line. I went into my room and collapsed on the bed. I have no idea how long I lay there when the phone rang, but I know this time it wasn't long.

When I picked it up, he was on the line. "How are you?" he said.

"I'm fine," I said, "but I miss you."

His voice was soft, gentle on the other end. "I miss you too."

We made small talk for a few moments, if one can make small talk from such distances. He told me about his work, the children. One of the boys was in trouble again. His ex-wife wanted the boy to live with him. He sounded weary, speaking of all the difficulties in his life. The demands people made on him. It occurred to me that this might not be the moment to tell him what I needed to say, but he would be departing for Sri Lanka soon. It would be many weeks before we'd speak again.

"I don't mean to add to your complexities," I told him, "but I'm going to have a child."

Transatlantic silence was deafening. Water seemed to fill the line, the cost of minutes ticking away. "Did you hear me? I'm going to have a child."

"Well, a child is a wonderful thing . . ." His voice was full of pauses, as if he'd lost the thread of his own ideas, something rare for him. "Of course," he added despondently, "I'm not sure I've had great luck with mine."

"Well, maybe you're being given another chance."

Again he said nothing, then I heard a soft, "Perhaps."

"I want to have this child," I said, emphatically now as if I had made up my mind. "And . . ." I hesitated, "and I think we should make it legal."

Again there was silence, oceans of water flowing between us. "Legal?" he said. "In what sense?"

I paused, taking a deep breath. "We've been together a long time now. I think we should get married."

"Well . . . let's wait and see," he said. "Why don't we discuss it when you get home."

When you spend years of your life with someone, you get to know their quirks. Their turns of phrase; their little habits. I'd heard him say "wait and see" to others. To ex-wives he was trying to placate, to children making too many demands. To people who wanted him to speak at their conferences. To all those he intended ultimately to disappoint or ignore.

We hung up, agreeing to discuss it later in the summer, though I knew what the outcome would be. Lying down on the bed in the alcove, I thought of my grandmother. I saw her as clearly as I ever had. It was a Saturday morning and I was fifteen years old. We sat in her darkened living room, a plate of prune strudel before us, and my grandmother asked me about boys. Was there a special one I was seeing? Did I like them at all?

Then she gave me her only piece of sex education, the only time she ever acknowledged the physical act. She told me that if a man touches a woman's body before marriage, she disintegrates. I can still see her as she told me this: her eyes wide, filled with admonition, a hand pointing into the air. "Disintegrates?" I asked, incredulous. She nodded in the assured way she did.

I had been warned about premarital relations, but never with the threat of disintegration. Never mind that boys had already held me close at school dances, that I had felt their hands slip stealthily beneath my blouse. A quarter of a century ago in her living room, the curtains drawn, the cakes uneaten between us, my grandmother held up her fingers as if they contained an exploding spore, and then let them go. "Puff," she said. "Nothing at all."

FROM 1764 the czars of Petersburg collected works of art and put them in the buildings beside the Winter Palace. These buildings, constructed at different times, have come to be known as the Hermitage. After the revolution, the Palace with its fifteen hundred rooms became the perfect spot for displaying the treasures of indigenous Russian artifacts and European painting (Russian painting can primarily be seen at the Russian Museum). Today the main entrance to the Hermitage is in fact the splendid former entrance to the Palace. It is one of the ironies of the revolution that it managed to either restore or keep intact the remarkable buildings of the imperial regimes it so abhorred. In a dazzling light of white marble and gold, the staircase where the Czar and Czarina once walked now welcomes the visitor who climbs it to get to the galleries.

Here the old masters—Leonardo, Titian, Rubens, Rembrandt—are on display. Enormous wall murals of great battle scenes leave one spellbound. For two hours I followed my guide, a necessity it seemed, until I was overwhelmed and could go on no more, my head reeling not only from the magnificence and intensity of the art, but also from trying to imagine the balls held in these malachite, agate, marble, and gold-gilt ballrooms, the dinners eaten in the grand dining room, which now housed one of the world's most remarkable collections of art.

I needed to walk. I crossed the river and headed along Nevsky Prospect, then crossed into the city until I found an open farmers' market *(kolkhoz)*. Here I purchased a small bag of apples and a sweet roll from a stocky, jovial farm woman. Then I made my way to the Dostoyevsky house and museum.

Dostoyevsky lived in a small apartment, the equivalent of a brownstone floor-through, and the contrasts to the wonders of the Hermitage or even the impressive Count Tolstoy house in Moscow surprised me. The ordered simplicity of this life was evident in the toys his children played with, the pen he used laid out across writing paper. His spectacles. The dark, austere furnishings. Under glass there are letters and manuscripts written in his tormented hand along with the careful accounts his wife kept, which enabled the family to stay afloat. It was startling to see Dostoyevsky functioning in the real, pragmatic world so far from his novels and stories. I was touched by the normalcy surrounding a mind so possessed, and felt relief to be away from the enormous successes of Peter to these more conceivable accomplishments, at least to me, of a great writer who lived as an ordinary man.

As I made my way slowly back to the hotel, I found myself in stride with Father Time. He had a long white beard that fell halfway to his chest. He wore a green army suit, vintage World War I, bedecked with every conceivable medal, and walked with a carved wood walking stick. An army cap sat on his head, setting his blue eyes in sharp relief against his white beard. He took me by the arm.

"You are French?" he asked.

"American."

"I am a Bolshevik. One of the original fighters for the revolution."

I looked at him, amazed. "How old are you?"

"I am almost a hundred years old."

"You are a hero," I said, touching the medals on his chest.

He smiled, a twinkle in his eye. "We are all heroes. Every Russian is a hero." We were crossing Nevsky Prospect now, walking toward Pushkin Park. Some people smiled at the old man. Others, tourists, looked at him as if they were seeing a ghost.

"You know when I was a boy, I saw them once, the Czar and the Czarina. They were in a carriage, going right down this road." He stopped to point. "The carriage stopped and I could see them. They were so beautiful and they looked so happy . . ." Then his eyes turned dark, "and we were all so hungry. Still," he said with a sigh, "it was so sad."

We had reached Pushkin Park and the old man now eased himself down onto a bench. "I am getting old." He sat, resting his hands on his walking stick. Someone stopped and asked if they could take his picture. He stood up solemnly and stared into the camera. Then someone else stopped. Then, weary, he sat back down again. "I have lived through everything," he said. "We are all heroes. Remember, I said so."

ON SATURDAY MORNING when Sasha, the waiter from the train, did not arrive, I made my way alone to 2 Lermontovsky Prospect, to one of the oldest synagogues in Russia. It was a brown, stone structure, crumbling it seemed, and though there were some young couples with children, most of the Jews who milled around, waiting for the service to begin, were older, stooped. While these people had perhaps not suffered the pogroms, the executions during the civil war, and the mass exterminations (the Jewish population of the Ukraine went from 2,400,000 in 1941 to 800,000 after the war), these were faces that lived through the siege of Leningrad, with Hitler's troops threatening at the door. They had also lived through the Stalinist purges and the ongoing persecution of the Soviet Jew. There was something dead in many of their eyes, something gone. I had read much on the suffering of the Soviet Jew, but seeing it here, outside the synagogue, in the flesh, stunned me.

Yet as I walked in, the faces of people seemed to light up. Hands reached out; strangers greeted me. They seemed to know right away that I was a visitor, not one of them. Many shook my hand. I assumed it was because they had never seen me before, but perhaps it was something else. A lilt to my step, the way I smiled. New York, I said, over and over again, and men with bloodhound eyes, women, heads wrapped, stopped me to shake my hand or embrace me.

I entered the synagogue and went upstairs to the balcony where the women prayed and immediately I was ashamed at myself for not bringing something to cover my head. All the women had colored babushkas, in bright floral silks with spangles; the men all wore hats or yarmulkes. Some of the women cried as they prayed. A woman beside me recited the Kaddish, the Prayer for the Dead, over and over again, beating her breast, crying. With them, I stood and recited the Kaddish, tears welling in my eyes as if I were praying for all the living, and the dead.

After perhaps half an hour a young woman turned to me. "You're American, right?" She was a foreign exchange student living in Leningrad for the summer, and she had met a group of medical students who were also visiting. As we left the synagogue, Sally introduced me to two of the medical students, Michael and Josh. I was speaking with Michael, a student from Yale who was touring the Soviet Union with Physicians for Social Responsibility, when a frail, blond man with ferret-like features approached us.

"I would like to take you to hear some music," the man said. Then he added quietly, "It is not near, but you will meet some interesting Jews. Refuseniks, like me."

I had not yet met any Jews who had dissented against the Soviet system and in exchange lost whatever small privileges they might have had. We agreed to go. David introduced himself and gave us instructions. "Do not walk in a group or speak English loudly," he said. "Don't look as if you don't know where you are going. We'll all hop on a trolley."

The four of us jumped on a trolley as it sped down the middle of the street. We paid our tickets while David stood a few feet behind us. His eyes kept shifting over the crowd. I had ballet tickets for that night to see the Kirov and I found myself concerned about the time since we had no idea how far we were going or when we might be back. I mentioned this to Sally and she turned to David who stood slightly behind us. "How far we are going?" she said. And when he did not reply, she said, "Is it very far?"

Suddenly we realized our mistake. He looked at us

strangely as if he had never seen us before. He turned his back to us. At the next stop David jumped off the trolley and never looked back.

THE VICE CONSUL of the U.S. Embassy, who was a friend of a friend, had invited me to go with him to the ballet that night and to dinner on the Gulf of Finland at a restaurant he knew. I was pleased to have the opportunity to go out, but when Scott Rothman picked me up he was not alone. The woman with him was a Finnish girl who had been working as a nanny in Leningrad for the past eight months. She hated Leningrad and she hated working as a nanny, she told me within five minutes of meeting her. It was also clear that she was infatuated with Scott. This was her last night in Leningrad and my presence was an inconvenience.

I sat in the back seat of the convertible as we sped to the Kirov Theater. This great ballet company had once been the pride of Russia, above the Bolshoi, but when Lenin moved the capital back to Moscow in 1918, the Kirov became little more than a training camp for the Bolshoi. Still, it had produced some of Russia's finest dancers, many of whom now danced in New York or had Hollywood careers.

For some reason Scott, who perhaps was not aware of the Finnish girl's intentions (or perhaps he was) put me in the middle between them. I could feel her scowling. Already I was wishing I had not come. The ballet they were dancing was *Giselle*, not my favorite, and I had hoped to see the Kirov dance a Russian ballet.

It was also a ballet about betrayal. Giselle, a peasant girl, falls in love with a disguised prince who cannot marry her because he is engaged to someone else. Upon learning this Giselle dies, presumably of a broken heart, and joins a group of betrayed spirits, the Wilis—women jilted en route to the altar who have died. The Wilis condemn the prince to dance to death, but Giselle's assistance and the crack of dawn break their spell. I watched this ballet in which women are viewed as wraiths, invisible and lithe, and at the same time vengeful, full of spite. Its meaning was not lost on me.

Later, en route to the Gulf of Finland, the white convertible careened along the Neva, moving through tree-lined residential streets of Leningrad. It was almost eleven o'clock at night but the sky was bright. I put my head back in the car and rested, the wind bracing my face while the Finnish girl, whose name I cannot recall, whispered into Scott's ear.

The restaurant, situated on the beach right on the Gulf, was huge and packed. Waiters in tuxedos carried steaming platters of dumplings, rice pilaf, skewered meat. From our table I could see the blue shores of the Gulf which fed into the Baltic, which eventually led to the North Sea and the Atlantic. The sun was still high in the sky as I peered across the vast body of sea. The Finnish girl sat next to Scott and while he made attempts to talk to me, she kept turning his attention away. Whenever he spoke to me she looked depressed, then managed to change the subject.

I told them I wasn't feeling well and wanted to take a walk along the beach while we waited for dinner. Scott was actually a gentle man with a soft manner about him. He said he would order what he knew was best here. I told him to please go ahead.

I walked down to the beach where there was a walkway along the sand. Taking off my shoes, I left the walkway and headed to the water. The sun glowed on my face and I smelled the sea breeze. It was fresh and salty and made me think of what lay across the water. For the first time, my feet in the water, I felt I had home in sight, though I still had miles and weeks left of travel. But its promise rose before me. I could see why this was where Peter wanted to build his city. It *was* like a window opening to another world.

I returned to the table just as a waiter, his arms stacked with food, brought in three silver platters, piping hot, of what Scott said was a real Russian specialty. Mushrooms in sour cream sauce. Scott and the Finnish girl had already made headway into a bottle of Georgian wine and the girl now had a blushed looked to her cheeks and seemed happier. They poured me a glass. Suddenly I was famished and the mushrooms looked delicious. As I picked up my fork to eat, Scott said, raising his glass as if in a toast, "Well, I hope no one is pregnant at this table."

I lowered my fork. "Why?"

"Because of the milk products. You know the cows ate the grass after Chernobyl and it goes right into their milk."

Imperceptibly I pushed my plate away. The Finnish girl was already eating, but Scott, with diplomatic panache, raised his hand. "Waiter," he said, "menu please."

It was two in the morning as we drove back along the canals and the banks of the Neva to my hotel. Scott dropped the Finnish girl off and seemed glad to be rid of her. She hardly said good-bye. We drove in silence to my hotel. When we reached it I got out, thanking him. "Look," he said, "if there's anything you need—if I can help you with anything—"

I thanked him for offering and said good night.

Once in my room, I placed a call to my parents. It took three hours, but at last I heard my mother's voice, tired on the other end. Then I blurted it all out, tearfully. "I'm not going to Kiev," I told her, "I'm not going into the Ukraine." I heard her breathe a sign of relief. "I would have gone," I said, "but I'm going to have a child," I told her, "so I'm not going."

"Good," she said, her voice seeming to wake up. And then, "A child. Well, I think that's good."

"You do? I'm not sure it's good," I muttered.

"When's the wedding?" she asked, her voice hopeful.

"There's not going to be a wedding." I told her about the phone call. "I'll probably have an abortion when I get home. I don't know. I can't go through with this. I can't do this on my own. Don't tell my father," I told her. "No matter what, don't tell him." Again the vision of the bluff down which I'd fling myself and my grandmother's hand releasing the dust of my body came to me.

"You sound confused," she said.

"I'm fine. I just needed to talk," I told her, "but promise me you won't tell anyone."

She promised.

SERGE, an "unofficial" Russian painter, lived on a quiet residential street of Leningrad. "Unofficial" meant he was not a member of the Union of Artists, yet he managed to live by selling his work. Through an introduction of a friend, I was invited to his studio. I made my way to the old building off a pleasant green square and into Serge's studio —a potpourri decorated with a collage of dead fish, wooden spoons, carved birds, snippets of fur, baskets of dried flowers, pictures of Marx, pine cones, mirrors, hats, pictures of Serge in strange costumes, all pinned to the wall.

Serge himself was a short but solid man in his mid-forties with a twinkle in his eye and a mole on his left cheek. He poured wine and spoke flamboyantly about his work. "Here," he told me, handing me a picture, "here, this is a watercolor I did of Nabokov's town." He handed me a lovely watercolor. "And here," he said with a laugh, showing me a semipolitical painting, "here is a bird who needs a visa to migrate. That's funny, don't you think? A bird who needs a visa."

"You see," Serge said, "I have managed to have a good life here for myself. I walk a thin line, it is true. I mean this painting, I suppose it could get me in trouble, but I am not in a union. They cannot stop me from painting, though they could put me in prison, but I go only so far and I know how far to go. I have never had a problem."

Serge had done the painting and design for the Banana Republic's Russian Safari catalogue and he displayed this proudly. Looking at the catalogue, I said, "You must have been well paid for this."

"I don't care," Serge shrugged, thinking my comment bourgeois. "I did it for fun. Everything I do, I do for fun. Otherwise, what is the point?"

At the synagogue the day before I had briefly made contact with a dissident named Vladimir Meyerhoff who asked me to meet him in a park the following day. While I did not anticipate that he would appear at this meeting, I went and to my surprise he was there. In contrast to Serge, Vladimir was dark, intense. Across his brow was furrowed a continuous groove. When he saw me crossing the park he rose, extending his hands. "You came," he said. "Please," he spoke quickly, "my house is only a few blocks from here, you must come. I'll fix you tea. But please. We can talk more easily there."

His house was on the canal Dostoyevsky used to roam, and Vladimir indeed reminded me of one of those dark heroes. En route to his house, we paused before a narrow three-story building. "This is the house where Raskolnikov killed the pawnbroker and her niece," he told me, as if this were historic fact. Then we crossed the canal, went a few blocks more, and began our climb up a dreary staircase in the building where Vladimir lived.

His apartment reminded me of the kind of rooms where my grandparents used to live. Grim oriental tapestries, gloomy landscape paintings on the walls, the furniture all large with dark wood frames, upholstered in red and brown vinyl. Darkness seemed to surround Vladimir. He told me his wife and children were in Estonia for the summer and he was here alone. He went into the kitchen and made tea. Then, for two hours, I sat listening almost without interruption as he told me the story of his life.

Sixteen years ago, he said, the Soviets convicted some Jews of a plot to hijack an airplane and fly to the West. Someone named Vladimir as a co-conspirator. Immediately he lost his job as a computer technician and had been working for sixteen years as a house electrician. "A job anyone with a high school degree can do," he told me despondently. Ten years ago he applied for a visa to emigrate to Israel. Nine years ago his parents left. He had not seen them since.

"Every year I reapply," Vladimir told me, "and every year it is a different story. They talk about reunification of families. You know, a year or so ago when I applied for a visa on the basis of reunification of my family, they said my parents were no longer close family members because I had not seen them in nine years. When I pointed out that I had not seen them in nine years because I had been denied a visa every year, they shrugged. Whenever you go for a visa, it is something else. You need this paper, you need that. You must wait for this person, then for that. They try to break you down, to wear you out. They tell you they will let your wife leave if you divorce her. Divorce her, they say, then she can leave. Then you can join her under reunification of families. But when you ask to be reunited with your wife, they say you divorced her so she is not your family anymore."

That spring, Vladimir said, a documentary had been made about enemies of the state. It was called *Mercenaries and Traitors*. It showed a map of Leningrad, and then the picture zoomed in on a street and finally on Vladimir's house. The movie said an enemy of the state lived in that house. Since then, his son had been persecuted at school and his daughter had been refused entry into the same private school as the son, which is standard in the Soviet Union. By Russian law she has the right to go to that school, yet she had been refused. "You know," he said, "I have 'Jew' stamped on my passport. Just like the Nazis. It's not different. That's how we are treated."

As I was leaving, Vladimir said to me, "In Russia when refuseniks toast, we don't say cheers. We say visa." I thought of Serge's painting—the bird who needs a visa. Freedom suddenly felt as precious as it ever had. Vladimir raised his teacup and I raised mine. "Visa," we said, clicking teacups. Then I said good-bye.

WHEN I RETURNED to my hotel, I found a message from the medical students, Michael and Josh, I'd met the other day at the synagogue. It said there was a party that evening at the place where they were staying and I should come. I took a cab in the early evening to the outskirts of Leningrad, a kind of dormitory complex which was part of the university. These students were on an exchange with Soviet medical students and doctors working on issues of world peace, in particular antinuclear. They were all members of their countries' affiliates of International Physicians for the Prevention of Nuclear War, the organization that had won the 1985 Nobel Peace Prize.

I walked into a small, smoke-filled room where a bottle of Stoli was being passed around from mouth to mouth, and the medical students in various states of inebriation were talking about medicine and the future of the world. Three Soviet doctors were present. One was a woman with short black hair, simple, dark features. When the Stoli came to her, she passed it without taking a sip. I sat down next to her. Her name was Tanya and she had been a doctor for four years. She was doing a residency in surgery in Moscow and her English was excellent.

Tanya told me that she lived with her mother in a flat with four other families. "It is not so bad," she said. "Some people have ten families in their flat. We each have our own room and a semiprivate bath. It could be a lot worse." She smiled softly and I liked her immediately.

Michael from Yale was moaning for his girlfriend who was back home. Every few minutes he picked up the phone and tried to place a call. Josh from the University of Chicago, with dark curly hair, kept putting the phone down. "Don't call her now, Michael," Josh kept saying, "You'll only make a fool of yourself."

Tanya said the smoke and the noise were bothering her and suggested we go outside and take a walk. We took the elevator down and began to walk on the sidewalk along a fairly active thoroughfare. "So you're a doctor," I muttered as we got outside. "I could use a doctor."

"Yes," she smiled, looking at me askance, "I believe you could."

"What do you mean?"

"I can tell."

"Tell what?"

"You are going to have a child, aren't you?"

"Yes, but how did you know?"

"You have a glow," she said. This did not sound like medically conclusive evidence to me. "I can just tell. I knew the minute you walked in the room."

"I don't know what I'm going to do. The circumstances," I said, "aren't great."

"They never seem to be. My mother raised me almost alone. Abortions were hard to come by then. But it has worked out all right."

"I don't know what I'm going to do."

"The father, you know him . . ."

"Very well. I thought we'd marry."

"Oh," she shook her head, "that *is* sad."

We followed the thoroughfare to a park where the trees made a nice cool breeze and we just kept walking.

"I was supposed to go to Kiev and then into the Ukraine," I told her.

"Oh, you made the right decision not to go. It isn't safe. Not for you, not for your child."

"Yes," I nodded, not quite comprehending the sense of "my child" since I was now deciding not to have this child.

"The Dnieper is probably contaminated. The water isn't safe." Later, when I returned to the States and called my doctor, I told him I was pregnant and that I had done a lot of drinking when I was in the Soviet Union. "God," he said, "I hope it wasn't water." "No, it was vodka," I told him. "Oh, vodka," he said, sounding relieved, "that's fine."

"Look," she said, "I'm going to Moscow tomorrow. I'll be there when you get back. Let's see one another. Maybe I can help you. Make things a little easier."

I took her phone number. "Tell the doctors I was tired and went home, would you?" I asked her. "Tell them I'll call them tomorrow."

I hailed a cab, waving good-bye to Tanya. In half an hour I was back at the hotel where I lay down on the bed, not falling asleep. I'm not sure how long it was before the phone rang. I heard my father's voice on the other end. He was eighty-six years old, but he sounded like a young man. "This is your father," he said.

"I know."

"How are you?"

"Great," I said, tears coming to my eyes.

"Well, I spoke with your mother," making it sound as if they were suddenly separated and living in different cities.

"She promised . . ." I blurted, realizing how foolish it had been to exact such a promise from her.

"Never mind. You know, you aren't getting any younger. I mean, you're going to be forty years old."

"Yes, I know . . ."

"Well," he said, "men come and go." He was right about that. "But, you know, a child is forever."

"You can live with this?" I asked timidly, never having imagined a conversation like this with my father.

"I can live with a lot worse," he said.

MY LAST NIGHT in Leningrad, Michael and Josh and their American guide, who Michael assured me was CIA, met for a walk along the canals. I promised I'd show them the house where Raskolnikov killed the pawnbroker and her niece, but as we moved along the canal, all the houses looked the same. It could have happened here, I said, or here. It could have happened anywhere, in any house. Realizing I had failed in my mission, I offered to introduce them to Vladimir, whose apartment didn't seem that far away.

It was eleven-thirty when we called, but Vladimir told me he doesn't sleep on White Nights and he invited us up. This time he took out a bottle of wine and poured drinks all around. Then he began to tell his story again, the same story he told me the day before, the same details. The co-conspirator charges, losing his job, the documentary, the persecution of his children. Everything. Indeed, he was Dostoyevskian in his suffering, which did seem monumental. He was compelled to repeat his story over and over again. "Visa" we said as we toasted; "visa," we raised our glasses dozens of times.

When we left, it was two in the morning and broad daylight. The medical students walked me back toward my hotel, but then I invited them to the bar where I'd gone my first night in Leningrad. The Finnish men had gone back to Finland and now the bar was filled with tired prostitutes, makeup faded or running down their eyes, stockings torn, like the wicked stepsisters after the ball.

This was no longer pick of the crop. The beautiful women, the impeccably dressed, the women who could model anywhere in the world, were asleep, having completed their weekend's work. In the morning they'd return to their jobs at desks where they sharpened pencils, filed their nails while sitting in the steno pool. What's left here were the derelicts. The fat ones, the ugly ones. The ones nobody wanted. Discarded and sad. I walked in with three men and all the women at the bar perked up like deer at the scent of the hunter and stared at me with envy and disgust. I could see their minds doing a quick calculation of how much I would make that night.

We had not been sitting down long when a young woman came over. She introduced herself as Veronica and pulled up a chair next to Michael, who was still moaning for his girlfriend back home. Veronica had a wedding ring on. She pointed to the ring and said she was married to a Finn. "But he never visits," she complained. "I never see him." She ran her hand over Michael's knee and he pushed her away. "I want a man," she said. "You have three and I have none. Can't I have one?" Veronica pleaded with me. "Just one." She put her head down on the table and sobbed, "Just give me one."

□   □   □   □

The next morning as I was leaving, a man helped me get my suitcase into the elevator. I thanked him in Russian. Then he asked me in broken English if he could buy my underwear. "My girlfriend likes American underwear." I told him I was wearing my underwear and what I was not wearing, I needed. He thanked me anyway, somewhat sadly, then helped me again with my suitcase as we reached the ground floor.

Moscow

ON THE PLANE back to Moscow, when fellow passengers realized that I was an American, traveling without a group, they gave me small souvenirs: the generic pins of Lenin, bits of hard candy. To the children beside me I gave my remaining pencils with the Statue of Liberty perched defiantly on the tip, and they squealed with delight. Still I felt dejected, as if the fact that I had decided not go to Kiev and into the Ukraine were an act of personal cowardice. For the first time in my life I found myself backtracking, taking a route I'd already taken, returning the way I'd come. But more than that sense of loss, something was gone, never to return.

The Ukraine was sprinkled with lethal dust. Many would die. Children, years from now, would languish in hospital beds, their bone marrow destroyed. My defeat did not seem personal, more global in a sense. I thought of my own child and wondered what kind of world she would be born into. A world divided, or one at peace. A world on the brink of destruction, or on its way to new solutions.

It was not long after I was back in Moscow before Ivan, the man I'd met in the embassy, called. I don't know how he knew when I was getting back, but my phone rang in the morning. He wanted to take me to a gallery run by a friend of his named Lev. Lev exhibited from his home the work of his friends, mostly dissidents, Jews, and those such as Ivan, who had been declared a parasite of the state.

Lev was a large, rather heavy man with obvious health problems. He chain-smoked the entire time I was there. The apartment was small and cluttered, but it had a big living room and on its walls were various photographs and paintings, none with very political or social themes, but most of it what one might term "bourgeois decadent"—portraits of women, men. And a few along social-realist themes, such as an impoverished-looking old man on a bench, carving wood.

Both Lev and Ivan had spent a good deal of time in Soviet prisons for various reasons. Lev because he was Jewish and because he ran a private art gallery where he exhibited "anti-Soviet art" and Ivan because of many things, including the fact that he was Jewish, had married an American, had refused factory work, but instead wanted to be a photographer and do his own work. He had in fact defied authorities consistently for years. Both men had been declared parasites.

"The worst sentence you can get," Lev told me, "is two weeks. If you are there longer, they give you something to do. But for two weeks, you do nothing. You sleep in a room that is about six yards by three yards with twenty-five men and at six-thirty in the morning the other prisoners go to work, but you stay in your cell. You have no blanket, no mattress, no pillow, nothing to read, nothing to do. You cannot wash. You go to the bathroom three times a day with an armed guard who won't speak and points a gun at you while you are on the toilet. Food is boiled grain and that makes it sound good. Imagine fifteen days spent this way."

"It seems terrible," I said feebly.

They both laughed as if I had made some kind of a joke. "Every day I am in a big prison," Ivan said. "For fifteen days I was in a smaller prison. What difference does it make which prison I'm in.

"In fact," Ivan said with a laugh, "I am sure they are listening to us right now. Once in a while I find a bug in this apartment. You know, some workman comes to plaster a wall, someone puts one in. So they know what we are saying. It is like being a fish in a bowl, all the time."

This was what the dream had dwindled to, the dream

that began the day Lenin stepped off the train at Finland Station to preach the tenets of Bolshevism—all power to the Soviets, the revolution of the people. When these former Russian Orthodox rose up, for they had been staunch believers, it was with a vision—the one Lenin promised. An exemplary community where all would be equal. A utopia that promised each and every one food, housing, work, merely in exchange that they turn themselves over to the state. Together they would build the society, each one laying stone upon stone. But it all went wrong. In oppression and intrigue, in the paranoia that created the police state. In bribes and privileges for Party members, in the end of incentive for the workers. Economic freedom turned into the monster of long lines, endless waits. They gave up their hope for freedom long before anyone knew what was happening.

Lev's wife, a large woman who breathed heavily, brought us some cakes. "You see my wife," he said, "her heart is ruined. She cannot breathe. They have broken her with worry."

I told them I was going to be seeing Andrei Voznesensky in two days and mentioned to them that I was going to ask Voznesensky about a woman poet, Irina Ratushinskaya, who was in prison. They looked at each other. "You know that poet you mentioned, Ratushinskaya," Ivan said, "he could probably get her out if he wanted. He doesn't risk anything. Or he risks just enough. He knows how to play the game perfectly." It was clear they thought little of him, but it was difficult to know whether this was based on real knowledge or some kind of aversion to Voznesensky's privileged position.

Later, as we were leaving, Lev said, "You might be in for some fun. The KGB has been following me. Perhaps they will follow us now." He took out a piece of paper. "These are the license plates they use. Always the same plates." We walked along but no car followed us; I must admit to a slight feeling of disappointment.

As we were about to go our separate ways, I said to Ivan, "And if you get your visa, what if you go to the States and your marriage falls apart and you have no work and you have nothing?"

Ivan smiled. He had beautiful blue eyes and they were sparkling. "The only thing I want," he said, "is to never see their faces again."

"I'd sleep in the street," Lev said, "just for one thing."

"Just for freedom," Ivan said, completing the thought.

We walked slowly because Lev's wife had difficulty walking and suddenly he paused. "You know," he said with a sweep of his hand, "sometimes I go outside in the morning and I see the trolleys and I think to myself, Why don't they just stop? Why doesn't all of this just stop."

That evening Tanya called and we went to eat in a small restaurant where the service was slow. We sat and talked. She told me about her mother, who was a medical doctor but because she was older, in her fifties, and because Moscow had too many doctors, she worked as a pharmacist. "Isn't that difficult for her?" I asked, trying to imagine anyone training for medicine and then working in a pharmacy.

"Oh no, she's happy they let her stay in Moscow. They could have sent her to practice medicine in the provinces. This way she can stay here. Of course, it has been difficult since my father left . . ."

"Oh, he left . . ."

"Well, actually he barely stayed. Not very much. I'm not even sure if they were married. For many years now it has been just my mother and me. We get along all right. It is best to get along with someone if you sleep in the same room."

"You share a room with your mother?"

"We used to share a bed," Tanya said with a laugh, "until

recently. I told her I was thirty and a medical doctor and it was time I had my own bed."

"In America we get our own apartments when we are twenty-two. No one goes back home, it seems."

"I couldn't live alone," Tanya pondered this. "I'm sure I'll stay with my mother until I get married. Maybe afterwards . . ."

"I could never sleep in a bed with my mother," I said.

"Oh, we all do what we have to. In some ways," she said, "our lives are easier than yours. Our jobs are guaranteed. Our housing, our medical care, our old-age benefits. We are taken care of."

It was true. I'd seen no homeless, no slums, no extremes of wealth and poverty. But it all seemed so dreary. No one seemed motivated. No one seemed to care very much.

"But we are . . ." I hesitated to say it, but then decided I could, "we are freer."

She reflected on this. "Yes," she said, "yes, you are. We are mirror images of one another, aren't we," meaning our two countries.

"Perhaps someday the world will find a way to combine the two systems."

"Yes," she sighed, "that's probably what we need."

After dinner we strolled through Red Square. Tanya told me a little more about her life. Marriage and children didn't really matter to her. She viewed them as fetters, things to tie her down. "Of course," she said, afraid she'd hurt my feelings, "I think for some people it is fine."

"Oh, I don't think marriage is coming my way," I said.

"You really don't think he will marry you?" She seemed saddened at this.

"No," I said, "I don't think he will."

We walked in silence back to my hotel. There we paused. In a short time we had grown very fond of each other. I felt as if Tanya had become a friend, almost as if she had been sent to help me. "Is there anything I can do for you? Is there anything you would like for your journey?"

I thought about this for a moment, then blurted out, "Oranges. I would love some oranges." I don't know what it was, but suddenly I felt overwhelmed by a desire for fresh fruit, for oranges specifically.

Tanya looked at me in dismay. "I will try . . ."

"Don't bother. It was just a thought." Now I was embarrassed by my wish, which seemed simple at the time but was clearly beyond Tanya's means. As I thought about it, I realized I hadn't seen oranges anywhere in the Soviet Union.

"It will be difficult," Tanya repeated as we said good night, "but I will see what I can do."

There was a small bar in my hotel and I went and ordered a Coke, not ready to go to bed. I had only been sitting for a moment when the man from Arkansas showed up. I'd forgotten his name, but he introduced himself again to me. "Bob," he said. "Long time no see." He pulled up a chair and sat down, beer in hand. "I've just had an incredible experience." He told me he had spent two nights with a Soviet woman. "You know, my hotel was costing $640 for four nights and I spent two of them, count them, two in bed with a Soviet woman in her apartment. Now she wants me to marry her and take her out of the Soviet Union, but I've got a wife. I kept trying to explain this to her. I've got a wife, I said, I've got a family. And she keeps saying she's going to get me arrested for spying or something."

It was clear that Bob was in a predicament, but I was somehow not in the mood. Women traveling alone seem to have two kinds of experiences. We are kept alone, isolated, like pariahs, or we attract crazy people with problems who are just drawn to us "for some reason." I seemed to specialize in the latter, but was not in the frame of mind to make the shift from pariah to social worker.

"I wish I could help you, Bob," I said, "but I can't."

His face looked red and puffy from lack of sleep, but

suddenly he seemed to wake up. "You seem kinda glum yourself. Nursing a Coke, I see."

"I'm pregnant."

"Oh," he sat back. "Is that good or bad?"

"Both."

"You keeping it?"

I am one of these people who believe that words are actions. Something said is something done. I hesitated. "Yes, I'm keeping it."

"That's right. You were off to the Ukraine when I met you. But I guess you didn't go."

"I didn't go."

"Look, if I can help you out, I've got lots of money. Why don't you come down to Little Rock? Have your baby there. I'll support you. If you want to put it up for adoption, I know some good people. If you want someone to take care of you, well, I could do that . . ."

"Thanks. I think I can take care of myself."

"Boy, you've made me forget about my own problems."

"Good," I said, "I'm glad.

"You sure you wouldn't like that back rub?"

"Not tonight, Bob." I got up and said good night.

A CONTACT had arranged a meeting with Andrei Voznesensky, the superstar Russian poet, at his dacha in a place where writers live outside of Moscow called Peredelkino. The contact was going to drive me, but I got stuck in the elevator for half an hour, and by the time I got downstairs he was gone. The only way to get there now was by taxi, which was going to be costly, but I felt the meeting would be an important one.

Outside the hotel where the taxis were assembled, I asked who would take me to Peredelkino. They all shook their heads, turned away. No one wanted to go.

"I am going to visit Mr. Andrei Voznesensky," I said. The drivers perked up. They negotiated among themselves. Finally a young man with a mustache named Alan stepped forward and said he would take me, but it would cost fifteen rubles an hour, or about twenty-five dollars. I estimated I would have to hire him for at least four hours. This would cost about a hundred dollars, but still I wanted to go. At about eight o'clock, we set out.

It was the night of the summer solstice as Alan and I sped in his small Volkswagen taxi into a crimson sunset toward the outskirts of Moscow. I had only sketchy directions and I communicated them as best I could. We drove and drove. Alan kept stopping people, asking directions. At last we reached Peredelkino, only to learn that Mr. Voznesensky's house is on the other side of some railroad tracks that could not be crossed. We drove back twenty miles.

An hour and a half after we left I reached Mr. Voznesensky's dacha, thinking how no New York City cab driver would put up with a bumbling tourist like me. Voznesensky, a rather pallid-looking man, came out of his dacha and kissed me flat on the mouth. "So," he said, "you have made it. It is wonderful that you have come. Tell me. How are my friends at P.E.N.? How is Karen Kennerly? How is Norman?" And in a moment we were catching up on New York gossip.

The dacha, or summer cottage, was a charming little house he and his wife, Zoja, shared with someone upstairs. I found it odd that a great Russian poet would have to share his dacha, but they seemed satisfied with the arrangement. The table in the country kitchen was spread with strawberries and chocolate, glasses and wine. "These are not Chernobyl strawberries," he assured me. "These come from these very woods. We pick them ourselves." I looked at the plump, delicious strawberries, amazed. He poured me a glass of wine that was filled with dead fruit flies. Raising my glass, I was forced to toast. "Cheers," he said. I drank a few dead bugs. Then discreetly I held my glass under the table, picking them out as we talked.

We talked about the upcoming Writers' Union Congress that would be taking place. "A revolution is happening here," he said. "Enormous changes. Like with the film industry. It is a miracle what has happened in that union. It will happen to the writers as well."

"What kind of changes?" I asked. Although I had a sense of what they'd be, I wanted him to say it.

"Less censorship, free expression, what you call your First Amendment rights."

"Really? You really think changes will occur?"

"You will see. Nothing will be like it was."

Then he led me into his studio. "Here," he said, "there are things I want you to see." The studio was a mess. Papers, books, pictures were everywhere, spilling onto the floor. It did not seem possible he could work at his desk. "Look," he said, "prints I collaborated on with Rauschenberg. They are very nice, aren't they. Ah, and this—" Then he dug around until he pulled out a sketch of a monument. He held it up to me with great pride. "This, you must see this. I designed it and had it built. It is a monument to Russian poets. But when you see it you will understand, you will see how things are changing, how it won't be as it was before. That time is past. Stalin, that's all over. Chernobyl," he said, "it is terrible, a terrible thing. But with Gorbachev, you'll see, it is getting better. At the Congress," he said, "I am going to make a speech. I am going to make a big speech."

It was almost midnight and all I could think about was how much the taxi was costing me. Alan sat waiting patiently, but I could not afford to stay any longer. Just as I was leaving, Zoja rushed out, bringing me a beautiful Russian scarf—a green-and-pink floral pattern with black fringe —and she wrapped it around me. "To remember us by," she said. Touched by her generosity, I kissed her on both cheeks.

Then Andrei walked me to the cab. When we reached the taxi, we paused.

"Andrei," I said, "there is someone I am concerned about. A poet. She has been in prison for a long time. Her health is very poor." He looked surprised as if he'd never heard of such a thing. I told him her name. Again he seemed surprised.

"I have never heard of her, but why don't you write down her name for me. I'll see what I can do." I wrote down her name, though I felt there was something theatrical about this. "I'll see if anything can be done." He slipped the piece of paper into his pocket. "But you know," he cocked his head, "this is Russia."

Six months later when I met Irina Ratushinskaya at a reception in New York, I wondered if it was Voznesensky who had somehow made this possible.

Andrei kissed me good-bye. Then, as I was getting in, he spoke to Alan for a while, telling him where to take me. Alan was half asleep, but managed to wake up as we drove. It was now almost dark and an incredible orange moon, full and shimmering, rose over Moscow. Few cars were out and we drove quickly but in silence. Once I asked where we were going, but Alan just smiled. He kept pointing straight ahead, saying something I could not quite make out, but which I think was telling me to be patient. To wait and see.

At last he pulled up to a small park lit by street lights, and in the middle stood a monument, tall, dark. Alan got out with me as we walked to the monument, barely visible but for the street lights. Then he began walking around the periphery, looking for something. Then he found it.

I went and stood beside him as he pointed. "Pasternak," he said softly. And there I could make out the word "Pasternak" at this monument to Russian poets. Voznesensky was right. Things were changing. For a long moment Alan and I stood beneath the eerie light, the name Pasternak before us like a promise of things to come. I did not have enough words in Russian to ask him what he felt, but his doe-like eyes seemed to soften in the light.

When we reached my hotel, some six hours after we'd set out, I asked him how much I owed him, thinking I'd have to change some money somewhere. He shook his head. It had been taken care of, he said. Voznesensky had paid him. Again I was amazed by this generosity. I gave him ten more rubles and said good night. "Good luck," he said to me in Russian, "and thank you."

On Sunday, my last day in Moscow, I decided to go to Novodevichy Monastery to attend mass. I walked through a garden where after church people would mill around and headed toward the stone building, which was in a state of disrepair. Old women, lacework around their heads, crossed themselves before the religious statues in the park. Others placed a kiss on the foot of the statue. Somber children dragged along. Men in dark suits and ties walked solemnly into the church.

Russian orthodoxy had reigned supreme until the time of Peter the Great, and then with dwindling power until the revolution, in which it was for all practical purposes institutionally eliminated, but here it flourished. It was Prince Vladimir of Kiev who in 987 brought orthodoxy to Russia from Byzantium intact. Vladimir had examined all the great religions of the world, sending emissaries out to bring back word, in order to determine what Russia's religion should be. He rejected the Muslims because the Russians could not live without drink, and he rejected Judaism because he could not accept the condemnation to wander. He rejected European Christianity because he saw "no glory there." But when his emissaries returned with word of Byzantium and its churches with thousands of shining lights, the richness of its ornaments and vestments, its mosaics and jewels, he determined that Eastern Orthodoxy should be the religion of Russia, because God dwells in beauty.

For the next thousand years the church played a major role in Russian political, spiritual and cultural life. Under Peter the role of the church was lessened, though the ordinary people turned to the church for their spiritual life. Then in the revolution this profoundly religious people suddenly found themselves with a new god thrust upon them in the guise of communism. By 1939 only a hundred churches were operating in the U.S.S.R. When I visited, 7,500, a fraction of what once existed, were open across the entire land. Still, though revolutionary zeal endeavored to replace spiritual belief, it had never quite succeeded.

People flocked into Novodevichy, filling the aisles. Covering my head with the scarf Zoja had given me, I entered the dark, cavelike church whose air was thick with incense. The cathedral was emblazoned by the light of thousands of candles, small beacons glowing in the darkness, just as the emissaries of Vladimir had promised. Flowers filled the naves. People milled about, children ran to and fro. Some knelt and crossed themselves. Others moved forward to take the eucharist. There was a remarkable sense of disorder. No one seemed to be sitting anywhere. Indeed, there seemed to be no chairs. People were talking, smiling, praying, lighting candles. They were pious but not austere. They prayed openly, freely, as anyone else would. The service reminded me of a Jewish service where people move about, come and go, talk, and no one seems to mind.

Neighbor leaned over to gossip with neighbor. A fleeing child was returned to its bewildered parent. It all seemed vibrant, full of life. I stayed for a long time. Then I lit a candle for my unborn child. Scarf over my head, I warmed my hands at the flame.

□   □   □   □

The next day, an hour before my train was to leave, Tanya stood in the lobby of my hotel, a bag of oranges in her hand. They were small and brown and hard, but they were oranges and only then, seeing her holding them, seeing what they looked like, did it occur to me what trouble she had gone through to procure them—the search, the hours spent in line. "Here," she said, holding them up. "It was the best I could do."

I would never see Tanya again. The letters I wrote never received replies. But these oranges sustained me. All the way to Berlin I sucked their bitter fruit, grateful for this gift.

The Border

BY NIGHT the train made its way west across Byelorussia, "White Russia," a land of timberland—of oaks, silver birch and pine. And of farmlands now covered with the fine dust of radioactive fallout which four years later would make the death rate of children in Minsk from leukemia leap from one a year to one a week. I missed its tragedy as the train snuck like a thief in the night across this tainted land.

I had boarded the train the late afternoon and to my relief had a two-person compartment to myself. There was no food service so I ate my last can of sardines and two of the oranges Tanya had brought me. The man in the compartment next to mine was Dutch, named Johan. He had purchased a fallout-proof tent in Tokyo and planned to sleep in it that evening. "Just as precaution," he said as I watched him set it up. "You know, Minsk, Byelorussia. That's the place where the cloud really settled." He was terrified by Chernobyl and said he had great fears about returning home.

I told him I was supposed to go to the Ukraine, but I learned I was pregnant on this trip. "Are you going to keep the baby?" he asked as if this were a rhetorical question.

"Yes," I said firmly, "I am."

Later in the evening he knocked on my door and invited me for a drink. I told him I wasn't drinking, but I joined him in his compartment. The only place to sit was under his tent, which seemed like little more than a strong scouting tent, though it had radioactive symbols with crosses through them etched on its side. Holding open the flap, I went in and sat in the fallout-proof tent with a stranger on a train. The air inside the tent had a heavy, almost mildewed smell as if something were festering, and the sudden shared

intimacy with a stranger added to my unease. "Are you going to stay in this all night?"

"Until I get home," he said.

I found him quite mad. "I am very tired," I told him.
"I've been traveling a long time." I gave him an orange,
then went back to my compartment.

All night long we chugged across White Russia. I kept
my shade up and watched as we moved through the cities
and towns of the northern European plain. I thought of
Johan sleeping in his tent and wondered about the air I
breathed as we crossed Eastern Europe. Suddenly in the
middle of the night I was gripped with a desire to crawl
inside Johan's tent, settle into its fetid darkness, but perhaps the Dutchman would not understand. I am not certain when I slept, but the next thing I knew it was morning
and the border was in sight.

Joseph Brodsky once said to me, as we sat in my little gar-
dener's shack built into the Roman Wall at the American
Academy in Rome—a good, safe distance from the
U.S.S.R.—that women make good novelists and customs
officials because they like to pick through the details of life.
Sitting at the Academy, this comment enraged me and con-
tinues to stir my ire. But the fact remains that when we
reached Brest and the border between the Soviet Union and
Poland and two women customs officials entered my compartment, Brodsky's words assumed a different meaning.

The women arrived at 9 A.M. They moved quickly
through most of the compartments on the train and
laughed at the Dutchman with his tent. They were of a
stocky, solid breed, the stereotypical Soviet female bureaucrat.

When they reached my compartment, they asked me to
take down my bags. Then they emptied them onto the bed.
They emptied everything I had—pills, cosmetics, my long-
forgotten diaphragm case, which they opened, then quickly

closed shut, earplugs, every article of clothing, dirty underwear, every souvenir, every roll of film (which they had me
remove from the canisters, fifty rolls in all), makeup, business cards, my address book, my journal and some other
writings. They laid to one side my journal, film and writings
as they slowly picked through my personal effects displayed
on the bed.

One of the women spoke English and she began translat-
ing an endless barrage of repetitive questions from the
other woman, older, larger, more severe. Why are you traveling alone? Why isn't your husband with you? What is this
writing? Why do you write so much? Why do you have
high heels? Why did you meet with this editor? How do
you know this poet? Does this roll of film show people's
faces? Did you photograph people?

I came to the land of the firebird, I told them, to find my
family's trace, to see the Easter eggs, the fresh-baked breads,
the villages my grandmother told me about, the ones that
made up my dream. I came alone because my husband
could not join me. He is in Berlin on important business.
He is waiting for me there. Employing the technique Mary
Kingsley used in Africa when she wanted to ensure herself
safe passage from one place to the next, I point in the
direction we are going. "He is over there."

The older, more austere woman who did not speak English was not satisfied with my responses. She barked an
order at her subordinate. "You must come with us," the one
who spoke English said gently. "Please bring your work."

I watched as the woman who did not speak English
flipped through my journal, which contained everything
that had happened on this trip. Tears came to my eyes. I
knew I was going to lose my writing and possibly my film.
And beyond that I was frightened, as frightened as I'd ever
been on the road. "I am going to have a baby," I told the
woman who spoke English. "I am very tired. I am feeling
sick." She said something to the older woman who did not

seem to care. Words went back and forth between them and it occurred to me that they were arguing on my account.

"Please," said the kinder woman, "come with us."

They told me to gather my things and follow them to the customs office. Brodsky had also said to me once that in the Soviet Union, unlike America, poetry matters. You can go to prison for it. Or as Ivan had said, "You can burn for it." I had written many things in my journals and I had no idea whom I might have implicated. Beyond this, I had written many personal things. I could live without my film, I told myself. I could even live without the drafts of some stories. But I could not let them confiscate my journal.

Though I did not know what it might cost me, I made a snap decision. As I trailed behind them, I slipped my journal under the blanket on the upper berth in my compartment. Already the women had spent an hour and a half with me. In half an hour the train would leave. The station was some distance from the train and there would not be time to send me back for the journal and so they would have to make a decision about detaining me or delaying the train, neither of which I thought they would do.

I tagged along, a delinquent child en route to the principal's office, my eyes laden with tears. Only this was not child's play. The cold station house was filled with Russian soldiers and a few Eastern European tourists, all of whom looked at me askance, some with ridicule, a few with concern. The soldiers seemed amused. We reached the customs office at the station where the chief of customs, another woman, asked me to spread my work out on the table, which looked like a butcher's slab. I was feeling faint as I put down my pack and displayed for them my film and some short stories with notes scribbled across them. "Where is your writing?" the woman who did not speak English asked, annoyed.

"Oh," I said dumbly. "I thought you wanted my work. That was just my personal diary. This is my work."

"Your diary? We asked you to bring your diary."

"I misunderstood. I thought it was my work . . ." Suddenly they seemed both annoyed and bored with me, which was what I'd hoped for. "Shall I go back to the train and get it?"

Simultaneously we glanced at the clock on the wall. Again they discussed what to do with me. It was a quarter to eleven and the train was to depart at eleven. If they detained me further, I'd miss my train. If I missed my train, they'd have to do something with me until the next train came along and they didn't seem to want to have to deal with this. The head of customs took the film out of its canisters again, all fifty rolls. What is on this roll? Where did you take this? I had no idea, but I answered the questions. Peking, Shanghai, my husband and me on the Yangtze, statues in Leningrad, pandas, the circus, architecture in Moscow. No people, no faces. No one.

At last, weary of me, they sent me to a window where a guard held my passport. He handed it to me, the visa removed, with no stamp in it. It was as if I had never been there at all.

I had to run to reach the train in time. The Dutchman who was still sitting in the fallout tent asked me if I was all right. I was, in fact, in tears. He invited me once more into his tent, but that warm seclusion with a stranger remained repellent to me and I felt hideously alone. Instead I sucked on one of Tanya's oranges for strength. It was not long before the train pulled out. As we crossed the river into Poland, I breathed a sigh of relief.

Divided City

ACROSS POLAND I stared at fields of wheat, miles and miles of grain, meadows of tall grass. Women in babushkas bent over their tomato plants, hoes in hand. Men trailed ox carts laden with cut hay. Children danced on the top of haystacks. Soon the light of the day shifted and the colors of the fields turned from a shimmering gold to late afternoon shades of pink and blue.

I recalled the dream I had had in China, a dream of being in a train, passing fields of colored wheat—red, blue, gray, and green—colors I had not understood at the time. Now all the emotions I had felt on this journey—from passion to sadness, from despair to hope—rushed past me in a rainbow of colors.

My grandmother had been buried alive as a child and I understood now, carrying my own child within me, why this image had stayed with me all this time, why it had sent me on this trip. I thought how we all bury the child within us or have it buried for us—through impoverishment and violence, through domestic strife and abuse, through the instilling of doubt or the creating of impossible expectations, through hatred and rage, prejudice and fear. In my own way I had buried a child of my own. Not the one I was going to have, but the one I had been. Now I felt her within me, scraping at the edges of her grave, beginning to dig her way out.

As a child, I could never do anything right. I could never set the table, make a bed, dress myself, turn in a report card that was just right. Try harder, my father always said. Reach for the stars. I reached until I thought my arms would break, until I could reach no more. I reached for love, for immortality, success. I wandered for years unsure and alone with dreams of home. I found lonely nights in a too-small apartment, sipping vodka, distractions that left me empty, the arms of men who didn't love me, the shunning of those who would.

And yet I am not a child of exile or war-torn grief. My parents were parents who loved me. They were good to us in the best way they knew how. Still, there are many ways, I thought, to hurt a child. Watching the wheat fly by as the train hurtled to the West, I felt somehow protected, yet I realized that many others had crossed this very terrain, thinking they were safe.

My parents' lives and those of my extended family were lived far away from the battlefields of Europe. Yet in 1947, when I was born, they named me Mary so no one, my mother told me years later, would know by my name that I was a Jew. Now I gazed outside my window again. The scene was peaceful, yet Poland's history lay strewn across its pasturelands. Between 1939 and 1945 six million Poles died on this plain I was crossing; half of them were Jews. Even now recent history hovered over these fields, planted yellow and green and tainted by the Chernobyl cloud.

In Warsaw on the station platform I bought sweet bread and munched on it, my supply of sardines at last depleted. For once when the train made a stop, I did not want to stay. My thoughts were of home. For the rest of the after-noon farmlands, small villages zipped by. I dozed and woke to a waning light. I was beginning to grow restless. In a matter of hours, I would cross into the West. This eight-week journey would come to an end. I thought how in a sense the trip had been short, the journey long. I paced the train. The Dutchman had folded up his tent and was sitting placidly staring at the monotonous landscape that rushed by.

At nine-thirty that night under a sea of floodlights we entered a kind of large concrete warehouse with huge platforms, room for many trains. We had reached the German border. For a long time the train just sat in this starkly illumined concrete structure. A few guards marched by, but no one came to inspect our passports. I had my transit visa in hand and did not expect any difficulties at this crossing, but still the wait made me uncomfortable and it was not long before I felt within me a growing sense of unease. Germany was a country I had avoided for many years and I wondered now why I had chosen to come this way.

Two guards arrived, blond and tall, and without much ceremony they inspected my transit visa. They were formal and efficient and within moments they were gone, but my heart was pounding. The train began to move again. I heard the endless clack of the wheels whose rhythmic sound I'd listened to for weeks now, but suddenly its sound took on another meaning.

In an hour we'd be in Berlin. With floodlights shining on my face, I lay back on my bunk and thought about the parents of two of my friends who had once taken similar train rides only going in the opposite direction. These were, you might say, the lucky ones, the ones who got out in the early days of Hitler's Reich. The ones who now attend their children's art openings and baby-sit for their grandchildren. People who have married, led the semblance of a normal life. But these are also people for whom the past is a closed book. There are things they will barely discuss.

When they were small children, their parents took them to the train station in Berlin where they put them on the train. Their parents told them that they were going to a summer camp in Britain, which was true, and that they would be home soon, which was not. Weeping mothers put their daughters on trains filled with laughing girls. Fathers embraced their sons, telling them to behave. The father of a friend of mine was put on a train when he was twelve years old and the boy never again saw anyone he'd known before.

The great-aunt of another friend recalls seeing her mother on the platform waving good-bye, sobbing. But her mother clung to her youngest, a four-year-old girl, declaring that she could not let all of her children go, and so she kept this one behind. Later they would die in Auschwitz.

Now on the train riding into Berlin, about to be a mother myself, I tried to imagine. What would I do? Would I let go? Or would I hold on? Would I put my daughter on a train bound for England, knowing I would never see her again, or would I keep her with me, as my friend's aunt had done, and hope against all probability. I tried to imagine my orphaned child growing up in England, thanking me for the gift of life I had given her. Or silently cursing me for sending her off, leaving her alone in the world. I knew which decision was the right one, but there for the first time as the trail hurtled toward Berlin, my unborn child became real to me, and I wept because I did not know for certain what I would do.

IN 1919 at the end of World War I Germany was a hungry, defeated, and bankrupt nation. Plagued by unemployment, a 33-billion-dollar war reparations bill, runaway inflation and general despair, the German people were searching for someone who would make Germany strong again. At about this time an extreme right-wing nationalist party that pledged a strong and unified Germany began to rise to power. This group, who called themselves the German Workers' Party, wanted to punish the "criminals" who had agreed to the Treaty of Versailles which had taken away much of defeated Germany's territories, forced the nation to disarm and pay huge reparations. This nationalist group called for the union into one nation of all German-speaking peoples. It favored strong government and cancellation of the Versailles Treaty. The leader of this group, which later changed its name to the National Socialist German Workers'—or Nazi—party, was a young Austrian named Adolf Hitler.

The son of a cruel, authoritarian father, Hitler was brought up to believe that order, obtained by any means, was the highest value. He had been taught at an early age harshness, coldness and a fierce wielding of power, as were his followers. Paranoid and unstable, Hitler deemed anything that smacked of creativity or vitality (even colors) a threat to society, a peril, Jewish. A vibrant speaker with piercing blue eyes, Hitler had a remarkable ability to rally people to the cause and the cause that made the German people cheer him was the return to Germany's past glory. He said he would build an empire that would last a thousand years, in words oddly reminiscent of a similar unstable historical figure, the first ruler of China and builder of the Great Wall, Qin.

In the Jew, Hitler found his true enemy. He managed to blame most of Germany's ills on the Jews and to equate the return to Germany's former greatness with their annihilation, not only in Germany but throughout Europe. German Jewry was among the most sophisticated and intellectual, not to mention assimilated, in the world. Hitler became Chancellor on January 30, 1933. Shortly afterward the travelers who met on the platforms at Anhalter Bahnhof (the main railroad station for westbound trains) included such left-wing and Jewish luminaries as Bertolt Brecht, Kurt Weill, Heinrich Mann, George Grosz, Albert Einstein, and the architects of the Bauhaus school, including Walter Gropius and Mies van der Rohe, all of whom managed to secure emigration papers out of Germany.

Upon coming to power in 1933 Hitler began to systematically deprive the Jews of their rights, starting with their exclusion from the Civil Service (which consisted of all teaching positions from grammar school through the university, and most areas of the entertainment industry, including opera, theater, radio and concerts). It was at this point that many Jews perceived the inevitable and fled. In 1935 the Nuremberg Laws made Jews no longer citizens, but subjects, and declared that all intimate relations between a Jew and an Aryan, including marriage and friendship, were forms of "racial pollution." In the next several years thirteen additional decrees, taking away their rights such as to attend universities (those who did attend were never permitted to graduate) and to own property, supplemented the Nuremberg Laws until the Jew would be outlawed entirely.

Jews were denied not only the amenities of life, but also the basic necessities. Grocery stores had signs that read, "Jews Not Admitted" and even milk was denied to mothers with babies. Brutal, inhuman daily anti-Semitism drove half of German Jewry—a quarter of a million people—into exile. In every town and village public slogans declared, "The Jew Is Our Misfortune." At a sharp bend in a road a sign read, "Drive carefully. Dangerous curve. Jews 75 miles an hour."

In the early years of the Reich, emigration was difficult, though not impossible. Jews were prevented from taking money out of the country or selling their property at a reasonable rate, though some with great wealth managed to do so. Those who did leave sometimes found they had no opportunities elsewhere in Europe and so they returned to the country of their birth, thinking the situation, while grim, would not worsen. Still there were those who continued to live in a kind of fool's paradise, believing that a legal solution would be found to the Jewish problem. This hope, along with any remaining illusion that the situation would somehow not worsen, was dispelled during the organized assaults of November 1938, referred to as *Kristallnacht,* or

Night of Broken Glass, when seventy-five hundred Jewish shop windows were shattered, all the synagogues went up in flames, and twenty thousand Jewish men were taken off to concentration camps.

On January 30, 1939, Hitler declared that the result of the war will be "the annihilation of the Jewish race in Europe." On September 1, he invaded Poland. And then the deportations, the construction of concentration camps, and ultimately in 1942 the "Final Solution" began.

The statistics of Hitler's insane atrocities against the Jews are appalling and beyond comprehension. Poland lost three million of its 3,300,000 Jews, the U.S.S.R. lost 1,100,000 of its 3,000,000, The Netherlands lost 100,000 of its 140,000, Hungary lost 559,000 of its 825,000, and Germany lost 141,000 of its 566,000 (half of Germany's Jews went into exile at the beginning of the war). Berlin, which began with 172,672 Jews in 1925, declared itself officially *Judenrein*—cleansed of Jews—on June 16, 1943. In 1967 Berlin had a total Jewish population of 7,500—6,000 in West Berlin and 1,500 in East Berlin.

There were some statistics that might revive one's hope in humankind. Italy resisted deportation and lost only 7,000 of its 44,500 Jews. Denmark lost only 60 of its 7,800 and the Danes were acclaimed for the rescuing of 7,220 of their Jews who found refuge in Sweden. And Bulgaria, though allied with Germany, lost none of its 50,000 Jews; Bulgaria simply refused to deport them. But for the most part the numbers are staggering, the human suffering and loss beyond comprehension.

At no time in history had anyone attempted to systematically destroy a people. Even Adolf Eichmann at his trial in Jerusalem referred to the annihilation of the Jews as "one of the greatest crimes in the history of humanity." In what Hannah Arendt so chillingly referred to as "the banality of evil," an entire system, operated by small-minded bureaucrats such as Eichmann who were only following the orders of their Führer, was put into place which allowed this to happen. Indeed it has been said that the only war Hitler actually won was the war against the Jews, a war which in fact helped contribute to Germany's military defeat. Hitler did manage to obliterate the Jew from Eastern Europe. He destroyed communities, towns. He had his officers kill naked women, children and old men in open pits. This collective assault upon humanity has come to be known as the Holocaust. From the Greek *holos* for whole and *kaustos* for burnt, meaning the complete destruction of people or animals by fire.

The complex psychological roots for Hitler's hatred of the Jews, the collusion of the German people as well as other European countries, and the roots of anti-Semitism in Europe have all been well documented elsewhere, but now I found myself entering Germany with great uncertainty, in a state of disbelief.

IN THE DARKNESS, the lights of the city appeared. Brilliant white flood lights shone on the stately classical buildings of East Berlin, those which had been left standing after the war. Beyond these, the city seemed cloaked in darkness. A sprinkling of lights here and there, but mainly these floodlights on the buildings of state.

And then I saw the wall, illumined by these same lights. It wended its white, serpentine form through the city, eerie monster that it was, stretching and extending for some 26 miles, pristine, silent, sinister in its whiteness. It was a scar across torn flesh. It bifurcated this city, split it in two.

And then, so quickly it startled me, we were on the other side. A shout, a sigh, seemed to go up from the train. And now the wall turned into a playful beast bedecked in brilliant colors, animated images dancing on its spine like a Chinese dragon on New Year's Day. The wall on the Western side stood, defiant and irreverent, a blaze of graffiti in contrast to the starkness of the East. I found myself ready for the open range, free flow, the unobstructed, the unconfined. I felt as if I had been holding my breath for weeks and now suddenly I could breathe again. Before me was West Berlin—neon-lit, noisy, decadent, materialistic and beckoning.

Soon we pulled into the station in West Berlin and everyone began to disperse. Johan, his tent folded beneath his arm, bade me good-bye. But I stayed where I was, gazing from the window of the train. For this was the place where child had been wrenched from mother, where sobbing parents had tried to explain their tears as they said good-bye. It was also the place of still more horrific scenes. It was in well-lit stations such as this that cattle cars had stood, their windowless darkness about to hold the Jews of Berlin, or of Paris, or Warsaw, or of dozens of other European centers.

The "Office for Jewish Emigration," administrated from beginning to end by an Austrian Nazi and native of Hitler's hometown of Linz, Karl Adolf Eichmann, was the agency in charge at first of Jewish emigration, and ultimately of deportation and extermination. The German Reichsbahn, or State Railroad, secured special trains, *Sonderzuge,* for the Jews who were booked as regular passengers. They paid their own passage (one-way group fare was provided. Children traveled half-price, infants under four traveled free). But for the most part the Jews were transported as cargo in freight cars. By the end, railways had carried three million people to obscure destinations in Poland and incorporated territories from which luggage and clothing but no people ever returned.

The Jews had been promised that they were going to live in another place where there would only be their own kind.

It was on the platforms from where tourists were now running off into the night to find taxis to take them to the bright lights of West Berlin that the deportees were processed and lined up and stuffed into the airless cars in which they rode standing for hours, sometimes days, without food or water, without sanitary facilities. Many—the old and infirm—died during the journey. Some were crushed to death.

Families had clasped one another, praying they would not be separated. Exhausted, they clutched small children in their weary arms, for if the child slipped from their hands he would be trampled under the feet of their fellow passengers, packed so tightly they could not bend down. Families were forced into trains that would take the route I had just taken, or routes south to Auschwitz, to Dachau, and never come back again. In this train station where my journey had ended, other people's nightmares had begun.

For the first time in weeks, with no Intourist official to greet me, I had to fend for myself. I got my bags down and dragged them through the deserted depot, with no destination in mind. Competition for cabs on the street was stiff but after about half an hour I found one. I had no idea where to go so I said "International Hotel," assuming there must be one and that it would have good rooms and a hot shower, and the cab sped through the streets of Berlin. I found myself bedazzled, the way I imagine a blindman must feel when suddenly he sees the light. Shops, discos, stores, restaurants, all the accoutrements of commercial capitalism missing in the East were alive here and the change startled me.

Checking into the hotel, which was in fact the nicest I'd been in in a long time, I went to the roof garden for a drink. It would be soft drinks from now on, so I sipped a Perrier with lime. From this darkened penthouse, the view of the city was dramatic, for the East was truly monochromatic, stark, pale, and the West aglow, like identical twins with opposite personalities, the only way their parents can tell them apart.

Beside me sat an American and an elegantly dressed German businessmen, both speaking English. The American was spouting off, his conversation shifting from the price of the dollar to television advertising. "Why doesn't Mercedes-Benz advertise on television," the American exclaimed. ("Because we don't have to," the elegant German replied.) "You know," the American said, "when you drive down the street in a Mercedes you look so cool. I just love to drive that car. But you guys should advertise. You don't know what your sales potential could be with TV." The German nodded, demurely. "America, we've got a great system," the American said. The German smiled wanly. "I do my own taxes. The government sends me just enough information so I can cheat them. You know how I know I'm living in a democracy?" the American went on. "Because there's always a way to get out of paying taxes, that's how I know." So at last it seemed I was back in the West.

Unable to sleep, I walked from my hotel into the heart of West Berlin, I strolled the Kurfürstendamm, West Berlin's main commercial street. I wandered past cafés, shops with their neon flashing, past bars and clubs, discos, restaurants. It was close to midnight, but the streets were filled with people—men and women dressed mostly in jet black, their hair spiked or heads shaved, chains and razor blades dangling from their ears, their necks. Laughter such as I had not heard in weeks came from everywhere, in part alcohol- or drug-induced, but laughter all the same.

Hungry, I stopped at an Italian restaurant and ordered spaghetti. Like a prisoner let free, I covered it with grated parmesan cheese and wolfed it down. I took huge bites out of the garlic bread. Around me couples dined, cigarette smoke circling around their heads.

Suddenly someone pulled back the extra chair at my table and sat down. "I see you are also in Berlin alone," he said in heavily accented English. "May I join you? For coffee?"

I looked up at a rather handsome man with bright green eyes. "I don't drink coffee at night," I said.

"Well then, a Cognac."

"I'm not drinking," I said, annoyed at this intrusion.

"Well, could I join you, just for a moment? I am a foreign correspondent. I am on assignment. I like my work, but it gets lonely sometimes."

I hadn't talked to anyone in a while, so I motioned for him to sit down. Samuel introduced himself. He was a reporter from Israel, stationed in Paris. He was here to cover the opening of the Jewish cemetery in East Berlin. "It was in ruins," he said, "but now they are opening it again. They have straightened out the headstones, planted flowers, trees. You should come with me on Thursday."

On Thursday I was leaving for New York. I thought that I could change my plans. "Perhaps," I said.

"So, are you married? What do you do?" I told him I was also a foreign correspondent and that my husband was waiting for me in New York.

"Is this your first time? In Germany?" he asked.

"It is my first time."

"And does it make you uncomfortable?"

"Yes," I said, glad to speak about it, "it does, though I didn't lose anyone, during the war."

"Ah, I was born in Palestine, but only because my parents were among the lucky ones. They got out on a boat in the first waves of emigration out of here. It takes some getting used to, Berlin."

I paid my bill and we walked the Kurfürstendamm. "Were they German Jews?"

"No, Rumanian. But they saw the handwriting on the wall. Their brothers and sisters, my aunts and uncles, they were not so lucky."

"Do you have any left?"

"Not a one, just my parents and my sister. There is no one else. Have you been to Israel?"

"Yes, in 1967, right after the war."

"And did you like it?"

I thought about my feelings carefully. I could not say that I liked it, but I tried to understand it. "There were things I liked and some things that I didn't like."

"Such as . . ."

I wasn't sure I wanted to get into this discussion. "I found it very militaristic. I didn't like the treatment of the Palestinians. I think Israel has made some mistakes . . ."

He nodded in agreement. "Yes, we have made mistakes, but what choice do we have?"

"You could treat the Palestinians differently, for one."

"Some people say that we learned well from the Nazis. What do you think?"

I shook my head. "I really don't know. I wouldn't say that. I just think there are ways in which you could be more humane."

"You don't know what it is like. Living where we do, surrounded by enemies."

"You're right, I don't. But maybe you have not tried to make friends of your enemies."

"Do you know what that means for Israel?"

"I have always lived in America. I have always felt safe. I can't know what you know."

Samuel sighed and for a moment we both seemed exhausted by politics. Now I found myself preoccupied, and for reasons that surprised me I told Samuel my entire story —my journey, the baby, everything—and he listened intently. "I could never bring myself to come to Germany before, even when I lived in Europe," I said, "but, well, I won't be traveling for a while and somehow it just seemed like the end of the line."

"Don't worry." he smiled. "Nothing bad will happen to you."

"You mean here? In Berlin?"

"No, I mean in general."

"How do you know?"

"Because I won't let it," lifting me into his arms.

I managed to get away and turned to go back to my hotel.

"Perhaps you'll come with me, to the cemetery."

I was tempted, but I was also ready to leave.

"On Thursday I'll be home. In New York." I said.

"Ah," he nodded. "Yes, home."

In her poem "Questions of Travel," Elizabeth Bishop writes, "Think of the long trip home./ Should we have stayed at home and thought of here?/ Where should we be today?"

I think of how long I sat at "home," wherever that is for me, because it is becoming more a concept than a reality. I dreamed of this journey to Russia and now, the journey incomplete, I think of home. Of what awaits me. What decisions, what trials, what choices must be made. There will be many and I know there is much pain ahead. And I am left with the fabric of this trip, the vision of my grandmother's stories unfinished, muddled with tragic historic circumstance and my own personal fate—a piece left to complete, a story perhaps left to tell, but for another time.

I feel like Chagall who all his life longed to return to his beloved Vitebsk, the town of his surreal paintings, birthplace of the floating cows, the sky-borne brides, but when the opportunity presented itself in his later years he refused to return. Perhaps he knew that the pictures that arose from his imagination were nurtured by what he remembered, not by what was real, and perhaps he even feared that a dose of reality would kill them off. But when I planned this journey I did not want to be like Chagall.

Rather like Oedipus, defying some ancient taboo, I needed to know. But circumstances would not allow it. And now at the end of the line I think that perhaps home is not a place. Perhaps, it is what we remember.

IF THE GREAT WALL of China was intended to keep people out, the Berlin Wall was built to keep them in. On August 13, 1961, the people of Berlin woke to find their movements truncated, their lives shattered, severed in two. In the night as they'd slept, unbeknownst to them or to their allies or even the CIA whose job it was to monitor such activity closely and who paid spies large sums of money for that purpose, a twenty-six-mile barrier of barbed wire was stretched, barbed wire that had been sitting in huge stacks in the middle of East German parade grounds.

This operation, ordered by Khrushchev and carried out by Erich Honecker, former leader of East Germany, was performed with as much secrecy as all the great surprises of history. Nowhere was it written what was planned. Almost nowhere had it been talked about. It had simply been accomplished with stealth and surprise. No intelligence agency of the West had predicted this event. "How the hell could they build that without our knowing about it in advance?" an angry Kennedy asked when he received word some seventeen hours after the wall had gone up while he was sailing in Hyannis. But the fact was, they had.

Khrushchev had said he would "bury" the West, referring to the use of nuclear weapons. In a secret meeting held on August 10, 1961, Khrushchev told his closest insiders, which included one spy for the West who felt reporting this would cause too much risk to his person and there was nothing the West could do (later he was arrested by the Soviets and executed), "We're going to close Berlin. We're just going to put up serpentine barbed wire and the West will stand there like dumb sheep. And while they're standing there, we'll finish the wall."

On August 13, the barbed wire was laid. The Iron Curtain, a once imaginary curtain, was made flesh. Children who had played in Tiergarten park would never return. Bridges across the Spree were blown up, Friedrichstrasse Station was closed, Brandenburg Gate was sealed. Families and friends who had easily moved in and out of one another's lives were irrevocably separated. And gradually construction began of a twenty-six-mile cinder-block wall that would zigzag through the city. Though appearing to be a makeshift obstacle, it was more ominous and escape-resistant than many could imagine. There would be ingenious attempts—tunnels, balloons, border crossings by East Germans dressed as Soviet soldiers—but these were treacherous. When they succeeded, the West was exuberant. When they failed, the results were tragic and all too palpable.

The Cold War had taken a new, icy turn. Its symbol became Berlin. When Kennedy came to Berlin in 1963, shortly before his death, he spoke the memorable words to three fifths of West Berlin's population: "Two thousand years ago the proudest boast was *Civis Romanus sum.* Today in the world of freedom, the proudest boast is *Ich bin ein Berliner.*" He challenged those who did not know the difference between communism, which he did not believe was the wave of the future, and freedom. "Let them come to Berlin," he said.

After a buffet breakfast of fruit salad and scrambled eggs, of which I had many helpings, I made my way to Checkpoint Charlie, the American entry point into East Berlin. It was there that American and Soviet tanks had faced one another in a stand-off on October 27, 1961, from which the Soviet tanks would eventually back down, before the world learned to live with the wall.

At the Museum of the Wall I stood in tears before pictures of brides waving across barbed wire at their grandparents, of riddled bodies, faces of the brokenhearted. I read unbearable accounts of families divided, of children taken from their escaping parents, never to be seen again. While the parents languished in East German prisons, the children were put up for adoption. To this day some parents and children are still searching for one another.

In a somewhat shaken state, I made my way back into the East one last time. Displaying my passport to the United States Customs official, I received a visa, a stamp, and wandered easily through the maze of tunnels where the East German border guard examined my passport and waved me in without a word.

It was as if I had stepped into a period piece, a Hollywood version of life in the 1950s. Fashion, cars, hairstyles had stepped back a quarter of a century. The architecture was classical, as opposed to West Berlin where much that had been bombed was now modern. I made my way to Unter den Linden, the broad main street of East Berlin, lined with the government buildings of the Reichstag as well as record and book shops. Music poured from old Victrolas. Beethoven, Haydn. There were no modern record shops, no video stores. The bookshops and map and magazine stores all seemed antiquarian, dated.

I walked slowly along Unter den Linden, whose name means "under the linden trees," once Berlin's greatest avenue. To Frederick the Great it was the centerpiece of his royal capital and for the wealthy and aristocratic it was the most prestigious address in the city. During the boom years of the industrial revolution, building speculation ruined some of the eighteenth-century splendor, but the avenue remained fashionable until the bombs of World War II reduced it to rubble. Now the linden trees had been replanted and many of the monumental buildings were restored or rebuilt. Still, it was along here on May 10, 1933, that thousands of students marched in a torchlight procession, carrying books by Thomas Mann, Albert Einstein, Proust, Zola, André Gide, H. G. Wells, and Jack London, to be burned as anti-German literature.

I walked slowly in the heat of the day until I came to the end of the avenue to the Pariser Platz. Here I stood with the grand Reichstag to my right and the closed Brandenburg Gate before me. The gate, once the supreme symbol of the city, was now stuck in the no-man's land between the end of Unter den Linden and the wall, its whiteness more stark to me than upon my arrival two days before. Built in 1791, the gate consists of two Doric columns crowned with a copper statue of Winged Victory and her four-horse chariot. With an irony in a city whose well of irony never runs dry, the Brandenburg Gate was baptized *Friedenstor,* Peace Gate, when it was built.

I moved to the grass where I stood beneath the shade of a tree. Here a young man, perhaps of college age, approached. He spoke in German. "Right here, where you are standing"—he pointed to a grassy spot beside me just off the sidewalk, a square plot of land where Unter den Linden meets Otto-Grotewohl Strasse (formerly Wilhelmstrasse)— "that is where his bunker was. That is where he killed himself. Right there, but you see, there is no marker. Nothing. But this is where it happened."

"Who?" I asked dumbly, surprised by his outburst.

"Hitler," he said, "the man who ruined my country."

"Right here?" I pointed to the ground where there was not a trace of what had happened, not a sign. As if it had never happened, as if it had vanished. "There should be something," I said. "A plaque."

"Perhaps we want to forget . . ."

"Maybe that's not such a good thing," I said, the words of Santayana looming within me but their translation elud-

ing me. "Those who do not remember the past are condemned to relive it."

"You are from . . ."

"America," I said, "New York."

"You are . . ." He hesitated, pushing his sandy hair,
straight and silky, off his face, "a Jew."

I nodded without speaking. Then I said, "Yes, I'm a
Jew."

"Yes," he said, nodding wearily it seemed, "I can understand . . . My country, my people, we have a terrible
thing to overcome. But we are not the same people who
did this, you understand. Hitler was, well, a monster, you
see, and now," he pointed at the wall, "this is what we must
live with. This is what we must understand. How this could
have happened . . . But then, you are a Jew. I do not
know how you must feel to be here . . . The world
should be a better place." He rambled, moving in and out
of German and English.

He grew excited, then sad, then weary all at once and I
couldn't help but feel how somehow he typified this new
generation of Germans, burdened with guilt, political
strain, the pressures of living this strange way of life in a
divided country, a divided city.

"You live in the East?" I asked.

"No, my grandmother lives here. She is sick. I am given
day passes once every few weeks. But I don't like to come
here. I hate going through the checkpoints. It is like coming to a zoo. Often I come to this place and try to piece it
all together . . ."

"You mean, what happened . . ."

"The war, the Jews, the wall. I try to make sense out of
what I am."

"There should be a plaque," I said. "People should not
forget."

"You are right. I will write a letter. There should be a way
of remembering."

"You are a student?" I asked.

He laughed. "Yes, a student of life. No, I am a laborer. I work with my hands," and he held them up for me to see. Once again he seemed so very weary, too old for his perhaps twenty years. I looked once more toward Brandenburg Gate, then at the wall. "Maybe they'll tear it down."

He looked for a moment with me, his eyes suddenly filled with a brightness I had not seen in our brief encounter. "*Ja,*" he said, "maybe they will. . . ."

I wandered along Unter den Linden and bought an ice cream cone which I sat on a bench eating, thinking about the young German and his hope for a better world. We have lost our innocence. Someone should give it back.

Mandelstam must have thought this when he wrote, in "The Last Supper": "Heaven . . . fell in love with the wall. It filled it with cracks. It fills them with light. It fell on the wall. It shines out there . . . And that's my night sky before me and I'm the child standing under it." I longed myself to be that child, gazing with wonder up at the night sky, innocent again, and I thought that perhaps, with a child of my own, this might be possible once more.

I made my way back through the matrix of concrete and chicken-wire tunnels, through assorted checkpoints with armed guards and serious patrol dogs, all of which made me feel I was on some peculiar initiation rite or perhaps some privileged visiting dignitary and not just another citizen of the world as I flashed my visa and passport. It was easy to get in, it occurred to me. Getting out was another matter.

Now I flashed my visa and passport to the American official who stamped it with a tired smile and sent me into the light where I left behind the world of old books and somber dresses and entered that world of discount drugs and neon nightlife. I emerged fatigued, somewhat abashed, into the side of freedom and democracy and crass capitalism, and inequality and poverty and so on, having left behind a dour, somber other reality. I pondered where I had been and what awaited me.

Meandering along the side of the wall, I passed an image. The shadow of a man escaping over the wall and tumbling into a giant can of Coca-Cola. What is better? I asked myself. What is worse? It should all blend together. Somehow this should all come down. Humpty Dumpty, painted in black and white, watched me, a startled look in his eyes, as he was about to fall.

I paused at the memorial for a boy, age eighteen, shot in the back. He had bled to death in the no-man's land between East and West. His name was written, his dates, a cross. There will be no walls in heaven, graffiti scrawled beside his memorial read. Here I lingered. My fingers touched the wall's cold façade, because any boy now was someone's child to me.

ABOUT THE AUTHOR

MARY MORRIS was born and raised in Chicago. Her previous books include *Vanishing Animals and Other Stories*, which was awarded the Rome Prize by the American Academy and Institute of Arts and Letters; the novel *Crossroads; The Bus of Dreams*, a book of stories awarded the Friends of American Writers Award; and, most recently, a novel, *The Waiting Room*. She is also the author of a previous work of nonfiction, *Nothing to Declare: Memoirs of a Woman Traveling Alone*. Mary Morris currently resides in New York City.

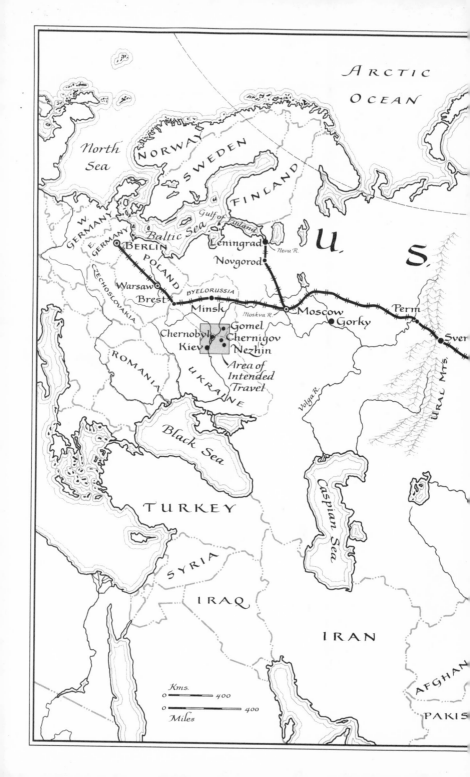